Workshop on Cognitive Aspects of Computational Language Acquisition 2007

Held in conjunction with ACL 2007

Prague, Czech Republic
29 June 2007

ISBN: 978-1-61738-528-5

Printed from e-media with permission by:

Curran Associates, Inc.
57 Morehouse Lane
Red Hook, NY 12571

Some format issues inherent in the e-media version may also appear in this print version.

Printed by Curran Associates, Inc. (2010)

For permission requests, please contact the Association for Computational Linguistics at the address below.

Association for Computational Linguistics
209 N. Eighth Street
Stroudsburg, Pennsylvania 18360

Phone: 1-570-476-8006
Fax: 1-570-476-0860

acl@aclweb.org

Additional copies of this publication are available from:

Curran Associates, Inc.
57 Morehouse Lane
Red Hook, NY 12571 USA
Phone: 845-758-0400
Fax: 845-758-2634
Email: curran@proceedings.com
Web: www.proceedings.com

Preface

This volume contains the papers accepted for presentation at the ACL 2007 Workshop on Cognitive Aspects of Computational Language Acquisition, held in Prague, Czech Republic on the 29th of June, 2007.

The past decades have seen a massive expansion in the application of statistical and machine learning methods to natural language processing (NLP). This work has yielded impressive results in numerous speech and language processing tasks including speech recognition, morphological analysis, parsing, lexical acquisition, semantic interpretation, and dialogue management.

Advances in these areas are generally viewed as engineering achievements but recently researchers have begun to investigate the relevance of computational learning techniques to research on human language acquisition. These investigations could have double significance since an improved understanding of human language acquisition will not only benefit cognitive sciences in general but may also feed back to the NLP community, placing researchers in a better position to develop new language models and/or techniques.

Success in this type of research requires close collaboration between NLP and cognitive scientists. The aim of this workshop is thus to bring together researchers from the diverse fields of NLP, machine learning, artificial intelligence, linguistics, psycho-linguistics, etc. who are interested in the relevance of computational techniques for understanding human language learning. The workshop is intended to bridge the gap between the computational and cognitive communities, promote knowledge and resource sharing, and help initiate interdisciplinary research projects.

In the call for papers we solicited papers describing cognitive aspects of computational language acquisition including:

- Computational learning theory and analysis of language learning
- Computational models of human (first, second and bilingual) language acquisition
- Computational models of various components of the language faculty and their impact on the acquisition task
- Computational models of the evolution of language
- Data resources and tools for investigating computational models of human language acquisition
- Empirical and theoretical comparisons of the learning environment and its impact on the acquisition task
- Computational methods for acquiring various linguistic information (related to e.g. speech, morphology, lexicon, syntax, semantics, and discourse) and their relevance to research on human language acquisition
- Investigations and comparisons of supervised, unsupervised and weakly-supervised methods for learning (e.g. machine learning, statistical, symbolic, biologically-inspired, active learning, various hybrid models) from the cognitive aspect

Of the 22 papers submitted, the programme committee selected 12 papers for publication that are representative of the state-of-the-art in this interdisciplinary area. Each full-length submission was independently reviewed by three members of the program committee, who then collectively faced the difficult task of selecting a subset of papers for publication from a very strong field. Among the accepted papers we see proposed techniques for creating, analysing and annotating data resources for research on language acquisition. We also see presentations of computational models for first and second language acquisition. These models investigate the acquisition of both syntactic and semantic phenomena, adopting different linguistic theories and formalisms, using varying levels of supervision.

We would like to thank all the authors who submitted papers, as well as the members of the programme committee for the time and effort they contributed in reviewing the papers. Our thanks go also to the organisers of the main conference, the publication chairs, and the conference workshop committee headed by Simone Teufel.

Paula Buttery, Aline Villavicencio, Anna Korhonen

Organizers

Chairs:

Paula Buttery (University of Cambridge, UK)
Aline Villavicencio (Federal University of Rio Grande do Sul, Brazil, University of Bath, UK)
Anna Korhonen (University of Cambridge, UK)

Program Committee:

Colin J Bannard (Max Planck Institute for Evolutionary Anthropology, Germany)
Robert C. Berwick (Massachusetts Institute of Technology, USA)
Jim Blevins (University of Cambridge, UK)
Antal van den Bosch (Tilburg University, The Netherlands)
Chris Brew (Ohio State University, USA)
Ted Briscoe (University of Cambridge, UK)
Alexander Clark (Royal Holloway, University of London, UK)
Robin Clark (University of Pennsylvania, USA)
Stephen Clark (University of Oxford, UK)
Matthew W. Crocker (Saarland University, Germany)
James Cussens (University of York, UK)
Walter Daelemans (University of Antwerp, Belgium and Tilburg University, The Netherlands)
Bruno Gaume (Universite Paul Sabatier, France)
Ted Gibson (Massachusetts Institute of Technology, USA)
Henriette Hendriks (University of Cambridge, UK)
Julia Hockenmaier (University of Pennsylvania, USA)
Marco Idiart (Federal University of Rio Grande do Sul, Brazil)
Mark Johnson (Brown University, USA)
Gea de Jong (University of Cambridge, UK)
Aravind Joshi (University of Pennsylvania, USA)
Gerard Kempen (Leiden University, Netherlands)
Brian MacWhinney (Carnegie Mellon University, USA)
Martin Pickering (University of Glasgow, UK)
Thierry Poibeau (University Paris 13, France)
Brechtje Post (University of Cambridge, UK)
Ari Rappoport (The Hebrew University of Jerusalem, Israel)
Kenji Sagae (University of Tokyo, Japan)
Sabine Schulte im Walde (University of Stuttgart, Germany)
Mark Steedman (University of Edinburgh, UK)
Suzanne Stevenson (University of Toronto, Canada)
Bert Vaux (University of Wisconsin, USA)
Charles Yang (University of Pennsylvania, USA)
Menno van Zaanen (Macquarie University, Australia)

Table of Contents

Conference Program

Friday, June 29, 2007

8:55–9:00 Opening Remarks

9:00–9:45 Invited Talk by Suzanne Stevenson

9.45–10:15 *A Linguistic Investigation into Unsupervised DOP*
Rens Bod

10:15–10:45 *Using Classifier Features for Studying the Effect of Native Language on the Choice of Written Second Language Words*
Oren Tsur and Ari Rappoport

Morning Coffee Break

11.15–11.45 *Phon 1.2: A Computational Basis for Phonological Database Elaboration and Model Testing*
Yvan Rose, Gregory Hedlund, Rod Byrne, Todd Wareham and Brian MacWhinney

11.45–12.15 *High-accuracy Annotation and Parsing of CHILDES Transcripts*
Kenji Sagae, Eric Davis, Alon Lavie, Brian MacWhinney and Shuly Wintner

12.15–12.45 *I will shoot your shopping down and you can shoot all my tins—Automatic Lexical Acquisition from the CHILDES Database*
Paula Buttery and Anna Korhonen

Lunch

14.15–14.45 *A Cognitive Model for the Representation and Acquisition of Verb Selectional Preferences*
Afra Alishahi and Suzanne Stevenson

14.45–15.15 *ISA meets Lara: An incremental word space model for cognitively plausible simulations of semantic learning*
Marco Baroni, Alessandro Lenci and Luca Onnis

15.15–15.45 *Simulating the acquisition of object names*
Alessio Plebe, Vivian De La Cruz and Marco Mazzone

Afternoon Break

Friday, June 29, 2007 (continued)

A Linguistic Investigation into Unsupervised DOP

Rens Bod
School of Computer Science
University of St Andrews
ILLC, University of Amsterdam
rb@cs.st-and.ac.uk

Abstract

Unsupervised Data-Oriented Parsing models (U-DOP) represent a class of structure bootstrapping models that have achieved some of the best unsupervised parsing results in the literature. While U-DOP was originally proposed as an engineering approach to language learning (Bod 2005, 2006a), it turns out that the model has a number of properties that may also be of linguistic and cognitive interest. In this paper we will focus on the original U-DOP model proposed in Bod (2005) which computes the most probable tree from among the shortest derivations of sentences. We will show that this U-DOP model can learn both rule-based and exemplar-based aspects of language, ranging from agreement and movement phenomena to discontiguous contructions, provided that productive units of arbitrary size are allowed. We argue that our results suggest a rapprochement between nativism and empiricism.

1 Introduction

This paper investigates a number of linguistic and cognitive aspects of the unsupervised data-oriented parsing framework, known as U-DOP (Bod 2005, 2006a, 2007). U-DOP is a generalization of the DOP model which was originally proposed for supervised language processing (Bod 1998). DOP produces and analyzes new sentences out of largest and most probable subtrees from previously analyzed sentences. DOP maximizes what has been called the 'structural analogy' between a sentence and a corpus of previous sentence-structures (Bod 2006b). While DOP has been successful in some areas, e.g. in ambiguity resolution, there is also a serious shortcoming to the approach: it does not account for the acquisition of *initial* structures. That is, DOP assumes that the structures of previous linguistic experiences are already given and stored in a corpus. As such, DOP can at best account for adult language use and has nothing to say about language acquisition.

In Bod (2005, 2006a), DOP was extended to unsupervised parsing in a rather straightforward way. This new model, termed U-DOP, again starts with the notion of tree. But since in language learning we do not yet know which trees should be assigned to initial sentences, it is assumed that a language learner will initially allow (implicitly) for all possible trees and let linguistic experience decide which trees are actually learned. That is, U-DOP generates a new sentence by reconstructing it out of the largest possible and most frequent subtrees from all possible (binary) trees of previous sentences. This has resulted in state-of-the-art performance for English, German and Chinese corpora (Bod 2007).

Although we do not claim that U-DOP provides any near-to-complete theory of language acquisition, we intend to show in this paper that it can learn a variety of linguistic phenomena, some of which are exemplar-based, such as idiosyncratic constructions, others of which are typically viewed as rule-based, such as auxiliary fronting and subject-verb agreement. We argue that U-DOP can be seen as a rapprochement between nativism and empiricism. In particular, we argue that there is a fallacy in the argument that for syntactic facets to be learned they must be either innate or in the input data: they can just as well emerge from an analogical process without ever hearing the particular facet and without assuming that it is hard-wired in the mind.

In the following section, we will start by reviewing the original DOP framework in Bod (1998). In section 3 we will show how DOP can be

Proceedings of the Workshop on Cognitive Aspects of Computational Language Acquisition, pages 1–8,
Prague, Czech Republic, June 2007 ©2007 Association for Computational Linguistics

generalized to language learning, resulting in U-DOP. Next, in section 4, we show that the approach can learn idiosyncratic constructions. In section 5 we discuss how U-DOP can learn agreement phenomena, and in section 6 we extend our argument to auxiliary movement. We end with a conclusion.

2 Review of 'supervised' DOP

In its original version, DOP derives new sentences by combining subtrees from previously derived sentences. One of the main motivations behind the DOP framework was to integrate rule-based and exemplar-based aspects of language processing (Bod 1998). A simple example may illustrate the approach. Consider an extremely small corpus of only two phrase-structure trees that are labeled by traditional categories, shown in figure 1.

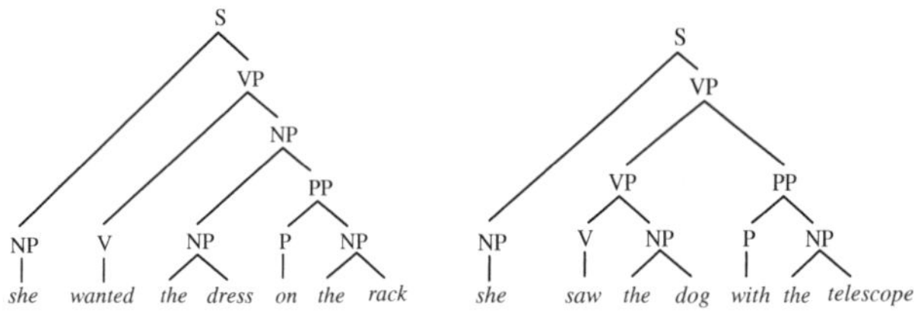

Figure 1. An extremely small corpus of two trees

A new sentence can be derived by combining subtrees from the trees in the corpus. The combination operation between subtrees is called *label substitution,* indicated as ∘. Starting out with the corpus of figure 1, for instance, the sentence *She saw the dress with the telescope* may be derived as shown in figure 2.

Figure 2. Analyzing a new sentence by combining subtrees from figure 1

We can also derive an alternative tree structure for this sentence, namely by combining three (rather than two) subtrees from figure 1, as shown in figure 3. We will write $(t \circ u) \circ v$ as $t \circ u \circ v$ with the convention that ∘ is *left*-associative.

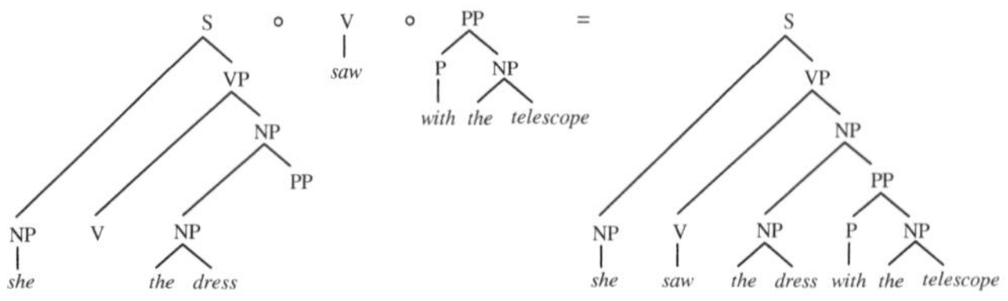

Figure 3. A different derivation for the same sentence

DOP's subtrees can be of arbitrary size: they can range from context-free rewrite rules to entire sentence-analyses. This makes the model sensitive to multi-word units, idioms and other idiosyncratic constructions, while still maintaining full productivity. DOP is consonant with the view, as expressed by certain usage-based and constructionist accounts in linguistics, that any string of words can function as a construction (Croft 2001; Tomasello 2003; Goldberg 2006; Bybee 2006). In DOP such constructions are formalized as lexicalized subtrees, which form the productive units of a *Stochastic Tree-Substitution Grammar* or *STSG*.

Note that an unlimited number of sentences can be derived by combining subtrees from the corpus in figure 1. However, virtually every sentence generated in this way is highly ambiguous, yielding several syntactic analyses. Yet, most of these analyses do not correspond to the structure humans perceive. Initial DOP models proposed an exclusively probabilistic metric to rank different candidates, where the 'best' tree was computed from the frequencies of subtrees in the corpus (see Bod 1998).

While it is well known that the frequency of a structure is a very important factor in language comprehension and production (Jurafsky 2003), it is not the only factor. Discourse context, semantics and recency also play an important role. DOP can straightforwardly take into account discourse and semantic information if we have corpora with such information from which we take our subtrees, and the notion of recency can be incorporated by a frequency-adjustment function (Bod 1998). There is, however, an important other factor which does not correspond to the notion of frequency: this is the *simplicity* of a structure (cf. Frazier 1978; Chater 1999). In Bod (2002), the simplest structure was formalized by the *shortest derivation* of a sentence consisting of the fewest subtrees from the corpus. Note that the shortest derivation will include the largest possible subtrees from the corpus, thereby *maximizing the structural overlap between a sentence and previous sentence-*

structures. Only in case the shortest derivation is not unique, the frequencies of the subtrees are used to break ties among the shortest derivations. This DOP model assumes that language users maximize what has been called the *structural analogy* between a sentence and previous sentence-structures by computing the most probable tree with largest structural overlaps between a sentence and a corpus. We will use this DOP model from Bod (2002) as the basis for our investigation of unsupervised DOP.

We can illustrate DOP's notion of structural analogy with the examples given in the figures above. DOP predicts that the tree structure in figure 2 is preferred because it can be generated by just two subtrees from the corpus. Any other tree structure, such as in figure 3, would need at least three subtrees from the training set in figure 1. Note that the tree generated by the shortest derivation indeed tends to be structurally more similar to the corpus (i.e. having a larger overlap with one of the corpus trees) than the tree generated by the longer derivation. Had we restricted the subtrees to smaller sizes -- for example to depth-1 subtrees, which makes DOP equivalent to a (probabilistic) context-free grammar -- the shortest derivation would not be able to distinguish between the two trees in figures 2 and 3 as they would both be generated by 9 rewrite rules.

When the shortest derivation is not unique, we use the subtree frequencies to break ties. The 'best tree' of a sentence is defined as the most probable tree generated by a shortest derivation of the sentence, also referred to as 'MPSD'. The probability of a tree can be computed from the relative frequencies of its subtrees, and the definitions are standard for Stochastic Tree-Substitution Grammars (STSGs), see e.g. Manning and Schütze (1999) or Bod (2002). Interestingly, we will see that the exact computation of probabilities is not necessary for our arguments in this paper.

3 U-DOP: from sentences to structures

DOP can be generalized to language learning by using the same principle as before: language users maximize the structural analogy between a new sentence and previous sentence-structures by computing the most probable shortest derivation. However, in language *learning* we cannot assume that the correct phrase-structures of previously heard sentences are already known. Bod (2005) therefore proposed the following generalization of DOP, which we will simply refer to as U-DOP: *if a language learner does not know which syntactic tree should be assigned to a sentence, s/he initially allows (implicitly) for all possible trees and let linguistic experience decide which is the 'best' tree by maximizing structural analogy (i.e. the MPSD).*

Although several alternative versions of U-DOP have been proposed (e.g. Bod 2006a, 2007), we will stick to the computation of the MPSD for the current paper. Due to its use of the shortest derivation, the model's working can often be predicted without any probabilistic computations, which makes it especially apt to investigate linguistic facets such as auxiliary fronting (see section 6).

From a conceptual perspective we can distinguish three learning phases under U-DOP, which we shall discuss in more detail below.

(i) Assign all unlabeled binary trees to a set of sentences

Suppose that a language learner hears the following two ('Childes-like') sentences: *watch the dog* and *the dog barks*. How could a rational learner figure out the appropriate tree structures for these sentences? U-DOP conjectures that a learner does so by allowing any fragment of the heard sentences to form a productive unit and to try to reconstruct these sentences out of most probable shortest combinations.

Consider the set of all unlabeled binary trees for the sentences *watch the dog* and *the dog barks* given in figure 4. Each node in each tree is assigned the same category label *X*, since we do not (yet) know what label each phrase will receive.

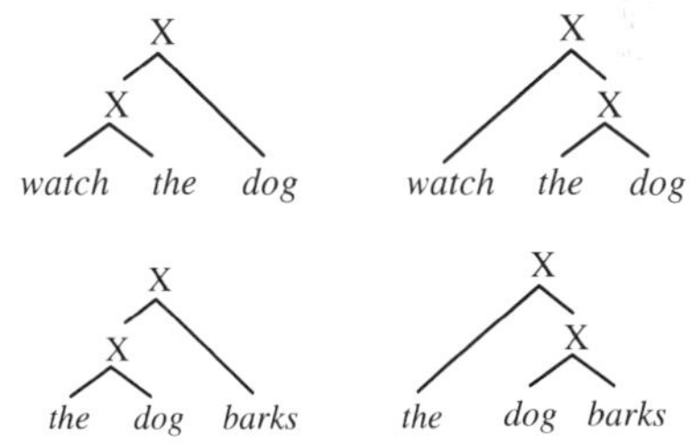

Figure 4. The unlabeled binary tree set for *watch the dog* and *the dog barks*

Although the number of possible binary trees for a sentence grows exponentially with sentence length, these binary trees can be efficiently represented by means of a chart or tabular diagram. By adding pointers between the nodes we obtain a structure known as a shared parse forest (Billot and Lang 1989).

(ii) Divide the binary trees into all subtrees

Figure 5 exhaustively lists the subtrees that can be extracted from the trees in figure 4. The first subtree in each row represents the whole sentence as a chunk, while the second and the third are 'proper' subtrees.

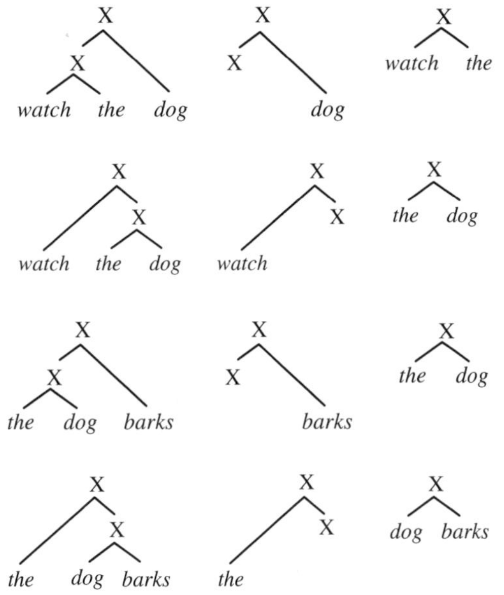

Figure 5. The subtree set for the binary trees in figure 4.

Note that while most subtrees occur once, the subtree [*the dog*]$_X$ occurs twice. There exist efficient algorithms to convert all subtrees into a compact representation (Goodman 2003) such that standard best-first parsing algorithms can be applied to the model (see Bod 2007).

(iii) Compute the 'best' tree for each sentence

Given the subtrees in figure 5, the language learner can now induce analyses for a sentence such as *the dog barks* in various ways. The phrase structure [*the* [*dog barks*]$_X$]$_X$ can be produced by two different derivations, either by selecting the large subtree that spans the whole sentence or by combining two smaller subtrees:

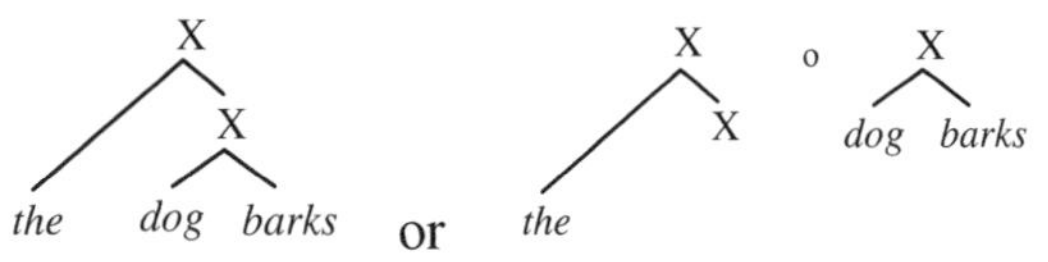

Figure 6. Deriving *the dog barks* from figure 5

Analogously, the competing phrase structure [[*the dog*]$_X$ *barks*]$_X$ can also produced by two derivations:

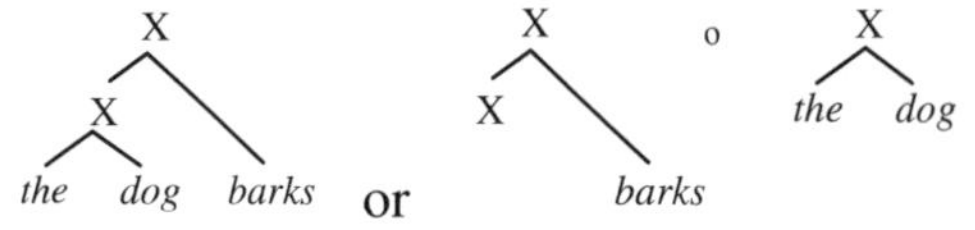

Figure 7. Other derivations for *the dog barks*

Note that the shortest derivation is not unique: the sentence *the dog barks* can be trivially parsed by any of its fully spanning trees. Such a situation does not usually occur when structures for *new* sentences are learned, i.e. when we induce structures for a held-out test set using all subtrees from all possible trees assigned to a training set. For example, the shortest derivation for the new 'sentence' *watch dog barks* is unique, given the set of subtrees in figure 5. But in the example above we need subtree frequencies to break ties, i.e. U-DOP computes the most probable tree from among the shortest derivations, the MPSD. The probability of a tree is compositionally computed from the frequencies of its subtrees, in the same way as in the supervised version of DOP (see Bod 1998, 2002). Since the subtree [*the dog*]$_X$ is the only subtree that occurs more than once, we can predict that the most probable tree corresponds to the structure [[*the dog*]$_X$ *barks*]$_X$ in figure 7 where *the dog* is a constituent. This can also be shown formally, but a precise computation is unnecessary for this example.

4 Learning constructions by U-DOP

For the sake of simplicity, we have only considered subtrees without lexical labels in the previous section. Now, if we also add an (abstract) label to each word in figure 4, then a possible subtree would the subtree in figure 9, which has a discontiguous yield *watch X dog*, and which we will therefore refer to as a "discontiguous subtree".

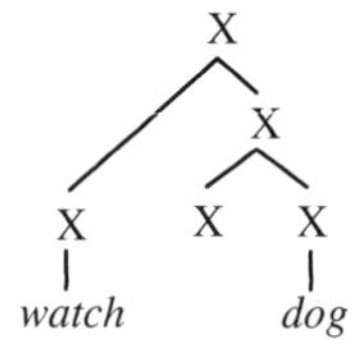

Figure 9. A discontiguous subtree

Thus lexical labels enlarge the space of dependencies covered by our subtree set. In order for U-DOP to take into account both contiguous and non-contiguous patterns, we will define the total tree-set of a sentence as the set of all unlabeled trees that are unary at the word level and binary at all higher levels.

Discontiguous subtrees, like in figure 9, are important for acquiring a variety of constructions as in (1)-(4):

(1) Show me the *nearest* airport *to* Leipzig.
(2) BA carried *more* people *than* cargo in 2005.
(3) *What is* this scratch *doing* on the table?
(4) Don't *take* him *by surprise*.

These constructions have been discussed at various places in the literature, and all of them are discontiguous in that the constructions do not appear as contiguous word strings. Instead the words are separated by 'holes' which are sometimes represented by dots as in *more* ... *than* ..., or by variables as in *What is X doing Y* (cf. Kay and Fillmore 1999). In order to capture the syntactic structure of discontiguous constructions we need a model that allows for productive units that can be partially lexicalized, such as subtrees. For example, the construction *more* ... *than* ... in (2) can be represented by a subtree as in figure 10.

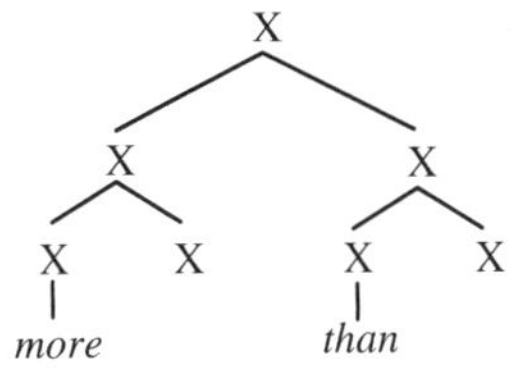

Figure 10. Discontiguous subtree for *more...than...*

U-DOP can learn the structure in figure 10 from a few sentences only, using the mechanism described in section 3. While we will go into the details of learning discontiguous subtrees in section 5, it is easy to see that U-DOP will prefer the structure in figure 10 over a structure where e.g. [*X than*] forms a constituent. First note that the substring *more X* can occur at the end of a sentence (in e.g. *Can I have more milk?)*, whereas the substring *X than* cannot occur at the end of a sentence. This means that [*more X*] will be preferred as a constituent in [*more X than X*]. The same is the case for *than X* in e.g. *A is cheaper than B*. Thus both [*more X*] and [*than X*] can appear separately from the construction and will win out in frequency, which means that U-DOP will learn the structure in figure 10 for the construction *more* ... *than* ....

Once it is learned, (supervised) DOP enforces the application of the subtree in figure 10 whenever a new form using the construction *more* ... *than* ... is perceived or produced because the particular subtree will directly cover it and lead to the shortest derivation.

5 Learning agreement by U-DOP

Discontiguous context is important not only for learning constructions but also for learning various syntactic regularities. Consider the following sentence (5):

(5) Swimming in rivers is dangerous

How can U-DOP deal with the fact that human language learners will perceive an agreement relation between *swimming* and *is*, and not between *rivers* and *is*? We will rephrase this question as follows: which sentences must be perceived such that U-DOP can assign as the best structure for *swimming in rivers is dangerous* the tree 16(a) which attaches the constituent *is dangerous* to *swimming in rivers*, and not an incorrect tree like 16(b) which attaches *is dangerous* to *rivers*? Note that tree (a) correctly represents the dependency between *swimming* and *is dangerous*, while tree (b) misrepresents a dependency between *rivers* and *is dangerous*.

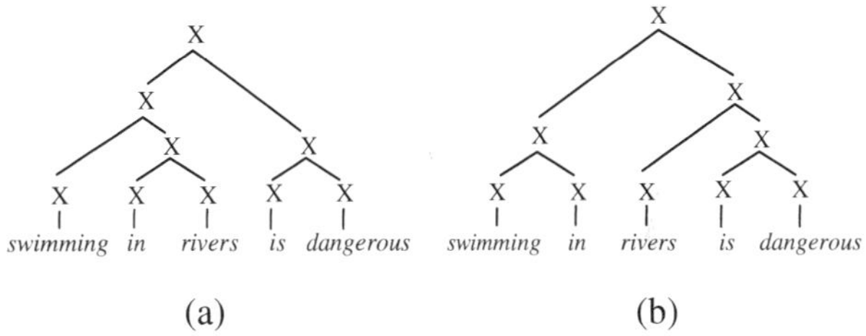

Figure 16. Two possible trees for *Swimming in rivers is dangerous*

It turns out that we need to observe only one additional sentence to overrule tree (b), i.e. sentence (6):

(6) Swimming together is fun

The word *together* can be attached either to *swimming* or to *is fun*, as illustrated respectively by 17(a) and 17(b) (of course, *together* can also be attached to *is* alone, and the resulting phrase *together is* to *fun*, but our argument still remains valid):

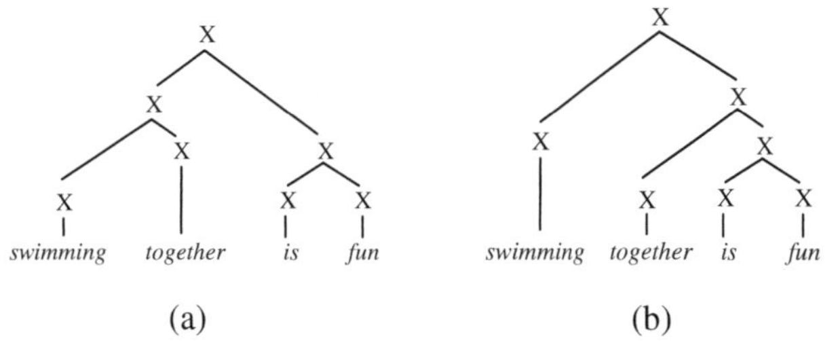

Figure 17. Two possible trees for *Swimming together is fun*

First note that there is a large common subtree between 16(a) and 17(a), as shown in figure 18.

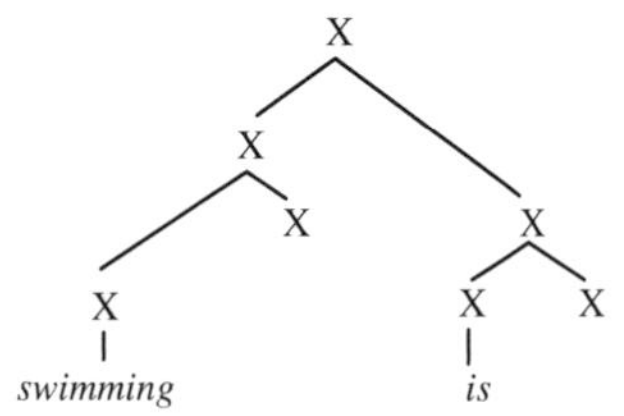

Figure 18. Common subtree in the trees 16(a) and 17(a)

Next note that there is not such a large common subtree between 16(b) and 17(b). Since the shortest derivation is not unique (as both trees can be produced by directly using the largest tree from the binary tree set), we must rely on the frequencies of the subtrees. It is easy to see that the trees 16(a) and 17(a) will overrule respectively 16(b) and 17(b), because 16(a) and 17(a) share the largest subtree. Although 16(b) and 17(b) also share subtrees, they cover a smaller part of the sentence than does the subtree in figure 18. Next note that for every common subtree between 16(a) and 17(a) there exists a corresponding common subtree between 16(b) and 17(b) except for the common subtree in figure 18 (and one of its sub-subtrees by abstracting from *swimming*). Since the frequencies of all subtrees of a tree contribute to its probability, if follows that figure 18 will be part of the most probable tree, and thus 16(a) and 17(a) will overrule respectively 16(b) and 17(b).

However, our argument is not yet complete: we have not yet ruled out another possible analysis for *swimming in rivers is dangerous* where *in rivers* forms a constituent together with *is dangerous*. Interestingly, it suffices to perceive a sentence like (7): *He likes swimming in river.* The occurrence of *swimming in rivers* at the end of this sentence will lead to a preference for 16(a) because it will get a higher frequency as a group. An implementation of U-DOP confirmed our informal argument.

We conclude that U-DOP only needs three sentences to learn the correct tree structure displaying the dependency between the subject *swimming* and the verb *is*, known otherwise as "agreement". Once we have learned the correct structure for subject-verb agreement by the subtree in figure 18, (U-)DOP enforces agreement by the shortest derivation.

It can also be shown that U-DOP still learns the correct agreement if sentences with incorrect agreement, like **Swimming in rivers are dangerous*, are heard as long as the *correct* agreement has a higher frequency than the incorrect agreement during the learning process.

6 Learning 'movement' by U-DOP

We now come to what is often assumed to be the greatest challenge for models of language learning, and what Crain (1991) calls the "parade case of an innate constraint": the problem of auxiliary movement, also known as auxiliary fronting or inversion. Let's start with the typical examples, which are similar to those used in Crain (1991), MacWhinney (2005), Clark and Eyraud (2006) and many others:

(8) The man is hungry

If we turn sentence (8) into a (polar) interrogative, the auxiliary *is* is fronted, resulting in sentence (9).

(9) Is the man hungry?

A language learner might derive from these two sentences that the first occurring auxiliary is fronted. However, when the sentence also contains a relative clause with an auxiliary *is*, it should not be the first occurrence of *is* that is fronted but the one in the main clause, as shown in sentences (11) and (12).

(11) The man who is eating is hungry
(12) Is the man who is eating hungry?

There is no reason that children should favor the correct auxiliary fronting. Yet children do produce the correct sentences of the form (12) and rarely if ever of the form (13) even if they have not heard the correct form before (see Crain and Nakayama 1987).

(13) *Is the man who eating is hungry?

How can we account for this phenomenon? According to the nativist view, sentences of the type in (12) are so rare that children must have innately specified knowledge that allows them to learn this facet of language without ever having seen it (Crain and Nakayama 1987). On the other hand, it has been claimed that this type of sentence is not rare at all and can thus be learned from experience (Pullum and Scholz 2002). We will not enter the controversy on this issue, but believe that both viewpoints overlook a very important alternative possibility, namely that auxiliary fronting needs neither be innate nor in the input data to be learned, but may simply be an emergent property of the underlying model.

How does (U-)DOP account for this phenomenon? We will show that the learning of auxiliary fronting can proceed with only *two* sentences:

(14) The man who is eating is hungry
(15) Is the boy hungry?

Note that these sentences do not contain an example of the fact that an auxiliary should be fronted from the main clause rather than from the relative clause.

For reasons of space, we will have to skip the induction of the tree structures for (14) and (15), which can be derived from a total of six sentences using similar reasoning as in section 5, and which are given in figure 20a,b (see Bod forthcoming, for more details and a demonstration that the induction of these two tree structures is robust).

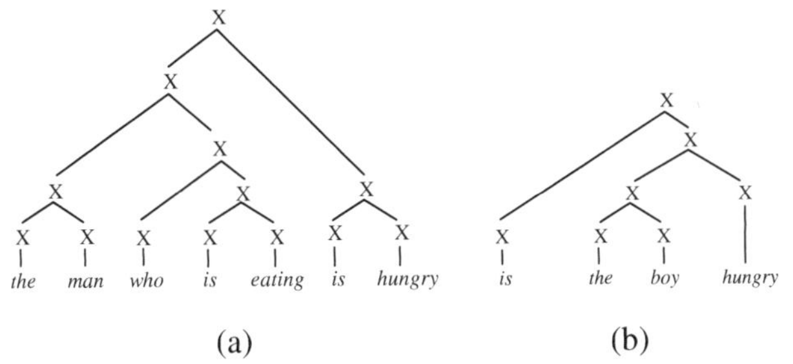

Figure 20. Tree structures for *the man who is eating is hungry* and *is the boy hungry?* learned by U-DOP

Given the trees in figure 20, we can now easily show that U-DOP's shortest derivation produces the correct auxiliary fronting, without relying on any probability calculations. That is, in order to produce the correct interrogative, *Is the man who is eating hungry*, we only need to combine the following two subtrees from the acquired structures in figure 20, as shown in figure 21 (note that the first subtree is discontiguous):

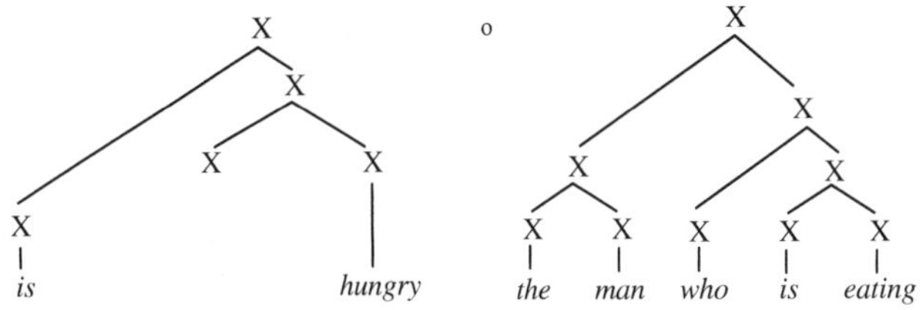

Figure 21. Producing the correct auxiliary fronting by combining two subtrees from figure 20

On the other hand, to produce the sentence with incorrect auxiliary fronting **Is the man who eating is hungry?* we need to combine many more subtrees from figure 20. Clearly the derivation in figure 21 is the shortest one and produces the correct sentence, thereby blocking the incorrect form.[1]

Thus the phenomenon of auxiliary fronting needs neither be innate nor in the input data to be learned. By using the notion of shortest derivation, auxiliary fronting can be learned from just a couple sentences only. Arguments about frequency and "poverty of the stimulus" (cf. Crain 1991; MacWhinney 2005) are therefore irrelevant – provided that we allow our productive units to be of arbitrary size. (Moreover, learning may be further eased once the syntactic categories have been induced. Although we do not go into category induction in the current paper, once unlabeled structures have been found, category learning turns out to be a relatively easy problem).

Auxiliary fronting has been previously dealt with in other probabilistic models of structure learning. Perfors et al. (2006) show that Bayesian model selection can choose the right grammar for auxiliary fronting. Yet, their problem is different in that Perfors et al. start from a set of given grammars from which their selection model has to choose the correct one. Our approach is more congenial to Clark and Eyraud (2006) who show that by distributional analysis in the vein of Harris (1954) auxiliary fronting can be correctly predicted. However, different from Clark and Eyraud, we have shown that U-DOP can also learn complex, discontiguous constructions. In order to learn both rule-based phenomena like auxiliary inversion and exemplar-based phenomena like idiosyncratic constructions, we believe we need

[1] We are implicitly assuming here an extension of DOP which computes the most probable shortest derivation given a certain meaning to be conveyed. This semantic DOP model was worked out in Bonnema et al. (1997) where the meaning of a sentence was represented by its logical form.

the richness of a probabilistic tree grammar rather than a probabilistic context-free grammar.

7 Conclusion

We have shown that various syntactic phenomena can be learned by a model that only assumes (1) the notion of recursive tree structure, and (2) an analogical matching algorithm which reconstructs a new sentence out of largest and most frequent fragments from previous sentences. The major difference between our model and other computational learning models (such as Klein and Manning 2005 or Clark and Eyraud 2006) is that *we start with trees*. But since we do not know which trees are correct, we initially allow for all of them and let analogy decide. Thus we assume that the language faculty (or 'Universal Grammar') has knowledge about the notion of tree structure but no more than that. Although we do not claim that we have developed any near-to-complete theory of all language acquisition, our argument to use only recursive structure as the core of language knowledge has a surprising precursor. Hauser, Chomksy and Fitch (2002) claim that the core language faculty comprises just 'recursion' and nothing else. If one takes this idea seriously, then U-DOP is probably the first fully computational model that instantiates it: U-DOP's trees encode the ultimate notion of recursion where every label can be recursively substituted for any other label. All else is analogy.

References

Billot, S. and B. Lang, 1989. The Structure of Shared Forests in Ambiguous Parsing. *Proceedings ACL 1989*.

Bod, R. 1998. *Beyond Grammar*. Stanford: CSLI Publications.

Bod, R. 2002. A Unified Model of Structural Organization in Language and Music, *Journal of Artificial Intelligence Research*, 17, 289-308.

Bod, R. 2005. Combining Supervised and Unsupervised Natural Language Processing. *The 16th Meeting of Computational Linguistics in the Netherlands (CLIN 2005)*.

Bod, R. 2006a. An All-Subtrees Approach to Unsupervised Parsing. *Proceedings ACL-COLING 2006*, 865-872.

Bod, R. 2006b. Exemplar-Based Syntax: How to Get Productivity from Examples. *The Linguistic Review* 23, 291-320.

Bod, 2007. Is the End of Supervised Parsing in Sight?. *Proceedings ACL 2007*, Prague.

Bod, forthcoming. From Exemplar to Grammar: How Analogy Guides Language Acquisition. In J. Blevins and J. Blevins (eds.) *Analogy in Grammar*, Oxford University Press.

Bonnema, R., R. Bod and R. Scha, 1997. A DOP Model for Semantic Interpretation. *Proceedings ACL/EACL 1997*, Madrid, Spain, 159-167.

Bybee, J. 2006. From Usage to Grammar: The Mind's Response to Repetition. *Language* 82(4), 711-733.

Chater, N. 1999. The Search for Simplicity: A Fundamental Cognitive Principle? *The Quarterly Journal of Experimental Psychology*, 52A(2), 273-302.

Clark, A. and R. Eyraud, 2006. Learning Auxiliary Fronting with Grammatical Inference. *Proceedings CONLL 2006*, New York.

Crain, S. 1991. Language Acquisition in the Absence of Experience. *Behavorial and Brain Sciences* 14, 597-612.

Crain, S. and M. Nakayama, 1987. Structure Dependence in Grammar Formation. *Language* 63, 522-543.

Croft, B. 2001. *Radical Construction Grammar*. Oxford University Press.

Frazier, L. 1978. On Comprehending Sentences: Syntactic Parsing Strategies. PhD. Thesis, U. of Connecticut.

Goldberg, A. 2006. Constructions at Work: the nature of generalization in language. Oxford University Press.

Goodman, J. 2003. Efficient algorithms for the DOP model. In R. Bod, R. Scha and K. Sima'an (eds.). *Data-Oriented Parsing*, CSLI Publications, 125-146.

Harris, Z. 1954. Distributional Structure. *Word* 10, 146-162.

Hauser, M., N. Chomsky and T. Fitch, 2002. The Faculty of Language: What Is It, Who Has It, and How Did It Evolve?, *Science* 298, 1569-1579.

Jurafsky, D. 2003. Probabilistic Modeling in Psycholinguistics. In Bod, R., J. Hay and S. Jannedy (eds.), *Probabilistic Linguistics*, The MIT Press, 39-96.

Kay, P. and C. Fillmore 1999. Grammatical constructions and linguistic generalizations: the What's X doing Y? construction. *Language*, 75, 1-33.

Klein, D. and C. Manning 2005. Natural language grammar induction with a generative constituent-context model. *Pattern Recognition* 38, 1407-1419.

MacWhinney, B. 2005. Item-based Constructions and the Logical Problem. *Proceedings of the Second Workshop on Psychocomputational Models of Human Language Acquisition*, Ann Arbor.

Manning, C. and H. Schütze 1999. *Foundations of Statistical Natural Language Processing*. The MIT Press.

Perfors, A., Tenenbaum, J., Regier, T. 2006. Poverty of the Stimulus? A rational approach. *Proceedings 28th Annual Conference of the Cognitive Science Society*. Vancouver

Pullum, G. and B. Scholz 2002. Empirical assessment of stimulus poverty arguments. *The Linguistic Review* 19, 9-50.

Tomasello, M. 2003. *Constructing a Language*. Harvard University Press.

Using Classifier Features for Studying the Effect of Native Language on the Choice of Written Second Language Words

Oren Tsur
Institute of Computer Science
The Hebrew University
Jerusalem, Israel
oren@cs.huji.ac.il

Ari Rappoport
Institute of Computer Science
The Hebrew University
Jerusalem, Israel
www.cs.huji.ac.il/~arir

Abstract

We apply machine learning techniques to study language transfer, a major topic in the theory of Second Language Acquisition (SLA). Using an SVM for the problem of native language classification, we show that a careful analysis of the effects of various features can lead to scientific insights. In particular, we demonstrate that character bi-grams alone allow classification levels of about 66% for a 5-class task, even when content and function word differences are accounted for. This may show that native language has a strong effect on the word choice of people writing in a second language.

1 Introduction

While advances in NLP achieve improved results for NLP applications such as machine translation, question answering and document summarization, there are other fields of research that can benefit from the methods used by the NLP community. Second Language Acquisition (SLA), a major area in Applied Linguistics and Cognitive Science, is one such field. In this paper we demonstrate how modern machine learning tools can contribute to SLA theory. In particular, we address the major SLA topic of language transfer, the effect of native language on second language learners. Using an SVM for the computational problem of native language classification, we study in detail the effects of various SVM features. Surprisingly, character bi-grams alone lead to a classification accuracy of about 66% in a 5-class task, even when accounting for differences in content and function words.

This result leads us to form a novel hypothesis on the role of language transfer in SLA: that the choice of words people make when writing in a second language is strongly influenced by the phonology of their native language.

As far as we know, this is the first time that such a hypothesis has beed formulated. Moreover, this is the first statistical learning-supported hypothesis in language transfer. Our results should be further substantiated by additional psycholinguistic and computational experiments; nonetheless, we provide a strong starting point.

The next section provides some essential background. In Section 3 we describe our experimental setup and feature selection, and in Section 4 we detail an array of variations of experiments for ruling out some possible types of bias that might have affected the results. In Section 5 we discuss our hypothesis in the context of psycho-linguistic theory. We conclude with directions for future research.

2 Background

Our hypothesis is tested within an algorithm addressing the practical problem of determining the native language of an anonymous writer writing in a foreign language. The problem is applicable to different fields, such as language instructing, tailored error correction, security applications and psycholinguistic research.

As background, we start from the somewhat related problem of authorship attribution. The authorship attribution problem was addressed by lin-

Proceedings of the Workshop on Cognitive Aspects of Computational Language Acquisition, pages 9–16,
Prague, Czech Republic, June 2007

guists and other literary experts trying to pinpoint an anonymous author, such as that of The Federalist Papers (Holmes and Forsyth, 1995). Traditionally, authorship experts analyzed topics, stylistic idiosyncrasies and personal information about the possible candidates in order to determine an author.

While authorship is usually addressed with deep human inspection of the texts in question, it has already been shown that automatic text analysis based on various stylistic features can identify the gender of an anonymous author with accuracy above 80% (Argamon et al, 2003). Various papers (Diedrich et al, 2003; Koppel and Schler, 2003; Koppel et al, 2005a; Stamatatos et al, 2004) report relative success in machine based authorship attribution tasks for small sets of known candidates.

Native language detection is a harder problem than the authorship attribution problem, since we wish to characterize the writing style of a set of writers rather than the unique style of a single person. There are several works presenting non-native speech recognition and dialect analysis systems (Bouselmi et al, 2005; Bouselmi et al, 2006; Hansen et al, 2004). However, all those works are based on acoustic signals, not on written texts.

Koppel et al (2005a) report an accuracy of 80% in the task of determining a writer's native language. To the best of our knowledge, this is the only published work on automated classification of an author's native language (along with another version of the paper by the same authors (Koppel et al, 2005b)). Koppel et al used an SVM (Schölkopf and Smola, 2002) and a combination of features in their system (such as errors analysis and POS-error co-occurrences, as described in section 2.2), but surprisingly, it appears that a very naive set of features achieves a relatively high accuracy. The character bi-gram frequencies feature performs rather well, and definitely outperforms the intuitive contribution of frequent bigrams in this type of task.

3 Experimental Setting

3.1 The Corpus

The corpus that served for all of the experiments described in this paper is the International Corpus of Learner English (ICLE) (Granger et al, 2002), which was also the one used by Koppel et al (2005a; 2005b). The corpus was compiled for the purpose of studying the English writing of non-native speakers. All contributors to the corpus are advanced English students and are roughly the same age. The corpus is combined from a number of sub-corpora, each containing one native language. The corpus was assembled in ten years of international collaboration between a number of universities and it contains more than 2 million words of writing by students from 19 different native language backgrounds. We followed Koppel et al (2005a) and worked on 5 sub-corpora, each containing 238 randomly selected essays by native speakers of the following languages: Bulgarian, Czech, French, Russian and Spanish. Each of the texts in the corpus was written by a different author and is of length between 500 to 1,000 words. Each of the sub corpora contains about 180,000 (unique) types, for a total of 886,677 tokens.

Essays in the corpus are of two types: argumentative essays and literature examination papers. Descriptive, narrative or technical subjects were not included in the corpus. The literature examination essays were restricted to no more than 25% of each sub-corpus. Each contributor was requested to fill a learner profile that was used to fine-proof the corpus as needed.

In order to verify our results we used another control corpus containing the Dutch and Italian sub-corpora contained in the ICLE instead of the Bulgarian and French ones.

3.2 Document Representation

In the original experiment by Koppel et al (2005a) each document was represented by a numerical vector of 1,035 dimensions. Each vector entry represented the frequency (relative to the document's length) of a given feature. The features were of 4 types:

- 400 function words
- 200 most frequent letter n-grams
- 250 rare POS bi-gram
- 185 error types

While the first three types of attributes are relatively straightforward, the fourth is more complex. It represents clusters of families of spelling errors as well as co-occurrences of errors and POS tags. Document representation is described in detail in (Koppel et al, 2005a; Koppel et al, 2005b).

A multi-class SVM (Witten and Frank, 2005) was employed for learning and evaluating the classification model. The experiment was run in a 10-fold cross validation manner in order to test the effectiveness of the model.

3.3 Previous Results

Koppel et al (2005a) report that when all features types were used in tandem, an accuracy of 80.2% was achieved. In the discussion section they analyze the frequency of a few function words, error types, the co-occurrences of POS tags and errors, and the co-occurrences of POS tags and certain function words that seem to have significance in the support vectors learnt by the SVM.

The goal of their research was to obtain the best classification, therefore the results obtained by using only bi-grams of characters were not particularly noted, although, surprisingly, representing each document by only using the relative frequency of the top 200 characters bi-grams achieves an accuracy of about 66%. We believe that this surprising fact exposes some fundamental phenomenon of human language behavior. In the next section we describe a set of experiments designed to isolate the causes of this phenomenon.

4 Experimental Variations and Results

Intuitively, we do not expect the most frequent character n-grams to serve as good native language predictors, expecting that these will only reflect the most frequent English words (and characters sequences). Accordingly, without language transfer effects, a naive baseline classifier based on an n-gram model is expected to achieve about 20% accuracy in a 5 native languages classification task. However, using classification based on the relative frequency of top 200 bi-grams achieves about 66%[1] in all experiments, substantially higher than the random baseline. These results are so surprising that they suggest that the characters bi-grams classification masks some other bias or noise in the corpus, or, conversely, that it mirrors other simple-to-

[1]Koppel et al did not report these results explicitly. However, they can be roughly estimated from their graph.

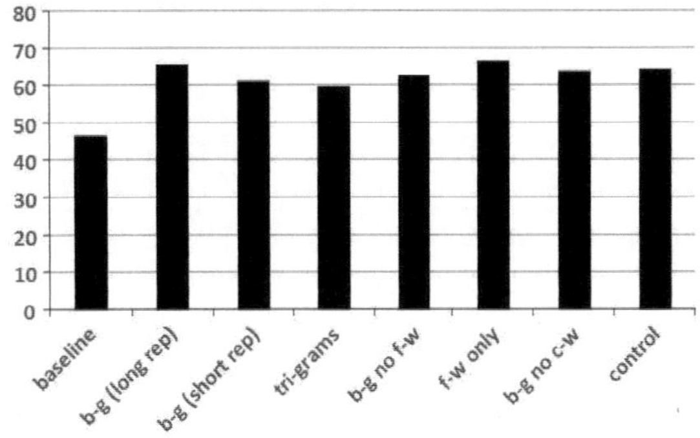

Figure 1: Classification accuracy of the different variations of document representation. b-g: bi-grams, f-w: function words, c-w: content words.

explain phenomena such as shallow language transfer through the use of function words, or content bias. The following sub-sections describe different variations of the experiment, ruling out the effect of these different types of bias.

4.1 Unigram Baseline

We first implemented a naive baseline classifier. We represented each document by the normalized frequencies of the (de-capitalized) letters it contains[2]. These frequencies are simply a unigram model of the sub-corpora. Using the multi-class SVM (Witten and Frank, 2005) we obtained 46.78% accuracy. This accuracy is more than twice the random baseline accuracy. This result is in accordance with our bi-grams results. Our discussion focuses on bi-grams rather than unigrams because the former's results are much higher and because bi-grams are much closer to the phonology of the language (for alphabetic scripts, of course).

4.2 Bi-grams Based Classification

Choosing the 200 most frequent character bi-grams in the corpus, we used a vector of the same dimension. Each vector entry contained the normalized frequency of one of the bi-grams. Using a multi-class SVM in a 10-fold cross validation manner we

[2]White spaces were considered a letter. However, sequences of white spaces and tabs were collapsed to a single white space. All the experiments that make use of character frequencies were performed twice, including and excluding punctuation marks. Results for both experiments are similar, therefore all the numbers reported in this paper are based on letters and punctuation marks.

	Bulg.	Czech	French	Russian	Spanish
dr	**170**	183	n/a	195	n/a
am	**117**	135	142	140	152
m_	121	120	133	**119**	139
iv	**104**	138	144	148	148
_y	**161**	181	196	183	166
la	122	123	122	142	**105**

Table 1: Some of the separating bi-grams found in the feature selection process. '_' indicates a white space. The numbers are the frequency ranking of the bi-grams in each sub-corpus (e.g., there are 103 bi-grams more frequent than 'iv' in the Bulgarian corpus). n/a indicates that this bi-gram is not one of the 200 most frequent bi-grams of the sub-corpus.

achieved 65.60% accuracy with standard deviation of 3.99.

The bi-grams features in the 200 dimensional vector are the 200 most frequent bi-grams in the whole corpus, regardless of their frequency in each sub-corpus. We note that the effect of misspelled words on the 200 most frequent bi-grams is negligible.

A more sophisticated feature selection could reduce the dimension of the representation vector without detracting from the results. Careful feature selection can also give a better intuition regarding the support vectors. We performed feature selection in the following manner: we chose the top 200 bi-grams of each sub-corpus, getting 245 unique bi-grams in total. We then chose all the bi-grams that were ranked significantly higher or significantly lower in one language than in at least one other language, assuming that those bi-grams have strong separating power. With the threshold of significance set to 20 we obtained 84 separating bi-grams. Table 1 shows some of the separating bi-grams thus found. For example, 'la' is a good separator between Russian and Spanish (its rank in the Spanish corpus is much higher than that in the Russian corpus), but not between other pairs.

Using only those 84 bigrams we obtained classification accuracy of 61.38%, a drop of only 4% compared to the results achieved with the 200 dimensional vectors. These results show that increasing the dimension of the representation vector using additional bi-grams contribute a marginal improvement while it does not introduce substantial noise.

4.3 Using Tri-gram Frequencies as Features

Repeating the same experiment with the top 200 tri-grams, we obtained an accuracy of 59.67%, which is 40% higher than the expected baseline and 15% higher than the uni-grams baseline. These results show that the texts in our corpus can be classified by only using naive n-gram models, while the optimal n of the n-gram is a different question that might be addressed in a different work (and might be language-dependent).

4.4 Function Words Based Classification

Function words are words that have a little lexical meaning but instead serve to express grammatical relations within a sentence or specify the attitude of the speaker (function words should not be confused with stopwords, although the lists of most frequent function words and the stopword list share a large subset). We used the same list of 460 function words used by Koppel et al (2005a). A partial list includes: {*a, afterward, although, because, cannot, do, enter, eventually, fifteenth, hither, hath, hence, lastly, occasionally, presumable, said, seldom, undoubtedly, was*}.

In this variation of the experiment, we represented each document only by the relative frequencies of the function words it contained. Using the same experimental setup as before, we achieved an accuracy of 66.7%. These results are less surprising than the results obtained by the character n-grams vectors, since we do expect native speakers of a certain language to use, misuse or ignore certain function words as a result from language transfer mechanisms (Odlin, 1989). For example, it is well known that native speakers of Russian tend to omit English articles.

4.5 Function Words Bias

The previous results suggest that the n-gram based classification is simply the result of the different uses of function words by speakers of different native languages. In order to rule out the effect of the function words on the bi-gram-based classification, we removed all function words from the corpus, recalculated the bi-gram frequencies and ran the experiment once again, this time achieving an accuracy of 62.92% in the 10-fold cross validation test.

These results, obtained on the function words-free corpus, clearly show that n-gram based classification is not a mere artifact masking the use of function words.

4.6 Content Bias

Bi-gram frequencies could also reflect content bias rather than language use. By content bias we mean that the subject matter of the documents in the different sub-corpora could exhibit internal sub-corpus uniformity and external sub-corpus disparity. In order to rule this out, we employed a variation on the Term Frequency – Inverted Document Frequency (*tf-idf*) content analysis metric.

The *tf-idf* measure is a statistical measure that is used in information retrieval tasks to evaluate how important a word/term is to a document in a collection or corpus (Salton and Buckley, 1988). Given a collection of documents D, the *tf-idf* weight of term t in a document $d \in D$ is computed as follows:

$$tfidf_t = f_{t,d} \times log\frac{|D|}{f_{t,D}}$$

where $f_{t,d}$ is the frequency of term t in document d, and $f_{t,D}$ is the number of documents in which t appears. Therefore, the weight of term $t \in d$ is maximal if it is a common term in d while the number of documents it appears in is relatively low.

We used the *tf-idf* weights in the information retrieval sense in order to discover the dominant content words of each sub-corpus. We treated each subcorpus (set of documents by writers who share a native language) as a single document and calculated the *tf-idf* of each word. In order to determine whether there is a content bias or not, we set a dominance threshold, and removed all words such that the difference between their *tf-idf* score in two different sub-corpora is higher than the dominance threshold. Given a threshold *t*, the *dominance* $D_{w,t}$, of a token w is given by:

$$D_{w,t} = max_{i,j}|tfidf_{w,i} - tfidf_{w,j}|$$

where $tfidf_{w,k}$ is the *tf-idf* score of token w in sub-corpus k. Changing the threshold in 0.0005 intervals, we removed from 1 to 340 unique content words (between 1,545 and 84,725 word tokens in total). However, the classification accuracy was essentially the same (see Figure 2), with a slight drop of only 2% after removing 51 content words (by using a threshold of 0.0015).

Word	Bulg.	Czech	Fr.	Rus.	Spa.
europe	0	0.3	2.7	0.2	0.2
european	0	0.3	3	0.1	0.5
imagination	4.3	2	0.8	1	0.8
television	0	3.6	1.9	3.1	0.3
women	0.4	1.7	1.2	5.5	2.6

Table 2: The *tf-idf* score of some of the most dominant words, multiplied by 1,000 for easier reading.

Subcorpus	content words	function words	unique stems
Bulgarian	1543	94685	11325
Czech	2784	110782	12834
French	2059	67016	9474
Russian	2730	112410	12338
Spanish	2985	108052	12627
Total	12101	492945	36474

Table 3: Numbers of dominant content words (with a threshold of 0.0025) and function words that were removed from each sub-corpus. The unique stems column indicates the number of unique stems (types) that remained after removal of *c-w* and *f-w*.

We calculated the *tf-idf* weights after stop-words removal and stemming (using a Porter stemmer (Porter, 1980)), trying to pinpoint dominant stems. The results were similar to the word's *tf-idf* and no significantly dominant stem was found in either of the sub-corpora.

A drop of only 3% in accuracy was noticed after removing both dominant content words and function words. These results show that if a content bias exists in the corpus it has only a minor effect on the SVM classification, and that the n-grams based clas-

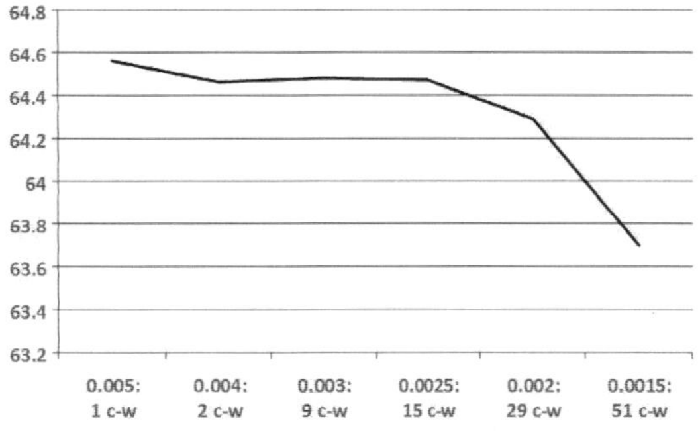

Figure 2: Classification accuracy as a function of the threshold (removed content words).

Thresh.	0.004 2 *c-w*	0.003 9 *c-w*	0.0025 15 *c-w*	0.0015 51 *c-w*	0.001 113 *c-w*
Bulg.	77	908	1543	3955	7426
Czech	306	1829	2784	5139	8588
French	665	1829	2059	3603	6205
Russian	781	1886	2730	6302	9918
Spanish	389	1418	2985	6548	10521
Total	2218	7970	12101	25547	42658

Table 4: Number of occurrences of content words that were removed from each sub-corpus for some of the thresholds. The numbers in the top row indicate the threshold and the number of unique content words that were found with this threshold.

sification is not an artifact of a content bias.

We ran the same experiment five more times, each time on 4 sub-corpora instead of 5, removing one (different) language each time. The results in all 5 4-class experiments were essentially the same, and similar to those of the 5 language task (beyond the fact that the random baseline for the former is 25% rather than 20%).

4.7 Suffix Bias

Bias might also be attributed to the use of suffixes. There are numerous types of English suffixes, which, roughly speaking, may be categorized as derivational or inflectional. It is reasonable to expect that just like a use of function words, use or misuse of certain suffixes might occur due to language transfer. Frequent use of a certain suffix or avoidance of the use of a certain suffix may influence the bi-grams statistics and thus the bi-grams classification may be only an artifact of the suffixes usage.

Checking the use of the 50 most productive suffixes taken from a standard list (e.g. *ing, ed, less, able, most, en*) we have found that only a small number of suffixes are not equally used by speakers of all 5 languages. Most notable are the differences in the use of *ing* between native French speakers and native Czech speakers and the differences of use of *less* between Bulgarian and Spanish speakers (Table 5). However, no real bias can be attributed to the use of any of the suffixes because their relative aggregate effect on the values in the support vector entries is very small.

Suffix	Bulg.	Czech	French	Russian	Spanish
ing	872	719	932	903	759
less	47	36	39	45	32

Table 5: Counts of two of the suffixes whose frequency of use differs the most between sub-corpora.

4.8 Control Corpus

Finally, we have also ran the experiment on a different corpus replacing the French and the Spanish sub-corpora by the Dutch and Italian ones, introducing a new Roman language and a new Germanic language to the corpus. We obtained 64.66% accuracy, essentially the same as in the original 5-language setting.

The corpus was compiled from works of advanced English students of the same level who write essays of approximately the same length, on a set of randomly and roughly equally distributed topics. We expected that these students will use roughly the same n-grams distribution. However, the results described above suggest that there exists some mechanism that influences the authors' choice of words. In the next section we present a computational psycholinguistic framework that might explain our results.

5 Statistical Learning and Language Transfer in SLA

5.1 Statistical Learning by Infants

Psychologists, linguists, and cognitive science researchers try to understand the process of language learning by infants. Many models for language learning and cognitive language modeling were suggested (Clark, 2003).

Infants learn their first language by a combination of speech streams, vocal cues and body gestures. Infants as young as 8 months old have a limited grasp of their native tongue as they react to familiar words. In that age they already understand the meaning of single words, they learn to spot these words in a speech stream, and very soon they learn to combine different words into new sentential units. Parental speech stream analysis shows that it is impossible to separate between words by identifying sequences of silence between words (Saffran, 2001). Recent studies of infant language learning are in favor of the statistical framework (Saffran, 2001; Saffran et al, 1996). Saffran (2002) examined 8 month-old to one year-old infants who were stimulated by speech sequences. The infants showed a significant discrimination between word and non-word stimuli. In a different experimental setup infants showed a significant discrimination between frequent syllable n-grams and non frequent syllable n-grams, heard as part of a gibberish speech sequence generated by a computer according to various statistical language models. In a third experimental setup infants showed a significant discrimination in favor of English-like gibberish speech sequences upon non-English-like gibberish speech sequences. These findings along with the established finding (Jusczyk, 1997) that infants prefer the sound of their native tongue suggest that humans learn basic language units in a statistical manner and that they store some statistical parameters pertaining to these units. We should note that some researchers doubt these conclusions (Yang, 2004).

5.2 Language Transfer in SLA

The role of the first language in second language acquisition is under a continuous debate (Ellis, 1999). *Language Transfer* between L1 and L2 is the process in which a language learner of L2 whose native language is L1, is influenced by L1 when using L2 (actually, when building his/her inter-language). This influence might appear helpful when L2 is relatively close to L1, but it interferes with the learning process due to over- and under-generalization or other problems. Although there is clear evidence that language learners use constructs of their first language when learning a foreign language (James, 1980; Odlin, 1989), it is not clear that the majority of learner errors can be attributed to the L1 transfer (Ellis, 1999).

5.3 Sound Transfer Hypothesis

For alphabetic scripts, character bi-grams reflect basic sounds and sound sequences of the language[3]. We have shown that native language strongly correlates with character bi-grams when people write in English as a second language. After ruling out usage of function words, content bias, and morphology-related influences, the most plausible explanation is that these are language transfer effects related to L1 sounds.

We hypothesize that there are language transfer effects related to L1 sounds and manifested by the words that people choose to use when writing in a second language. (We say 'writing' because we have only experimented with written texts; a more general hypothesis covering speaking and writing can be formulated as well.)

Furthermore, since the acquisition and representation of phonology is strongly influenced by statistical considerations (Section 5.1), we speculate that the general language transfer phenomenon might be related to frequency. This does not directly follow from our findings, of course, but is an exciting direction to investigate, and it is in accordance with the growing body of work on the effects of frequency on language learning and the emergence of syntax (Ellis, 2002; Bybee, 2006).

We note that there is one obvious and well-known lexical transfer effect: the usage of cognates (words that have similar form (sound) and meaning in two different languages). However, the languages we used in our experiments contain radically differing amounts of cognates of English words (just consider French vs. Bulgarian, for example), while the classification results were about the same for all 5 languages. Hence, cognates might play a role, but they do not constitute a single major explaining factor for our findings.

We note that the hypothesis put forward in the present paper is the first that attributes a language transfer phenomenon to a cognitive representation (phonology) whose statistical nature has been seriously substantiated.

6 Conclusion

In this paper we have demonstrated how modern machine learning can aid other fields, here the important field of Second Language Acquisition (SLA). Our analysis of the features useful for a multi-class SVM in the task of native language classification has resulted in the formulation of a hypothesis of potential significance in the theory of language transfer in SLA. We hypothesize language transfer effects at the level of basic sounds and short sound sequences, manifested by the words that people choose when

[3]Note that for English, they do not directly correspond to phonemes or syllables. Nonetheless, they do reflect English phonology to some extent.

writing in a second language. In other words, we hypothesize that use of L2 words is strongly influenced by L1 sounds and sound patterns.

As noted above, further experiments (psychological and computational) must be conducted for validating our hypothesis. In particular, construction of a wide-scale learners' corpus with tight control over content bias is essential for reaching stronger conclusions.

Additional future work should address sound sequences vs. the orthographic sequences that were used in this work. If our hypothesis is correct, then using spoken language corpora should produce even stronger results, since (1) writing systems rarely show a 1-1 correspondence with how words are at the phonological level; and (2) writing allows more conscious thinking that speaking, thus potentially reduces transfer effects. Our eventual goal is creating a unified model of statistical transfer mechanisms.

References

Argamon S., Koppel M. and Shimoni A. 2003. *Gender, Genre, and Writing Style in Formal Written Texts*. Text 23(3).

Bouselmi G., Fohr D., Illina, I., and Haton J.P. 2005. *Fully Automated Non-Native Speech Recognition Using Confusion-Based Acoustic Model*. Eurospeech/Interspeech '05.

Bouselmi G., Fohr D., Illina I., and Haton J.P. 2006. *Fully Automated Non-Native Speech Recognition Using Confusion-Based Acoustic Model Integration and Graphemic Constraints*. IEEE International Conference on Acoustics, Speech and Signal Processing, 2006.

Bybee J. 2006. *Frequency of Use and the Organization of Language*. Oxford University Press.

Clark, E. 2003. *First Language Acquisition*. Cambridge University Press.

Diederich J., Kindermann J., Leopold E. and Paass G. 2004. *Authorship Attribution with Support Vector Machines*. Applied Intelligence, 109–123.

Ellis N. 2002. *Frequency Effects in Language Processing*. Studies in Second Language Acquisition, 24(2):143–188.

Ellis R. 1999. *Understanding Second Language Acquisition*. Oxford University Press.

Granger S., Dagneaux E. and Meunier F. 2002. *International Corpus of Learner English*. Presses universitaires de Louvain.

Hansen J. H., Yapanel U., Huang, R. and Ikeno A. 2004. *Dialect Analysis and Modeling for Automatic Classification*. Interspeech-2004/ICSLP-2004: International Conference Spoken Language Processing. Jeju Island, South Korea.

Holmes D. and Forsyth R. 1995. *The Federalist Revisited: New Directions in Authorship Attribution*. Literary and Linguistic Computing, pp. 111–127.

James C. E. 1980. *Contrastive Analysis*. New York: Longman.

Jusczyk P. W. 1997. *The Discovery of Spoken Language*. MIT Press.

Koppel M. and Schler J. 2003. *Exploiting Stylistic Idiosyncrasies for Authorship Attribution*. In Proceedings of IJCAI '03 Workshop on Computational Approaches to Style Analysis and Synthesis. Acapulco, Mexico.

Koppel M., Schler J. and Zigdon K. 2005(a). *Determining an Author's Native Language by Mining a Text for Errors*. Proceedings of KDD '05. Chicago IL.

Koppel M., Schler J. and Zigdon K. 2005(b). *Automatically Determining an Anonymous Author's Native Language*. In Intelligence and Security Informatics (pp. 209–217). Berlin / Heidelberg: Springer.

Odlin T. 1989. *Language Transfer: Cross-Linguistic Influence in Language Learning*. Cambridge University Press.

Porter F. M. 1980. *An Algorithm for Suffix Stripping*. Program, 14(3):130–137.

Saffran J. R. 2001. *Words in a Sea of Sounds: The Output of Statistical Learning*. Cognition, 81, 149–169.

Saffran J. R. 2002. *Constraints on Statistical Language Learning*. Journal of Memory and Language, 47, 172–196.

Saffran J. R., Aslin R. N. and Newport E. N. 1996. *Statistical Learning by 8-month Old Infants*. Science, issue 5294, 1926–1928.

Salton G. and Buckley C. 1988. *Term Weighing Approaches in Automatic Text Retrieval*. Information Processing and Management, 24(5):513–523.

Schölkopf B,. Smola A 2002. *Learning with Kernels*. MIT Press.

Stamatatos E,. Fakotakis N. and Kokkinakis G. 2004. *Computer-Based Authorship Attribution Without Lexical Measures*. Computers and the Humanities, 193–214.

Witten I. H. and Frank E. 2005. *Data Mining: Practical Machine Learning Tools and Techniques*. San Francisco: Morgan Kaufmann.

Yang C. 2004. *Universal Grammar, Statistics, or Both?*. Trends in Cognitive Science 8(10):451–456, 2004.

Phon 1.2: A Computational Basis for Phonological Database Elaboration and Model Testing

Yvan Rose[1], Gregory J. Hedlund[1], Rod Byrne[2], Todd Wareham[2], Brian MacWhinney[3]

[1]Department of Linguistics
Memorial University of Newfoundland

[2]Department of Computer Science
Memorial University of Newfoundland

[3]Department of Psychology
Carnegie Mellon University

yrose@mun.ca, ghedlund@cs.mun.ca, rod@cs.mun.ca, harold@cs.mun.ca, macw@cmu.edu

Abstract

This paper discusses a new, open-source software program, called Phon, that is designed for the transcription, coding, and analysis of phonological corpora. Phon provides support for multimedia data linkage, segmentation, multiple-blind transcription, transcription validation, syllabification, alignment of target and actual forms, and data analysis. All of these functions are available through a user-friendly graphical interface. Phon, available on most computer platforms, supports data exchange among researchers with the TalkBank XML document format and the Unicode character set.. This program provides the basis for the elaboration of PhonBank, a database project that seeks to broaden the scope of CHILDES into phonological development and disorders.

1 Introduction

Empirical studies of natural language and language acquisition will always be required in most types of linguistic research. These studies provide the basis for describing languages and linguistic patterns. In addition to providing us with baseline data, empirical data allow us to test theoretical, neurological, psychological and computational models. However, the construction of natural language corpora is an extremely tedious and resource-consuming process, despite tremendous advances in data recording, storage, and coding methods in recent decades.

Thanks to corpora and tools such as those developed in the context of the CHILDES project (http://childes.psy.cmu.edu/), researchers in areas such as morphology and syntax have enjoyed a convenient and powerful method to analyze the morphosyntactic properties of adult languages and their acquisition by first and second language learners. In the area of phonetics, the Praat system (http://www.fon.hum.uva.nl/praat/) has expanded our abilities to conduct phonological modeling, computational simulations based on a variety of theoretical approaches, and articulatory synthesis.

In this rapidly-expanding software universe, phonologists interested in the organization of sound systems (e.g. phones, syllables, stress and intonational patterns) and their acquisition have not yet enjoyed the same level of computational support. There is no developed platform for phonological analysis and no system for data-sharing parallel to that found in CHILDES. Unfortunately, this situation negatively affects the study of natural language phonology and phonological development. It also undermines potential studies pertaining to interfaces between various components of the grammar or the elaboration of computational models of language or language development.

It is largely accepted that the grammar is hierarchically organized such that larger domains (e.g. a sentence or a phrase) provide the conditioning environments for patterns occurring in the domains

Proceedings of the Workshop on Cognitive Aspects of Computational Language Acquisition, pages 17–24,
Prague, Czech Republic, June 2007

located lower in the hierarchy (e.g. the word or the syllable), as indicated in Figure 1.

Syntax (e.g. word order)
|
Morphology (e.g. stems, affixes)
|
Phonology (e.g. syllables, sounds)
|
Phonetics (e.g. FØ, formant structure)

Figure 1: General grammatical hierarchy

This hierarchical view of grammatical organization allows us to make reference to factors that link phonology to syntax. For example, in English, the phonological phrase, a domain that constrains phonological phenomena such as intonation, is best described using syntactic criteria (e.g. Selkirk 1986). Data on the acquisition of these grammatical structures and their phonological consequences can help us understand how they are learned and assimilated by the learner.

In this paper we discuss Phon 1.2, the current version of an open-source software program that offers significant methodological advances in research in phonology and phonological development. On the one hand, Phon provides a powerful and flexible solution for phonological corpus elaboration and analysis. On the other hand, its ability to integrate with other open-source software will facilitate the construction of complete analyses across all levels of grammatical organization represented in Figure 1.

The paper is organized as follows. In section 2, we discuss the general motivation behind the Phon project. In section 3, we discuss the current functionality supported in Phon 1.2. In section 4, we offer a glance at future plans for this project. Section 5 provides a final summary.

2 The PhonBank Project

PhonBank, the latest initiative within the CHILDES project, focuses on the construction of corpora suitable for phonological and phonetic analysis. In this section we first describe the goals and orientations of PhonBank. We then describe Phon, the software project designed to facilitate this endeavor.

2.1 PhonBank

The PhonBank project seeks to broaden the scope of the current CHILDES system to include the analysis of phonological development in first and second languages for language learners with and without language disorders. To achieve this goal, we will create a new phonological database called PhonBank and a program called Phon to facilitate analysis of PhonBank data. Using these tools, researchers will be in position to conduct a series of developmental, crosslinguistic, and methodological analyses based on large-scale corpora.

2.2 Phon

Phon consists of inter-connected modules that offer functionality to assist the researcher in important tasks related to corpus transcription, coding and analysis. (The main functions supported are discussed in the next section.)

The application is developed in Java and is packaged to run on Macintosh (Mac OS X 10.4+) and Windows (Vista not tested yet) platforms.[1] Phon is Unicode-compliant, a required feature for the sharing of data transcribed with phonetic symbols across computer platforms. Phon can share data with programs which utilize the TalkBank XML schema for their documents such as those provided by the TalkBank and CHILDES projects. Phon is available as free download directly from CHILDES (http://childes.psy.cmu.edu/phon/).

At the time of writing these lines, Phon is available in its version 1.1, an iteration of the program that offered a proof of concept for the application envisioned (see Rose et al., 2006). Over the past year, however, we have thoroughly revised significant portions of the code to refine the functionality, ensure further compatibility with other TalkBank-compliant applications, and streamline the interface for better user experience and improved workflow. Despite what the minor version increment (1.1 to 1.2) may imply, the new version, which is currently being tested internally and due for public release in June 2007, offers significant improvements as well as novel and innovative functionality.

[1] Support for the Unix/Linux platform is currently compromised, primarily because of licensing issues related to the multimedia functions of the application.

3 Phon 1.2

As illustrated in Figure 2, the general interface of Phon 1.2 consists of a media centre (top left of the interface), a section for metadata (e.g. recorded participants and their linguistic profiles; bottom left) and a Transcript Editor, the interface that provides access to most of the functionality (right).

Figure 2: Phon 1.2 General Interface

One of the most significant improvements brought to version 1.2 comes from the integration of common tasks within the same user interface. In the previous version, completely separate interfaces had to be accessed to achieve the following tasks, all of which are required in the elaboration of any corpus:

- Media linkage and segmentation.
- Data transcription and validation (including support for multiple-blind transcriptions).
- Segmentation of transcribed utterances (into e.g. phrases, words).
- Labeling of transcribed forms for syllabification.
- Phone and syllable alignment between target (expected) and actual (produced) forms.

As a result the user often had to navigate between various modules in order to accomplish relatively simple operations. For example, a simple modification to a transcription required, in addition to the modification itself, revalidation of the data, and then a verification of the syllabification and alignment data generated from this revised transcription, each of these steps requiring access to and subsequent exit from a separate module.

In Phon 1.2, most of this hurdle has been alleviated through an integration of most of the functions into the Transcript Editor, while the others (e.g. media linkage and segmentation; transcript validation) are accessed directly from the general interface, without a need to exit the Transcript Editor. In the next subsections, we describe the main functions supported by the application.[2]

3.1 Media linkage and segmentation

As mentioned above, linkage of multimedia data and subsequent identification of the portions of the recorded media that are relevant for analysis are now available directly from the application's main interface. These tasks follow the same logic as similar systems in programs like CLAN (http://childes.psy.cmu.edu/clan/). In addition to its integrated interface, Phon 1.2 offers support for linking different portions to a single transcript to different media files.

3.2 Data transcription

The Transcript Editor now incorporates in a single interface access to data transcription and annotation, transcription segmentation, syllabification and alignment. This module is illustrated in more detail with the screen shot of a data record (corresponding to an utterance) in Figure 3.

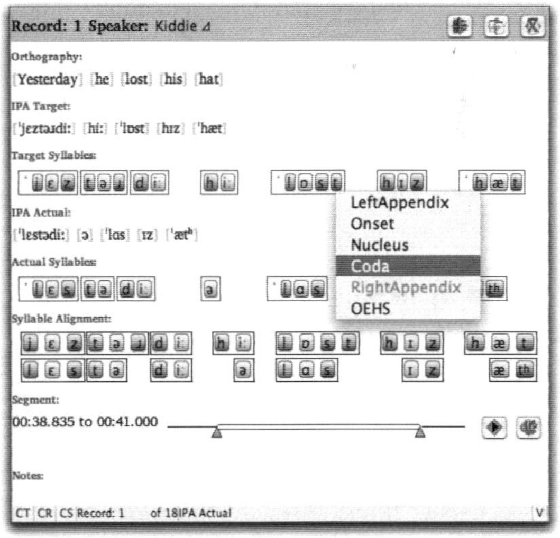

Figure 3: Data record in Transcript Editor

[2] Additional functions, such as user management, are also supported by Phon; we will however restrict ourselves to the most central functions of the program.

As can be seen, the interface incorporates tiers for orthographic and phonetic transcriptions as well as other textual annotations. Phon also provides support for an unlimited number of user-defined fields that can be used for all kinds of textual annotations that may be relevant to the coding of a particular dataset. All fields can be ordered to accommodate specific data visualization needs. Phonetic transcriptions are based on the phonetic symbols and conventions of the International Phonetic Association (IPA). A useful IPA character map is easily accessible from within the application, in the shape of a floating window within which IPA symbols and diacritics are organized into intuitive categories. This map facilitates access to the IPA symbols for which there is no keyboard equivalent.

Target and actual IPA transcriptions are stored internally as strings of phonetic symbols. Each symbol is automatically associated with a set of descriptive features generally accepted in the fields of phonetics and phonology (e.g. bilabial, alveolar, voiced, voiceless, aspirated) (Ladefoged and Maddieson, 1996). These features are extremely useful in the sense that they provide series of descriptive labels to each transcribed symbol. The availability of these labels is essential for research involving the grouping of various sounds into natural classes (e.g. voiced consonants; non-high front vowels). The built-in set of features can also be reconfigured as needed to fit special research needs.

Phon 1.2 is also equipped with functionality to automatically insert IPA Target transcriptions based on the orthographic transcriptions. Citation form IPA transcriptions of these words are currently available for English and French. The English forms were obtained from the CMU Pronouncing Dictionary (www.speech.cs.cmu.edu/cgi-bin/cmudict); the French forms were obtained from the Lexique Project database (www.lexique.org).

In cases when more than one pronunciation are available from the built-in dictionaries for a given written form (e.g. the present and past tense versions of the English word 'read'), the application provides a quick way to select the wanted form.

Of course, idealized citation forms do not provide accurate fine-grained characterizations of variations in the target language (e.g. dialect-specific pronunciation variants; phonetic details such as degree of aspiration in obstruent stops). They however typically provide a useful general baseline against which patterns can be identified.

1.1 Media playback and exporting

Actual forms (e.g. the forms produced by a language learner) must be transcribed manually. Transcript validation, the task described in the next section, also requires access to the recorded data. To facilitate these tasks, Phon provides direct access to the segmented portions of the media for playback in each record (see the 'Segment' tier in Figure 3). The beginning and end times of these segments can be edited directly from the record, which facilitates an accurate circumscription of the relevant portions of the recorded media. Finally, Phon can export the segmented portions of the media into a sound file, which enables quick acoustic verifications using sound visualizing software such as Praat (http://www.fon.hum.uva.nl/praat/), SFS (http://www.phon.ucl.ac.uk/resource/sfs/), Signalyze (http://www.signalyze.com/) or CSL (http://www.kayelemetrics.com/).

1.2 Transcript validation

In projects where only a single transcription of the recorded data is utilized, this transcription can be entered directly in the Transcript Editor. In projects that rely on a multiple-blind transcription method, each transcription for a given form is stored separately. To appear in the Transcript Editor, a blind transcription must be selected through the Transcript Validation mode. This interface allows the transcription supervisor (or, in a better setting, a team of supervisors working together) to compare competing transcriptions and resolve divergences. Alternative, non-validated transcriptions are preserved for data recoverability and verification purposes. They are however unavailable for further processing, coding or analysis.

1.3 Transcription segmentation

Researchers often wish to divide transcribed utterances into specific domains such as the phrase or the word. Phon fulfills this need by incorporating a text segmentation module that enables the identification of strings of symbols corresponding to such morphosyntactic and phonological domains. For example, using the syllabification module described immediately below, the researcher can test hypotheses about what domains are relevant for resyllabification processes across words. Word-level segmentation is exemplified in Figure 3, as can be seen from the gray bracketing circumscribing each word. Not readily visible from this interface however is the important fact that the bracketing enforces a logical organization between Orthographic, IPA Target and IPA Actual forms, the latter two being treated as daughter nodes directly related to their corresponding parent bracketed form in the Orthography tier. This system of tier dependency offers several analytical advantages, for example for the identification of patterns that can relate to a particular grammatical category or position within the utterance.

In addition to the textual entry fields just described, the Transcript Editor contains color-coded graphical representations of syllabification information for both IPA Target and IPA Actual forms as well as for the segmental and syllabic alignment of these forms.

1.4 Syllabification algorithm

Once the researcher has identified the domains that are relevant for analysis, segmentation at the level of the syllable is performed automatically: segments are assigned descriptive syllable labels (visually represented with colors) such as 'onset' or 'coda' for consonants and 'nucleus' for vowels. The program also identifies segmental sequences within syllable constituents (e.g. complex onsets or nuclei). Since controversy exists in both phonetic and phonological theory regarding guidelines for syllabification, the algorithm is parameterized to allow for analytical flexibility. The availability of different parameter settings also enables the researcher to test hypotheses on which analysis makes the best prediction for a given dataset. Phon 1.2 contains built-in syllabification algorithms for both English and French. The algorithm for English incorporates fine distinctions such as those proposed by Davis and Hammond (1995) for the syllabification of on-glides. Both algorithms are based on earlier work by, e.g. Selkirk (1982) and Kaye and Lowenstamm (1984), the latter also documenting the most central properties of French syllabification. While these algorithms use specific syllable positions such as the left appendix (utilized to identify strident fricatives at the left-edge of triconsonantal onset clusters; e.g. 'strap'), a simple syllabification algorithm is also supplied, which restricts syllable position to onset, nucleus and coda only. Additional algorithms (for other languages or assuming different syllable constructs) can easily be added to the program.

Our currently-implemented syllabification algorithms use a scheme based on a composition-cascade of seven deterministic FSTs (Finite State Tools). This cascade takes as input a sequence of phones and produces a sequence of phones and associated syllable-constituent symbols, which is subsequently parsed to create the full multi-level metrical structure. The initial FST in the cascade places syllable nuclei and the subsequent FSTs establish and adjust the boundaries of associated onset- and coda-domains. Changes in the definition of syllable nuclei in the initial FST and/or the ordering and makeup of the subsequent FSTs give language-specific syllabification algorithms. To ease the development of this cascade, initial FST prototypes were written and tested using the Xerox Finite-State Tool (xFST) (Beesley and Karttunen 2003). However, following the requirements of easy algorithm execution within and integration into Phon, these FSTs were subsequently coded in Java. To date, the implemented algorithm has been tested on corpora from English and French, and has obtained accuracies of almost 100%.

Occasionally, the algorithm may produce spurious results or flag symbols as unsyllabified. This is particularly true in the case of IPA Actual forms produced by young language learners, which sometimes contain strings of sounds that are not attested in natural languages. Syllabification is generated on the fly upon transcription of IPA forms; the researcher can thus quickly verify all results and modify them through a contextual menu (represented in Figure 3) whenever needed. Segments that are left unsyllabified are available for all queries on segmental features and strings of segments, but are not available for queries referring to aspects of syllabification (see also Figure 4 for a closer look at the display of syllabification).

The syllabification labels can then be used in database query (for example, to access specific information about syllable onsets or codas). In addition, because the algorithm is sensitive to main and secondary stress marks and domain edges (i.e. first and final syllables), each syllable identified is given a prosodic status and position index. Using the search functions, the researcher can thus use search criteria as precisely defined as, for example, complex onsets realized in word-medial, secondary-stressed syllables. This level of functionality is central to the study of several phenomena in phonological acquisition that are determined by the status of the syllable as stressed or unstressed, or by the position of the syllable within the word (e.g. Inkelas and Rose 2003).

1.5 Alignment algorithm

After syllabification, a second algorithm performs automatic, segment-by-segment and syllable-by-syllable alignment of IPA-transcribed target and actual forms. Building on featural similarities and differences between the segments in each syllable and on syllable properties such as stress, this algorithm automatically aligns corresponding segments and syllables in target and actual forms. It provides alignments for both corresponding sounds and syllables. For example, in the target-actual word pair 'apricot' > 'a_cot', the algorithm aligns the first and final syllables of each form, and identifies the middle syllable ('pri') as truncated. This is illustrated in Figure 4. Similarly, in cases of renditions such as 'blow' > 'bolow' the alignment algorithm relates both syllables of the actual form to the only syllable of the target form and diagnoses a case of vowel epenthesis.

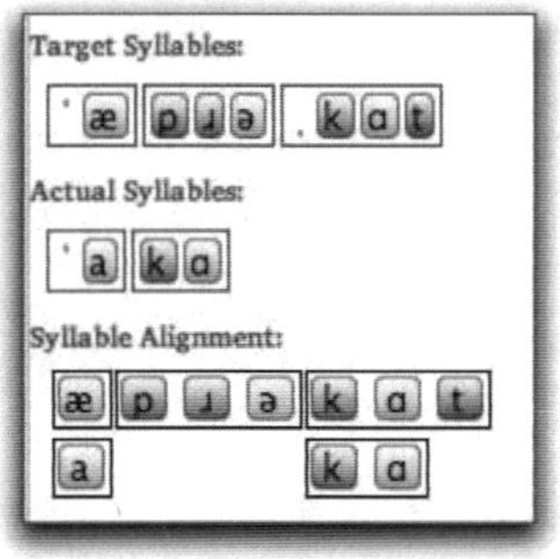

Figure 4: Syllabification and Alignment

In this alignment algorithm, forms are viewed as sequences of phones and syllable-boundary markers and the alignment is done on the phones in a way that preserves syllable integrity. This algorithm is a variant of the standard dynamic programming algorithm for pairwise global sequence alignment (see Sankoff and Kruskal 1983 and references therein); as such, it is similar to but extends the phone-alignment algorithm described in Kondrak (2003). At the core of the Phon alignment algorithm is a function *sim(x, y)* that assesses the degree of similarity of a symbol *x* from the first given sequence and a symbol *y* from the second given sequence. In our *sim()* function, the similarity value of phones *x* and *y* is a function of a basic score (which is the number of phonetic features shared by *x* and *y*) and the associated values of various applicable reward and penalty conditions, each of which encodes a linguistically-motivated constraint on the form of the alignment. There are nine such reward and penalty conditions, and the interaction of these rewards and penalties on phone matchings effectively simulates syllable integrity and matching constraints. Subsequent to this enhanced phone alignment, a series of rules is invoked to reintroduce the actual and target form syllable boundaries.

A full description of the alignment algorithm is given in Maddocks (2005) and Hedlund et al. (2005). Preliminary tests on attested data from the published literature on Dutch- and English-learning children (Fikkert, 1994; Pater, 1997) indicate an accuracy rate above 95% (96% for a Dutch corpus and 98% for an English corpus). As it is the case with the other algorithms included in the program, the user is able to perform manual adjustments of the computer-generated syllable alignments whenever necessary. This process was made as easy as possible: it consists of clicking on the segment that needs to be realigned and moving it leftward or rightward using keyboard arrows.

The alignment algorithm, as well as the data processing steps that precede it (especially, syllabification), are essential to any acquisition study that requires pair-wise comparisons between target and actual forms, from both segmental and syllabic perspectives.

Implicit to the description of the implementation of the syllabification and alignment functions is a careful approach whereby the algorithms implemented at this stage are used to assist data compilation; because every result generated by the algorithms can be modified by the user, no data analysis directly depends on them. The user thus has complete control on the processing of the data being readied for analysis. After extensive testing on additional types of data sets, we will be able to optimize their degree of reliability and then determined how they can be used in truly automated analyses.

1.6 Database query

Phon sports a simple search function built directly in the main interface (see Figure 2 above). More complex queries are now supported through a series of built-in analysis and reporting functions.

Using these functions, the research can identify records that contain:

- Phones and phone sequences (defined with IPA symbols or descriptive feature sets).
- Syllable types (e.g. CV, CVC, CGV, …).[3]
- Word types (e.g. number of syllables and the stress patterns that they compose).
- Segmental processes (obtained through featural comparisons between Target-Actual aligned phones; e.g. devoicing, gliding).
- Syllabic processes (obtained through comparisons between target-actual aligned syllables e.g. complex onset reduction).

Using these functions, the researcher can quickly identify the records that match the search criteria within the transcript. The reported data are visualized in tables which can be saved as comma-separated value text files (.csv) that can subsequently be open in statistical or spreadsheet applications. Using an expression builder, i.e. a system to combine simple searches using functions such as intersection and union, the researcher can also take advantage of more elaborate search criteria. The expression builder thus enables the study of interaction between factors such as feature combinations, stress, position within the syllable, word or any other larger domain circumscribed through the utterance segmentation function described above.

2 Future projects

Phon 1.2 now provides all the functionality required for corpus elaboration, as well as a versatile system for data extraction. In future versions, we will incorporate an interface for the management of acoustic data and fuller support for data querying and searching. At a later stage, we will construct a system for model testing. We discuss these plans briefly in the next subsections.

2.1 Interface for acoustic data

In order to facilitate research that requires acoustic measurements, Phon will also incorporate full interfacing with Praat and Speech Filing System, two software programs designed for acoustic analysis of speech sounds. As a result, researchers that utilize these programs will be able to take advantage of some of Phon's unique functions and, similarly, researchers using Phon will be able to take advantage of the functionality of these two applications.

2.2 Extension of database query functionality

The search and report functions described in section 3.8 provide simple and flexible tools to generate general assessments of the corpus or detect and extract particular phonological patterns. However, to take full advantage of all of the research potential that Phon offers, a more powerful query system will be designed. This system will take the form of a query language supplemented with statistical functions.

Such a system will enable precise assessments of developmental data within and across corpora of language learners or learning situations. The query language will also offer the relevant functionality to take full advantage of the module for management of acoustic data described in the preceding subsection.

2.3 Platform for model testing

As presently implemented, Phon will allow us to continue with the construction of PhonBank and will provide tools for analyzing the new database. Once this system is in place, we will begin to develop additional tools for model testing. These new systems will formalize learning algorithms in ways that will allow users to run these algorithms on stored data, much as in the "Learn" feature in Praat. This new model-testing application will include functions such as:

- Run an arbitrary language learning algorithm.
- Compare the results of the grammar produced by such a language learning algorithm against actual language data.
- In the event that the learning algorithm provides a sequence of grammars corresponding to the stages of human language learning, compare the results of this sequence of grammars against actual longitudinal language data.

By virtue of its software architecture, form-comparison routines, and stored data, Phon provides an excellent platform for implementing such an application. Running arbitrary language learn-

[3] C=consonant; V=vowel; G=glide.

ing algorithms could be facilitated using a Java API/interface-class combination specifying subroutines provided by Phon. The outputs of a given computational model could be compared against adult productions stored in Phon using the alignment algorithm described in Section 3.7 (which internally produces but does not output a score giving the similarity of the two forms being aligned). Finally, the outputs of a sequence of algorithm-produced grammars relative to a given target word could be compared against the sequence of productions of that word made over the course of acquisition by a particular learner by aligning these production sequences. Such an alignment could be done using the alignment algorithm described in Section 3.7 as a *sim()* function for matching up production-pairs in these sequences. In this case, more exotic forms of alignment such as local alignment or time-warping may be more appropriate than the global alignment used in Section 3.7. For a full description of such alignment options, see Gusfield (1997) and Sankoff and Kruskal (1983).

3 Discussion

In its current form, Phon 1.2 provides a powerful system for corpus transcription, coding and analysis. It also offers a sound computational foundation for the elaboration of the PhonBank database and its incorporation to the CHILDES system. Finally, it sets the basis for further improvements of its functionality, some of which was discussed briefly in the preceding section.

The model-testing tool design sketched above is ambitious and perhaps premature in some aspects —for example, should we expect the current (or even next) generation of language learning algorithms to mimic the longitudinal behavior of actual language learners? This question is especially relevant given that some language behaviors observed in learners can be driven by articulatory or perceptual factors, the consideration of which implies relatively more complex models. That being said, the above suggests how Phon, by virtue of its longitudinal data, output-form comparison routines, and software architecture, may provide an excellent platform for implementing the next generation of computational language analysis tools.

References

Beesley, K.R. and L. Karttunen (2003) *Finite-State Morphology*. Stanford CA: CSLI Publications.

Davis, S. and M. Hammond (1995). On the Status of Onglides in American English. *Phonology* 12:159-182.

Fikkert, P. (1994). *On the Acquisition of Prosodic Structure*. Dordrecht: ICG Printing.

Gusfield, D. (1997) *Algorithms on Strings, Trees, and Sequences: Computer Science and Computational Biology*. Cambridge: Cambridge University Press.

Hedlund, G.J., K. Maddocks, Y. Rose, and T. Wareham (2005) Natural Language Syllable Alignment: From Conception to Implementation. *Proceedings of the Fifteenth Annual Newfoundland Electrical and Computer Engineering Conference* (NECEC 2005).

Inkelas, S. and Y. Rose (2003). Velar Fronting Revisited. *Proceedings of the 27th Boston University Conference on Language Development*. Somerville, MA: Cascadilla Press. 334-345.

Kaye, J. and J. Lowenstamm (1984). De la syllabicité. *Forme sonore du langage*. Paris: Hermann, 123-161.

Kondrak, G. (2003) Phonetic alignment and similarity. *Computers and the Humanities* 37: 273-291.

Ladefoged, P. and I. Maddieson (1996). *The Sounds of the World's Languages*. Cambridge, MA: Blackwell.

Maddocks, K. (2005) An Effective Algorithm for the Alignment of Target and Actual Syllables for the Study of Language Acquisition. B.Sc.h. Thesis. Department of Computer Science, Memorial University of Newfoundland.

Pater, J. (1997). Minimal Violation and Phonological Development. *Language Acquisition* 6, 201-253.

Rose, Y., B. MacWhinney, R. Byrne, G. Hedlund, K. Maddocks, P. O'Brien and T. Wareham (2006). Introducing Phon: A Software Solution for the Study of Phonological Acquisition. *Proceedings of the 30th Boston University Conference on Language Development*. Somerville, MA: Cascadilla Press. 489-500.

Sankoff, D. and J.B. Kruskal (eds., 1983) *Time Warps, String Edits, and Macromolecules: The Theory and Practice of String Comparison*. Reading, MA: Addison-Wesley.

Selkirk, E. (1982) The Syllable. *The Structure of Phonological Representation*. Dordrecht: Foris, 337-385.

___ (1986) On Derived domains in Sentence Phonology. *Phonology* 3: 371-405.

High-accuracy Annotation and Parsing of CHILDES Transcripts

Kenji Sagae
Department of Computer Science
University of Tokyo
Hongo 7-3-1, Bunkyo-ku, Tokyo, Japan
sagae@is.s.u-tokyo.ac.jp

Eric Davis
Language Technologies Institute
Carnegie Mellon University
Pittsburgh, PA 15213
dhdavis@cs.cmu.edu

Alon Lavie
Language Technologies Institute
Carnegie Mellon University
Pittsburgh, PA 15213
alavie@cs.cmu.edu

Brian MacWhinney
Department of Psychology
Carnegie Mellon University
Pittsburgh, PA 15213
macw@cmu.edu

Shuly Wintner
Department of Computer Science
University of Haifa
31905 Haifa, Israel
shuly@cs.haifa.ac.il

Abstract

Corpora of child language are essential for psycholinguistic research. Linguistic annotation of the corpora provides researchers with better means for exploring the development of grammatical constructions and their usage. We describe an ongoing project that aims to annotate the English section of the CHILDES database with grammatical relations in the form of labeled dependency structures. To date, we have produced a corpus of over 65,000 words with manually curated gold-standard grammatical relation annotations. Using this corpus, we have developed a highly accurate data-driven parser for English CHILDES data. The parser and the manually annotated data are freely available for research purposes.

1 Introduction

In order to investigate the development of child language, corpora which document linguistic interactions involving children are needed. The CHILDES database (MacWhinney, 2000), containing transcripts of spoken interactions between children at various stages of language development with their parents, provides vast amounts of useful data for linguistic, psychological, and sociological studies of child language development. The raw information in CHILDES corpora was gradually enriched by providing a layer of morphological information. In particular, the English section of the database is augmented by part of speech (POS) tags for each word. However, this information is usually insufficient for investigations dealing with the syntactic, semantic or pragmatic aspects of the data.

In this paper we describe an ongoing effort aiming to annotate the English portion of the CHILDES database with syntactic information based on grammatical relations represented as labeled dependency structures. Although an annotation scheme for syntactic information in CHILDES data has been proposed (Sagae et al., 2004), until now no significant amount of annotated data had been made publicly available. In the process of manually annotating several thousands of words, we updated the annotation scheme, mostly by extending it to cover syntactic phenomena that occur in real data but were unaccounted for in the original annotation scheme.

The contributions of this work fall into three main categories: revision and extension of the annotation scheme for representing syntactic information in CHILDES data; creation of a manually annotated 65,000 word corpus with gold-standard syntactic analyses; and implementation of a complete parser that can automatically annotate additional data with high accuracy. Both the gold-standard annotated data and the parser are freely available. In addition to introducing the parser and the data, we report on many of the specific annotation issues that we encountered during the manual annotation pro-

Proceedings of the Workshop on Cognitive Aspects of Computational Language Acquisition, pages 25–32,
Prague, Czech Republic, June 2007

cess, which should be helpful for those who may use the annotated data or the parser. The annotated corpora and the parser are freely available from `http://childes.psy.cmu.edu/`.

We describe the annotation scheme in the next section, along with issues we faced during the process of manual annotation. Section 3 describes the parser, and an evaluation of the parser is presented in section 4. We analyze the remaining parsing errors in section 5 and conclude with some applications of the parser and directions for future research in section 6.

2 Syntactic annotation

The English section of the CHILDES database is augmented with automatically produced ambiguous part-of-speech and morphological tags (MacWhinney, 2000). Some of these data have been manually disambiguated, but we found that some annotation decisions had to be revised to facilitate syntactic annotation. We discuss below some of the revisions we introduced, as well as some details of the syntactic constructions that we account for.

2.1 The morphological annotation scheme

The English morphological analyzer incorporated in CHILDES produces various part-of-speech tags (there are 31 distinct POS tags in the CHILDES tagset), including ADJective, ADVerb, COmmunicator, CONJunction, DETerminer, FILler, Noun, NUMeral, ONomatopoeia, PREPosition, PROnoun, ParTicLe, QuaNtifier, RELativizer and Verb[1]. In most cases, the correct annotation of a word is obvious from the context in which the word occurs, but sometimes a more subtle distinction must be made. We discuss some common problematic issues below.

Adverb vs. preposition vs. particle The words *about, across, after, away, back, down, in, off, on, out, over, up* belong to three categories: ADVerb, PREPosition and ParTicLe. To correctly annotate them in context, we apply the following criteria.

First, a preposition must have a prepositional object, which is typically realized as a noun phrase (which may be topicalized, or even elided). Second, a preposition forms a constituent with its noun phrase object. Third, a prepositional object can be fronted (for example, *he sat on the chair* becomes *the chair on which he sat*), whereas a particle-NP sequence cannot (**the phone number up which he looked* cannot be obtained from *he looked up the phone number*). Finally, a manner adverb can be placed between the verb and a preposition, but not between a verb and a particle.

To distinguish between an adverb and a particle, the meaning of the head verb is considered. If the meaning of the verb and the target word, taken together, cannot be predicted from the meanings of the verb and the target word separately, then the target word is a particle. In all other cases it is an adverb.

Verbs vs. auxiliaries Distinguishing between Verb and AUXiliary is often straightforward, but special attention is given when tagging the verbs *be, do* and *have*. If the target word is accompanied by an non-finite verb in the same clause, as in *I have had enough* or *I do not like eggs*, it is an auxiliary. Additionally, in interrogative sentences, the auxiliary is moved to the beginning of the clause, as in <u>*have*</u> *I had enough?* and <u>*do*</u> *I like eggs?*, whereas the main verb is not. However, this test does not always work for the verb *be*, which may head a non-verbal predicate, as in *John* <u>*is*</u> *a teacher*, vs. *John* <u>*is*</u> *smiling*. In verb-participle constructions headed by the verb *be*, if the participle is in the progressive tense, then the head verb is labeled as auxiliary.

Communicators vs. locative adverbs COmmunicators can be hard to distinguish from locative adverbs, especially at the beginning of a sentence. Our convention is that CO must modify an entire sentence, so if a word appears by itself, it cannot be a CO. For example, utterances like *here* or *there* are labeled as ADVerb. However, if these words appear at the beginning of a sentence, are followed by a break or pause, and do not clearly express a location, then they are labeled CO. Additionally, in *here/there you are/go, here* and *there* are labeled CO.

2.2 The syntactic annotation scheme

Our annotation scheme for representing grammatical relations, or GRs (such as subjects, objects and adjuncts), in CHILDES transcripts is a slightly extended version of the scheme proposed by Sagae et al. (2004), which was inspired by a general annota-

[1]We use capital letters to denote the actual tag names in the CHILDES tagset.

tion scheme for grammatical relations (Carroll et al., 1998), but adapted specifically for CHILDES data. Our scheme contains 37 distinct GR types. Sagae et al. reported 96.5% interannotator agreement, and we do not believe our minor updates to the annotation scheme should affect interannotator agreement significantly.

The scheme distinguishes among SUBJects, (finite) Clausal SUBJects[2] (e.g., *that he cried moved her*) and XSUBJects (*eating vegetables is important*). Similarly, we distinguish among OBJects, OBJect2, which is the second object of a ditransitive verb, and IOBjects, which are required verb complements introduced by prepositions. Verb complements that are realized as clauses are labeled COMP if they are finite (*I think that was Fraser*) and XCOMP otherwise (*you stop throwing the blocks*). Additionally, we mark required locative adjectival or prepositional phrase arguments of verbs as LOCatives, as in *put the toys in the box/back*.

PREDicates are nominal, adjectival or prepositional complements of verbs such as *get*, *be* and *become*, as in *I'm not sure*. Again, we specifically mark Clausal PREDicates (*This is how I drink my coffee*) and XPREDicates (*My goal is to win the competition*).

Adjuncts (denoted by JCT) are optional modifiers of verbs, adjectives or adverbs, and we distinguish among non-clausal ones (*That's much better*; *sit on the stool*), finite clausal ones (CJCT, *Mary left after she saw John*) and non-finite clausal ones (XJCT, *Mary left after seeing John*).

MODifiers, which modify or complement nouns, again come in three flavors: MOD (*That's a nice box*); CMOD (*the movie that I saw was good*); and XMOD (*the student reading a book is tall*).

We then identify AUXiliary verbs, as in *did you do it?*; NEGation (*Fraser is not drinking his coffee*); DETerminers (*a fly*); QUANTifiers (*some juice*); the objects of prepositions (POBJ, *on the stool*); verb ParTicLes (*can you get the blocks out?*); ComPlementiZeRs (*wait until the noodles are cool*); COMmunicators (*oh, I took it*); the INfinitival *to*; VOCatives (*Thank you, Eve*); and TAG questions (*you know how to count, don't you?*).

[2]As with the POS tags, we use capital letters to represent the actual GR tags used in the annotation scheme.

Finally, we added some specific relations for handling problematic issues. For example, we use ENUMeration for constructions such as *one, two, three, go* or *a, b, c*. In COORDination constructions, each conjunct is marked as a dependent of the conjunction (e.g., *go and get your telephone*). We use TOPicalization to indicate an argument that is topicalized, as in *tapioca, there is no tapioca*. We use SeRiaL to indicate serial verbs as in *come see if we can find it* or *go play with your toys*. Finally, we mark sequences of proper names which form the same entity (e.g., *New York*) as NAME.

The format of the grammatical relation (GR) annotation, which we use in the examples that follow, associates with each word in a sentence a triple $i|j|g$, where i is the index of the word in the sentence, j the index of the word's syntactic head, and g is the name of the grammatical relation represented by the syntactic dependency between the i-th and j-th words. If the topmost head of the utterance is the i-th word, it is labeled `i|0|ROOT`. For example, in:

```
a          cookie      .
1|2|DET    2|0|ROOT    3|2|PUNCT
```

the first word *a* is a DETerminer of word 2 (*cookie*), which is itself the ROOT of the utterance.

2.3 Manual annotation of the corpus

We focused our manual annotation on a set of CHILDES transcripts for a particular child, Eve (Brown, 1973), and we refer to these transcripts, distributed in a set of 20 files, as the Eve corpus. We hand-annotated (including correcting POS tags) the first 15 files of the Eve corpus following the GR scheme outlined above. The annotation process started with purely manual annotation of 5,000 words. This initial annotated corpus was used to train a data-driven parser, as described later. This parser was then used to label an additional 20,000 words automatically, followed by a thorough manual checking stage, where each syntactic annotation was manually verified and corrected if necessary. We retrained the parser with the newly annotated data, and proceeded in this fashion until 15 files had been annotated and thoroughly manually checked.

Annotating child language proved to be challenging, and as we progressed through the data, we noticed grammatical constructions that the GRs could not adequately handle. For example, the original GR scheme did not differentiate between locative arguments and locative adjuncts, so we created a new GR label, LOC, to handle required verbal locative arguments such as *on* in *put it on the table*. *Put* licenses a prepositional argument, and the existing JCT relation could not capture this requirement.

In addition to adding new GRs, we also faced challenges with telegraphic child utterances lacking verbs or other content words. For instance, *Mommy telephone* could have one of several meanings: *Mommy this is a telephone*, *Mommy I want the telephone*, *that is Mommy's telephone*, etc. We tried to be as consistent as possible in annotating such utterances and determined their GRs from context. It was often possible to determine the VOC reading vs.the MOD (*Mommy's telephone*) reading by looking at context. If it was not possible to determine the correct annotation from context, we annotated such utterances as VOC relations.

After annotating the 15 Eve files, we had 18,863 fully hand-annotated utterances, 10,280 adult and 8,563 child. The utterances consist of 84,226 GRs (including punctuation) and 65,363 words. The average utterance length is 5.3 words (including punctuation) for adult utterances, 3.6 for child, 4.5 overall. The annotated Eve corpus is available at `http://childes.psy.cmu.edu/data/Eng-USA/brown.zip`. It was used for the *Domain adaptation task* at the CoNLL-2007 dependency parsing shared task (Nivre, 2007).

3 Parsing

Although the CHILDES annotation scheme proposed by Sagae et al. (2004) has been used in practice for automatic parsing of child language transcripts (Sagae et al., 2004; Sagae et al., 2005), such work relied mainly on a statistical parser (Charniak, 2000) trained on the Wall Street Journal portion of the Penn Treebank, since a large enough corpus of annotated CHILDES data was not available to train a domain-specific parser. Having a corpus of 65,000 words of CHILDES data annotated with grammatical relations represented as labeled dependencies allows us to develop a parser tailored for the CHILDES domain.

Our overall parsing approach uses a best-first probabilistic shift-reduce algorithm, working left-to-right to find labeled dependencies one at a time. The algorithm is essentially a dependency version of the data-driven constituent parsing algorithm for probabilistic GLR-like parsing described by Sagae and Lavie (2006). Because CHILDES syntactic annotations are represented as labeled dependencies, using a dependency parsing approach allows us to work with that representation directly.

This dependency parser has been shown to have state-of-the-art accuracy in the CoNLL shared tasks on dependency parsing (Buchholz and Marsi, 2006; Nivre, 2007)[3]. Sagae and Tsujii (2007) present a detailed description of the parsing approach used in our work, including the parsing algorithm. In summary, the parser uses an algorithm similar to the LR parsing algorithm (Knuth, 1965), keeping a stack of partially built syntactic structures, and a queue of remaining input tokens. At each step in the parsing process, the parser can apply a *shift* action (remove a token from the front of the queue and place it on top of the stack), or a *reduce* action (pop the two topmost stack items, and push a new item composed of the two popped items combined in a single structure). This parsing approach is very similar to the one used successfully by Nivre et al. (2006), but we use a maximum entropy classifier (Berger et al., 1996) to determine parser actions, which makes parsing extremely fast. In addition, our parsing approach performs a search over the space of possible parser actions, while Nivre et al.'s approach is deterministic. See Sagae and Tsujii (2007) for more information on the parser.

Features used in classification to determine whether the parser takes a shift or a reduce action at any point during parsing are derived from the parser's current configuration (contents of the stack and queue) at that point. The specific features used are:[4]

- Word and its POS tag: $s(1)$, $q(2)$, and $q(1)$.
- POS: $s(3)$ and $q(2)$.

[3]The parser used in this work is the same as the probabilistic shift-reduce parser referred to as "Sagae" in the cited shared task descriptions. In the 2007 shared task, an ensemble of shift-reduce parsers was used, but only a single parser is used here.

[4]$s(n)$ denotes the n-th item from the top of the stack (where $s(1)$ is the item on the top of the stack), and $q(n)$ denotes the n-th item from the front of the queue.

- The dependency label of the most recently attached dependent of: $s(1)$ and $s(2)$.
- The previous parser action.

4 Evaluation

4.1 Methodology

We first evaluate the parser by 15-fold cross-validation on the 15 manually curated gold-standard Eve files (to evaluate the parser on each file, the remaining 14 files are used to train the parser). Single-word utterances (excluding punctuation) were ignored, since their analysis is trivial and their inclusion would artificially inflate parser accuracy measurements. The size of the Eve evaluation corpus (with single-word utterances removed) was 64,558 words (or 59,873 words excluding punctuation). Of these, 41,369 words come from utterances spoken by adults, and 18,504 come from utterances spoken by the child. To evaluate the parser's portability to other CHILDES corpora, we also tested the parser (trained only on the entire Eve set) on two additional sets, one taken from the MacWhinney corpus (MacWhinney, 2000) (5,658 total words, 3,896 words in adult utterances and 1,762 words in child utterances), and one taken from the Seth corpus (Peters, 1987; Wilson and Peters, 1988) (1,749 words, 1,059 adult and 690 child).

The parser is highly efficient: training on the entire Eve corpus takes less that 20 minutes on standard hardware, and once trained, parsing the Eve corpus takes 18 seconds, or over 3,500 words per second.

Following recent work on dependency parsing (Nivre, 2007), we report two evaluation measures: labeled accuracy score (LAS) and unlabeled accuracy score (UAS). LAS is the percentage of tokens for which the parser predicts the correct head-word and dependency label. UAS ignores the dependency labels, and therefore corresponds to the percentage of words for which the correct head was found. In addition to LAS and UAS, we also report precision and recall of certain grammatical relations.

For example, compare the parser output of *go buy an apple* to the gold standard (Figure 1). This sequence of GRs has two labeled dependency errors and one unlabeled dependency error. `1|2|COORD` for the parser versus `1|2|SRL` is a labeled error because the dependency label produced by the parser (COORD) does not match the gold-standard annotation (SRL), although the unlabeled dependency is correct, since the headword assignment, `1|2`, is the same for both. On the other hand, `5|1|PUNCT` versus `5|2|PUNCT` is both a labeled dependency error and an unlabeled dependency error, since the headword assignment produced by the parser does not match the gold-standard.

4.2 Results

Trained on domain-specific data, the parser performed well on held-out data, even though the training corpus is relatively small (about 60,000 words). The results are listed in Table 1.

	LAS	UAS
Eve cross-validation	92.0	93.8

Table 1: Average cross-validation results, Eve

The labeled dependency error rate is about 8% and the unlabeled error rate is slightly over 6%. Performance in individual files ranged between the best labeled error rate of 6.2% and labeled error rate of 4.4% for the fifth file, and the worst error rates of 8.9% and 7.8% for labeled and unlabeled respectively in the fifteenth file. For comparison, Sagae et al. (2005) report 86.9% LAS on about 2,000 words of Eve data, using the Charniak (2000) parser with a separate dependency-labeling step. Part of the reason we obtain levels of accuracy higher than usually reported for dependency parsers is that the average sentence length in CHILDES transcripts is much lower than in, for example, newspaper text. The average sentence length for adult utterances in the Eve corpus is 6.1 tokens, and 4.3 tokens for child utterances[5].

Certain GRs are easily identifiable, such as DET, AUX, and INF. The parser has precision and recall of nearly 1.00 for those. For all GRs that occur more than 1,000 times in the Eve corpus (which contrains more than 60,000 tokens), precision and recall are above 0.90, with the exception of COORD, which

[5] This differs from the figures in section 2.3 because for the purpose of parser evaluation we ignore sentences composed only of a single word plus punctuation.

```
          go            buy           an          apple        .
parser:   1|2|COORD     2|0|ROOT      3|4|DET     4|2|OBJ      5|1|PUNCT
gold:     1|2|SRL       2|0|ROOT      3|4|DET     4|2|OBJ      5|2|PUNCT
```

Figure 1: Example output: parser vs. gold annotation

occurs 1,163 times in the gold-standard data. The parser's precision for COORD is 0.73, and recall is 0.84. Other interesting GRs include SUBJ, OBJ, JCT (adjunct), COM, LOC, COMP, XCOMP, CJCT (subordinate clause acting as an adjunct), and PTL (verb particle, easily confusable with prepositions and adverbs). Their precision and recall is shown in table 2.

GR	Precision	Recall	F-score
SUBJ	0.96	0.96	0.96
OBJ	0.93	0.94	0.93
JCT	0.91	0.90	0.90
COM	0.96	0.95	0.95
LOC	0.95	0.90	0.92
COMP	0.83	0.86	0.84
XCOMP	0.86	0.87	0.87
CJCT	0.61	0.59	0.60
PTL	0.97	0.96	0.96
COORD	0.73	0.84	0.78

Table 2: Precision, recall and f-score of selected GRs in the Eve corpus

We also tested the accuracy of the parser on child utterances and adult utterances separately. To do this, we split the gold standard files into child and adult utterances, producing gold standard files for both child and adult utterances. We then trained the parser on 14 of the 15 Eve files with both child and adult utterances, and parsed the individual child and adult files. Not surprisingly, the parser performed slightly better on the adult utterances due to their grammaticality and the fact that there was more adult training data than child training data. The results are listed in Table 3.

	LAS	UAS
Eve - Child	90.0	91.7
Eve - Adult	93.1	94.8

Table 3: Average child vs. adult results, Eve

Our final evaluation of the parser involved testing the parser on data taken from a different parts of the CHILDES database. First, the parser was trained on all gold-standard Eve files, and tested on manually annotated data taken from the MacWhinney transcripts. Although accuracy was lower for adult utterances (85.8% LAS) than on Eve data, the accuracy for child utterances was slightly higher (92.3% LAS), even though child utterances were longer on average (4.7 tokens) than in the Eve corpus.

Finally, because a few aspects of the many transcript sets in the CHILDES database may vary in ways not accounted for in the design of the parser or the annotation of the training data, we also report results on evaluation of the Eve-trained parser on a particularly challenging test set, the Seth corpus. Because the Seth corpus contains transcriptions of language phenomena not seen in the Eve corpus (see section 5), parser performance is expected to suffer. Although accuracy on adult utterances is high (92.2% LAS), accuracy on child utterances is very low (72.7% LAS). This is due to heavy use of a GR label that does not appear at all in the Eve corpus that was used to train the parser. This GR is used to represent relations involving *filler syllables*, which appear in nearly 45% of the child utterances in the Seth corpus. Accuracy on the sentences that do not contain filler syllables is at the same level as in the other corpora (91.1% LAS). Although we do not expect to encounter many sets of transcripts that are as problematic as this one in the CHILDES database, it is interesting to see what can be expected from the parser under unfavorable conditions.

The results of the parser on the MacWhinney and Seth test sets are summarized in table 4, where *Seth (clean)* refers to the Seth corpus without utterances that contain filler sylables.

5 Error Analysis

A major source for parser errors on the Eve corpus (112 out of 5181 errors) was telegraphic speech,

	LAS	UAS
MacWhinney - Child	92.3	94.8
MacWhinney - Adult	85.8	89.4
MacWhinney - Total	88.0	91.2
Seth - Child	72.7	82.0
Seth - Adult	92.2	94.4
Seth - Total	84.6	89.5
Seth (clean) - Child	91.1	92.7
Seth (clean) - Total	92.0	93.9

Table 4: Training on Eve, testing on MacWhinney and Seth

as in *Mommy telephone* or *Fraser tape+recorder floor*. Telegraphic speech may be the most challenging, since even for a human annotator, determining a GR is difficult. The parser usually labeled such utterances with the noun as the ROOT and the proper noun as the MOD, while the gold annotation is context-dependent as described above.

Another category of errors, with about 150 instances, is XCOMP errors. The majority of the errors in this category revolve around dropped words in the main clause, for example *want eat cookie*. Often, the parser labels such utterances with COMP GRs, because of the lack of *to*. Exclusive training on utterances of this type may resolve the issue. Many of the errors of this type occur with *want*: the parser could be conditioned to assign an XCOMP GR with *want* as the ROOT of an utterance.

COORD and PRED errors would both benefit from more data as well. The parser performs admirably on simple coordination and predicate constructions, but has troubles with less common constructions such as PRED GRs with *get*, e.g., *don't let your hands get dirty* (69 errors), and coordination of prepositional objects, as in *a birthday cake with Cathy and Becky* (154 errors).

The performance drop on the Seth corpus can be explained by a number of factors. First and foremost, Seth is widely considered in the literature to be the child who is most likely to invalidate any theory (Wilson and Peters, 1988). He exhibits false starts and filler syllables extensively, and his syntax violates many "universal" principles. This is reflected in the annotation scheme: the Seth corpus, following the annotation of Peters (1983), is abundant with *filler syllables*. Because there was no appropriate GR label for representing the syntactic relationships involving the filler syllables, we annotated those with a special GR (not used during parser training), which the parser is understandably not able to produce. Filler syllables usually occur near the start of the sentence, and once the parser failed to label them, it could not accurately label the remaining GRs. Other difficulties in the Seth corpus include the usage of *dates*, of which there were no instances in the Eve corpus. The parser had not been trained on the new DATE GR and subsequently failed to parse it.

6 Conclusion

We described an annotation scheme for representing syntactic information as grammatical relations in CHILDES data, a manually curated gold-standard corpus of 65,000 words annotated according to this GR scheme, and a parser that was trained on the annotated corpus and produces highly accurate grammatical relations for both child and adult utterances. These resources are now freely available to the research community, and we expect them to be instrumental in psycholinguistic investigations of language acquisition and child language.

Syntactic analysis of child language transcripts using a GR scheme of this kind has already been shown to be effective in a practical setting, namely in automatic measurement of syntactic development in children (Sagae et al., 2005). That work relied on a phrase-structure statistical parser (Charniak, 2000) trained on the Penn Treebank, and the output of that parser had to be converted into CHILDES grammatical relations. Despite the obvious disadvantage of using a parser trained on a completely different language genre, Sagae et al. (2005) demonstrated how current natural language processing techniques can be used effectively in child language work, achieving results that are close to those obtained by manual computation of syntactic development scores for child transcripts. Still, the use of tools not tailored for child language and extra effort necessary to make them work with community standards for child language transcription present a disincentive for child language researchers to incorporate automatic syntactic analysis into their work. We hope that the GR representation scheme and the parser presented here will make it possible and convenient for the child language community to take advantage of some of the recent developments in natural language parsing, as was the case with part-of-speech tagging when CHILDES specific tools were first made available.

Our immediate plans include continued improvement of the parser, which can be achieved at least in part by the creation of additional training data from other English CHILDES corpora. We also plan to release automatic syntactic analyses for the entire English portion of CHILDES.

Although we have so far focused exclusively on English CHILDES data, dependency schemes based on functional relationships exist for a number of languages (Buchholz and Marsi, 2006), and the general parsing techniques used in the present work have been shown to be effective in several of them (Nivre et al., 2006). As future work, we plan to adapt existing dependency-based annotation schemes and apply our current syntactic annotation and parsing framework to other languages in the CHILDES database.

Acknowledgments

We thank Marina Fedner for her help with annotation of the Eve corpus. This work was supported in part by the National Science Foundation under grant IIS-0414630.

References

A. Berger, S. A. Della Pietra, and V. J. Della Pietra. 1996. A maximum entropy approach to natural language processing. *Computational Linguistics*, 22(1):39–71.

Roger Brown. 1973. *A first language: the early stages*. George Allen & Unwin Ltd., London.

Sabine Buchholz and Erwin Marsi. 2006. Conll-x shared task on multilingual dependency parsing. In *Proceedings of the Tenth Conference on Computational Natural Language Learning (CoNLL-X)*, pages 149–164, New York City, June. Association for Computational Linguistics.

John Carroll, Edward Briscoe, and Antonio Sanfilippo. 1998. Parser evaluation: a survey and a new proposal. In *Proceedings of the 1st International Conference on Language Resources and Evaluation*, pages 447–454, Granada, Spain.

Eugene Charniak. 2000. A maximum-entropy-inspired parser. In *Proceedings of the first conference on North American chapter of the Association for Computational Linguistics*, pages 132–139, San Francisco, CA, USA. Morgan Kaufmann Publishers Inc.

D. Knuth. 1965. On the translation of languages from left to right. *Information and Control*, 8(6):607–639.

Brian MacWhinney. 2000. *The CHILDES Project: Tools for Analyzing Talk*. Lawrence Erlbaum Associates, Mahwah, NJ, third edition.

Joakim Nivre, Johan Hall, Jens Nilsson, Gulsen Eryigit, and Svetoslav Marinov. 2006. Labeled pseudo-projective dependency parsing with support vector machines. In *Proceedings of the Tenth Conference on Computational Natural Language Learning*.

Joakim Nivre, editor. 2007. *CoNLL-XI Shared Task on Multilingual Dependency Parsing*, Prague, June. Association for Computational Linguistics.

Ann M. Peters. 1983. *The Units of Language Acquisition*. Monographs in Applied Psycholinguistics. Cambridge University Press, New York.

Ann M. Peters. 1987. The role of immitation in the developing syntax of a blind child. *Text*, 7:289–311.

Kenji Sagae and Alon Lavie. 2006. A best-first probabilistic shift-reduce parser. In *Proceedings of the COLING/ACL 2006 Main Conference Poster Sessions*, pages 691–698, Sydney, Australia, July. Association for Computational Linguistics.

Kenji Sagae and Jun'ichi Tsujii. 2007. Dependency parsing and domain adaptation with lr models and parser ensembles. In *Proceedings of the Eleventh Conference on Computational Natural Language Learning*.

Kenji Sagae, Alon Lavie, and Brian MacWhinney. 2004. Adding syntactic annotations to transcripts of parent-child dialogs. In *Proceedings of the Fourth International Conference on Language Resources and Evaluation (LREC 2004)*, Lisbon, Portugal.

Kenji Sagae, Alon Lavie, and Brian MacWhinney. 2005. Automatic measurement of syntactic development in child language. In *Proceedings of the 43rd Annual Meeting of the Association for Computational Linguistics (ACL'05)*, pages 197–204, Ann Arbor, Michigan, June. Association for Computational Linguistics.

B. Wilson and Ann M. Peters. 1988. What are you cookin' on a hot?: A three-year-old blind child's 'violation' of universal constraints on constituent movement. *Language*, 64:249–273.

I will shoot your shopping down and you can shoot all my tins Automatic Lexical Acquisition from the CHILDES Database

Paula Buttery and Anna Korhonen
RCEAL, University of Cambridge
9 West Road, Cambridge, CB3 9DB, UK
pjb48, alk23@cam.ac.uk

Abstract

Empirical data regarding the syntactic complexity of children's speech is important for theories of language acquisition. Currently much of this data is absent in the annotated versions of the CHILDES database. In this perliminary study, we show that a state-of-the-art subcategorization acquisition system of Preiss et al. (2007) can be used to extract large-scale subcategorization (frequency) information from the (i) child and (ii) child-directed speech within the CHILDES database without any domain-specific tuning. We demonstrate that the acquired information is sufficiently accurate to confirm and extend previously reported research findings. We also report qualitative results which can be used to further improve parsing and lexical acquisition technology for child language data in the future.

1 Introduction

Large empirical data containing children's speech are the key to developing and evaluating different theories of child language acquisition (CLA). Particularly important are data related to syntactic complexity of child language since considerable evidence suggests that syntactic information plays a central role during language acquisition, e.g. (Lenneberg, 1967; Naigles, 1990; Fisher et al., 1994).

The standard corpus in the study of CLA is the CHILDES database (MacWhinney, 2000)[1] which provides 300MB of transcript data of interactions between children and parents over 25 human languages. CHILDES is currently available in raw, part-of-speech-tagged and lemmatized formats. However, adequate investigation of syntactic complexity requires deeper annotations related to e.g. syntactic parses, subcategorization frames (SCFs), lexical classes and predicate-argument structures.

Although manual syntactic annotation is possible, it is extremely costly. The alternative is to use natural language processing (NLP) techniques for annotation. Automatic techniques are now viable, cost effective and, although not completely error-free, are sufficiently accurate to yield annotations useful for linguistic purposes. They also gather important qualitative and quantitative information, which is difficult for humans to obtain, as a side-effect of the acquisition process.

For instance, state-of-the-art statistical parsers, e.g. (Charniak, 2000; Briscoe et al., 2006), have wide coverage and yield grammatical representations capable of supporting various applications (e.g. summarization, information extraction). In addition, lexical information (e.g. subcategorization, lexical classes) can now be acquired automatically from parsed data (McCarthy and Carroll, 2003; Schulte im Walde, 2006; Preiss et al., 2007). This information complements the basic grammatical analysis and provides access to the underlying predicate-argument structure.

Containing considerable ellipsis and error, spoken child language can be challenging for current NLP techniques which are typically optimized for written adult language. Yet Sagae et al. (2005) have recently demonstrated that existing statistical parsing techniques can be usefully modified to analyse CHILDES

[1] See http://childes.psy.cmu.edu for details.

Proceedings of the Workshop on Cognitive Aspects of Computational Language Acquisition, pages 33–40,
Prague, Czech Republic, June 2007 ©2007 Association for Computational Linguistics

with promising accuracy. Although further improvements are still required for optimal accuracy, this research has opened up the exciting possibility of automatic grammatical annotation of the entire CHILDES database in the future.

However, no work has yet been conducted on automatic acquisition of lexical information from child speech. The only automatic lexical acquisition study involving CHILDES that we are aware of is that of Buttery and Korhonen (2005). The study involved extracting subcategorization information from (some of) the adult (child-directed) speech in the database, and showing that this information differs from that extracted from the spoken part of the British National Corpus (BNC) (Burnard, 1995).

In this paper, we investigate whether state-of-the-art subcategorization acquisition technology can be used—without any domain-specific tuning—to obtain large-scale verb subcategorization frequency information from CHILDES which is accurate enough to show differences and similarities between child and adult speech, and thus be able to provide support for syntactic complexity studies in CLA.

We use the new system of Preiss et al. (2007) to extract SCF frequency data from the (i) child and (ii) child-directed speech within CHILDES. We show that the acquired information is sufficiently accurate to confirm and extend previously reported SCF (dis)similarities between the two types of data. In particular, we demonstrate that children and adults have different preferences for certain types of verbs, and that these preferences seem to influence the way children acquire subcategorization. In addition, we report qualitative results which can be used to further improve parsing and lexical acquisition technology for spoken child language data in the future.

2 Subcategorization Acquisition System

We used for subcategorization acquisition the new system of Preiss, Briscoe and Korhonen (2007) which is essentially a much improved and extended version of Briscoe and Carroll's (1997) system. It incorporates 168 SCF distinctions, a superset of those found in the COMLEX Syntax (Grishman et al., 1994) and ANLT (Boguraev et al., 1987) dictionaries. Currently, SCFs abstract over specific lexically governed particles and prepositions and specific predicate selectional preferences but include some derived semi-predictable bounded dependency constructions, such as particle and dative movement—this will be revised in future versions of the SCF system.

The system tokenizes, tags, lemmatizes and parses input sentences using the recent (second) release of the RASP (Robust Accurate Statistical Parsing) system (Briscoe et al., 2006) which parses arbitrary English text with state-of-the-art levels of accuracy. SCFs are extracted from the grammatical relations (GRs) output of the parser using a rule-based classifier. This classifier operates by exploiting the close correspondence between the dependency relationships which the GRs embody and the head-complement structure which subcategorization acquisition attempts to recover. Lexical entries of extracted SCFs are constructed for each word in the corpus data. Finally, the entries may be optionally filtered to obtain a more accurate lexicon. This is done by setting empirically determined thresholds on the relative frequencies of SCFs.

When evaluated on cross-domain corpora containing mainly adult language, this system achieves 68.9 F-measure[2] in detecting SCF types—a result which compares favourably to those reported with other comparable SCF acquisition systems.

3 Data

The English (British and American) sections of the CHILDES database (MacWhinney, 2000) were used to create two corpora: 1) CHILD and 2) CDS. Both corpora contained c. 1 million utterances which were selected from the data after some utterances containing un-transcribable sections were removed. Speakers were identified using speaker-id codes within the CHAT transcriptions of the data:[3] CHILD contained the utterances of speakers identified as target children; CDS contained input from speakers identified as parents/caretakers. The mean utterance length (measured in words) in CHILD and CDS were 3.48 and 4.61, respectively. The mean age of the child speaker in CHILD is around 3 years 6 months.[4]

[2] See Section 4 for details of F-measure.

[3] CHAT is the transcription and coding format used by all the transcriptions within CHILDES.

[4] The complete age range is from 1 year and 1 month up to 7 years.

3.1 Test Verbs and SCF Lexicons

We selected a set of 161 verbs for experimentation. The words were selected at random, subject to the constraint that a sufficient number of SCFs would be extracted (> 100) from both corpora to facilitate maximally useful comparisons. All sentences containing an occurrence of one of the test verbs were extracted from the two corpora and fed into the SCF acquisition system described earlier in section 2.

In some of our experiments the two lexicons were compared against the VALEX lexicon (Korhonen et al., 2006)—a large subcategorization lexicon for English which was acquired automatically from several cross-domain corpora (containing both written and spoken language). VALEX includes SCF and frequency information for 6,397 English verbs. We employed the most accurate version of the lexicon here (87.3 F-measure)—this lexicon was obtained by selecting high frequency SCFs and supplementing them with lower frequency SCFs from manually built lexicons.

4 Analysis

4.1 Methods for Analysis

The similarity between verb and SCF distributions in the lexicons was examined. To maintain a robust analysis in the presence of noise, multiple similarity measures were used to compare the verb and SCF distributions (Korhonen and Krymolowski, 2002). In the following $p = (p_i)$ and $q = (q_i)$ where p_i and q_i are the probabilities associated with SCF_i in distributions (lexicons) P and Q:

- Intersection (IS) - the intersection of non-zero probability SCFs in p and q;
- Spearman rank correlation (RC) - lies in the range $[1; 1]$, with values near 0 denoting a low degree of association and values near -1 and 1 denoting strong association;
- Kullback-Leibler (KL) distance - a measure of the additional information needed to describe p using q, KL is always ≥ 0 and $= 0$ only when $p \equiv q$;

The SCFs distributions acquired from the corpora for the chosen words were evaluated against: (i) a gold standard SCF lexicon created by merging the SCFs in the COMLEX and ANLT syntax dictionaries—this enabled us to determine the accuracy of the acquired SCFs; (ii) another acquired SCF lexicon (as if it were a gold standard)—this enabled us to determine similarity of SCF types between two lexicons. In each case we recorded the number of *true positives* (TPs), correct SCFs, *false positives* (FPs), incorrect SCFs, and *false negatives* (FNs), correct SCFs not in the gold standard.

Verb	CHILD	CDS
go	1	1
want	2	2
get	3	3
know	4	4
put	5	6
see	6	5
come	7	10
like	8	7
make	9	11
say	10	8
take	11	13
eat	12	14
play	13	15
need	14	16
look	15	12
fall	16	22
sit	17	21
think	18	9
break	19	27
give	20	17

Table 1: Ranks of the 20 most frequent verbs in CHILD and in CDS

Using these counts, we calculated type precision (the percentage of SCF types in the acquired lexicon which are correct), type recall (the percentage of SCF types in the gold standard that are in the lexicon) and F-measure:

$$F = \frac{2 \cdot precision \cdot recall}{precision + recall} \quad (1)$$

4.2 Verb Analysis

Before conducting the SCF comparisons we first compared (i) our 161 test verbs and (ii) all the 1212 common verbs and their frequencies in CHILD and CDS using the Spearman rank correlation (RC) and the Kullback-Leibler distance (KL). The result was a strong correlation between the 161 test verbs (RC = 0.920 ± 0.0791, KL = 0.05) as well as between all the 1212 verbs (RC = 0.851 ± 0.0287, KL = 0.07) in the two corpora.

These figures suggest that the child-directed speech (which is less diverse in general than speech between adults, see e.g. the experiments of Buttery and Korhonen (2005)) contains a very similar distribution of verbs to child speech. This is to be expected since the corpora essentially contain separate halves of the same interactions.

However, our large-scale frequency data makes it possible to investigate the cause for the apparently small differences in the distributions. We did this by examining the strength of correlation throughout the ranking. We compared the ranks of the individual verbs and discovered that the most frequent verbs in the two corpora have indeed very similar ranks. Table 1 lists the 20 most frequent verbs in CHILD (starting from the highest ranked verb) and shows their ranks in CDS. As illustrated in the table, the top 4 verbs are identical in the two corpora (*go, want, get, know*) while the top 15 are very similar (including many action verbs e.g. *put, look, sit, eat,* and *play*).

Yet some of the lower ranked verbs turned out to have large rank differences between the two corpora. Two such relatively highly ranked verbs are included in the table—*think* which has a notably higher rank in CDS than in CHILD, and *break* which has a higher rank in CHILD than in CDS. Many other similar cases were found in particular among the medium and low frequency verbs in the two corpora.

To obtain a better picture of this, we calculated for each verb its rank difference between CHILD vs. CDS. Table 2 lists 40 verbs with substantial rank differences between the two corpora. The first column shows verbs which have higher ranks in CHILD than in CDS, and the second column shows verbs with higher ranks in CDS than in CHILD. We can see e.g. that children tend to prefer verbs such as *shoot, die* and *kill* while adults prefer verbs such as *remember, send* and *learn*.

To investigate whether these differences in preferences are random or motivated in some manner, we classified the verbs with the largest differences in ranks (>10) into appropriate Levin-style lexical-semantic classes (Levin, 1993) according to their predominant senses in the two corpora.[5] We discovered that the most frequent classes among the verbs that children prefer are HIT (e.g. *bump, hit, kick*), BREAK (e.g. *crash, break, rip*), HURT (e.g. *hurt, burn, bite*) and MOTION (e.g. *fly, jump, run*) verbs. Overall, many of the preferred verbs (regardless of the class) express negative actions or feelings (e.g. *shoot, die, scare, hate*).

[5]This classification was done manually to obtain a reliable result.

CHILD		CDS	
shoot	*tie*	*remember*	*hope*
hate	*wish*	*send*	*suppose*
die	*cut*	*learn*	*bet*
write	*crash*	*wipe*	*kiss*
use	*kick*	*pay*	*smell*
bump	*scare*	*feed*	*guess*
win	*step*	*ask*	*change*
lock	*burn*	*feel*	*set*
fight	*stand*	*listen*	*stand*
jump	*care*	*wait*	*wonder*

Table 2: 20 verbs ranked higher in (i) child speech and (ii) child-directed speech.

In contrast, adults have a preference for verbs from classes expressing cognitive processes (e.g. *remember, suppose, think, wonder, guess, believe, hope, learn*) or those that can be related to the education of children, e.g. the WIPE verbs *wash, wipe* and *brush* and the PERFORMANCE verbs *draw, dance* and *sing*. In contrast to children, adults prefer verbs which express positive actions and feelings (e.g. *share, help, love, kiss*).

It is commonly reported that child CLA is motivated by a wish to communicate desires and emotions, e.g. (Pinker, 1994), but a relative preference in child speech over child-directed speech for certain verb types or verbs expressing negative actions and feelings has not been explicitly shown on such a scale before. While this issue requires further investigation, our findings already demonstrate the value of using large scale corpora in producing novel data and hypotheses for research in CLA.

4.3 SCF Analysis

4.3.1 Quantitative SCF Comparison

The average number of SCFs taken by studied verbs in the two corpora proved quite similar. In unfiltered SCF distributions, verbs in CDS took on average a larger number of SCFs (29) than those in CHILD (24), but in the lexicons filtered for accuracy the numbers were identical (8–10, depending on the filtering threshold applied). The intersection between the CHILD / CDS SCFs and those in the VALEX lexicon was around 0.5, indicating that the two lexicons included only 50% of the SCFs in the lexicon extracted from general (cross-domain) adult language corpora. Recall against VALEX was consequently low (between 48% and 68% depending on the filtering threshold) but precision was around 50-60% for both CHILDES and CDS lexicons

Measures	Unfilt.	Filt.
Precision (%)	82.9	88.7
Recall (%)	69.3	44.5
F-measure	75.5	59.2
IS	0.73	0.62
RC	0.69	0.72
KL	0.33	0.46

Table 3: Average results when SCF distributions in CHILD and CDS are compared against each other.

(also depending on the filtering threshold), which is a relatively good result for the challenging CHILDES data. However, it should be remembered that with this type of data it would not be expected for the SCF system to achieve as high precision and recall as it would on, for instance, adult written text and that the missing SCFs and/or misclassified SCFs are likely to provide us with the most interesting information.

As expected, there were differences between the SCF distributions in the two lexicons. Table 3 shows the results when the CHILD and CDS lexicons are compared against each other (i.e. using the CDS as a gold standard). The comparison was done using both the unfiltered and filtered (using relative frequency threshold of 0.004) versions of the lexicons. The similarity in SCF types is 75.5 according to F-measure in the unfiltered lexicons and 59.2 in filtered ones.[6]

4.3.2 Qualitative SCF Comparison

Our qualitative analysis of SCFs in the two corpora revealed reasons for the differences. Table 4 lists the 10 most frequent SCFs in CHILD (starting from the highest ranked SCF), along with their ranks in CDS and VALEX. The top 3 SCFs (NP, INTRANSITIVE and PP frames) are ranked quite similarly in all the corpora. Looking at the top 10 SCFs, CHILD appears, as expected, more similar to CDS than with VALEX, but large differences can be detected in lower ranked frames.

To identify those frames, we calculated for each SCF its difference in rank between CHILD vs. CDS. Table 5 exemplifies some of the SCFs with the largest rank differences. Many of these concern frames involving sentential complementation. Children use more frequently than adults SCFs involving THAT and HOW complementation, while adults have a preference for SCFs involving WHETHER, ING and IF complementation.

Although we have not yet looked at SCF differences across ages, these discoveries are in line with previous findings, e.g. (Brown, 1973), which indicate that children master the sentential complementation SCFs preferred by adults (in our experiment) fairly late in the acquisition process. With a mean utterance length for CHILD at 3.48, we would expect to see relatively few of these frames in the CHILD corpus—and consequently a preference for the simpler THAT constructions.

4.4 The Impact of Verb Type Preferences on SCF Differences

Given the new research findings reported in Section 4.2 (i.e. the discovery that children and adults have different preferences for many medium-low frequency verbs) we investigated whether verb type preferences play a role in SCF differences between the two corpora. We chose for experimentation 10 verbs from 3 groups:

1. Group 1 – verbs with similar ranks in CHILD and CDS: *bring, find, give, know, need, put, see, show, tell, want*
2. Group 2 – verbs with higher ranks in CDS: *ask, feel, guess, help, learn, like, pull, remember, start, think*
3. Group 3 – verbs with higher ranks in CHILD: *break, die, forget, hate, hit, jump, scare, shoot, burn, wish*

The test verbs were selected randomly, subject to the constraint that their absolute frequencies in the two corpora were similar.[7] We first correlated the unfiltered SCF distributions of each test verb in the two corpora against each other and calculated the similarity in the SCF types using the F-measure. We then evaluated for each group, the accuracy of SCFs in unfiltered distributions against our gold standard (see Section 4.1). Because the gold standard was too ambitious in terms of recall, we only calculated the precision figures: the average number of TP and FP SCFs taken by test verbs.

The results are included in Table 6. Verbs in Group 1 show the best SCF type correlation (84.7 F-measure) between the two corpora although they are the richest in terms of subcategorization (they take the highest number of SCFs out of the three groups). The SCF correlation is clearly lower in Groups 2 and 3, although

[6]The fact that the unfiltered lexicons appear so much more similar suggests that some of the similarity is due to similarity in incorrect SCFs (many of which are low in frequency, i.e. fall under the threshold).

[7]This requirement was necessary because frequency may influence subcategorization acquisition performance.

SCF	Example sentence	CHILD	CDS	VALEX
NP	*I love rabbits*	1	1	1
INTRANS	*I sleep with a pillow and blanket*	2	2	2
PP	*He can jump over the fence*	3	4	3
PART	*I can't give up*	4	7	9
TO-INF-SC	*I want to play with something else*	5	3	6
PART-NP/NP-PART	*He looked it up*	6	6	7
NP-NP	*Ask her all these questions*	7	5	18
NP-INF-OC	*Why don't you help her put the blocks in the can ?*	8	9	60
INTR-RECIP	*So the kitten and the dog won't fight*	9	8	48
NP-PP	*He put his breakfast in the bin*	10	10	4

Table 4: 10 most frequent SCFs in CHILD, along with their ranks in CDS and VALEX.

	SCF	Example sentence
CHILD	MP	*I win twelve hundred dollars*
	INF-AC	*You can help me wash the dishes*
	PP-HOW-S	*He explained to her how she did it*
	HOW-TO-INF	*Daddy can you tell me how to spell Christmas carols?*
	NP-S	*He did not tell me that it was gonna cost me five dollars*
CDS	ING-PP	*Stop throwing a tantrum*
	NP-AS-NP	*I sent him as a messenger*
	NP-WH-S	*I'll tell you whether you can take it off*
	IT WHS, SUBTYPE IF	*How would you like it if she pulled your hair?*
	NP-PP-PP	*He turned it from a disaster into a victory*

Table 5: Typical SCFs with higher ranks in (i) CHILD and (ii) CDS.

	Measures	Group1	Group2	Group3
SCF similarity	F-measure	84.7	72.17	75.60
SCF accuracy	TPs CDS	12	11	7
	TPs CHILD	10	9	8
	FPs CDS	36	29	13
	FPs CHILD	32	18	15

Table 6: Average results for 3 groups when (i) unfiltered SCF distributions in CHILD and CDS are compared against each other (SCF similarity) and when (ii) the SCFs in the distributions are evaluated against a gold standard (SCF accuracy).

the verbs in these groups take fewer SCFs. Interestingly, Group 3 is the only group where children produce more TPs and FPs on average than adults do, i.e. both correct and incorrect SCFs which are not exemplified in the adult speech. The frequency effects controlled, the reason for these differences is likely to lie in the differing relative preferences children and adults have for verbs in groups 2 and 3, which we think may impact the richness of their language.

4.5 Further Analysis of TP and FP Differences

We looked further at the interesting TP and FP differences in Group 3 to investigate whether they tell us something about (i) how children learn SCFs (via both TPs and FPs), and (ii) how the parsing / SCF extraction system could be improved for CHILDES data in the future (via the FPs).

We first made a quantitative analysis of the relative difference in TPs and FPs for all the SCFs in both corpora. The major finding of this high level analysis was a significantly high FP rate for some ING frames (e.g. PART-ING-SC, ING-NP-OMIT, NP-ING-OC) within CHILD (e.g. *"car going hit"*, *"I hurt hand moving"*). This agrees with many previous studies, e.g. (Brown, 1973), which have shown that children overextend and incorrectly use the "ing" morpheme during early acquisition.

A qualitative analysis of the verbs from Group 3 was then carried out, looking for the following scenarios:

- SCF is a FP in both CHILD and CDS - either i) the gold standard is incomplete, or ii) there is error in the parser/subcategorization system with respect to the CHILDES domain.
- SCF is a TP in CDS and not present in CHILD - children have not acquired the frame despite exposure to it (perhaps it is complicated to acquire).
- SCF is a TP in CHILD but not present in CDS - adults are not using the frame but the children have acquired it. This indicates that either i) children are acquiring the frame from elsewhere in their environment (perhaps from a television),

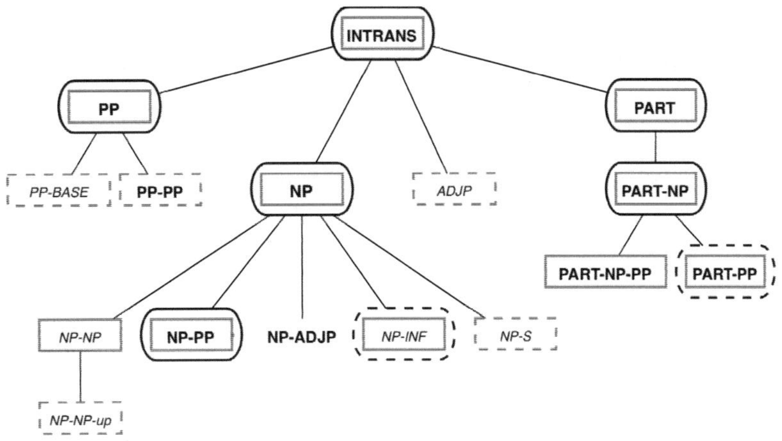

Figure 1: SCFs obtained for the verb *shoot*

or ii) there is a misuse of the verb's semantic class in child speech.

- SCF is a FP in CHILD but not present in CDS - children should not have been exposed to this frame but they have acquired it. This indicates either i) a misuse of the verb's semantic class, or ii) error in the parsing/subcategorization technology with respect to the child-speech domain.

These scenarios are illustrated in Figure 1 which graphically depicts the differences in TPs and FPs for the verb *shoot*. The SCFs have been arranged in a complexity hierarchy where complexity is defined in terms of increasing argument structure.[8] SCFs found within our ANLT-COMLEX gold standard lexicon for *shoot* are indicated in bold-face. A right-angled rectangle drawn around a SCF indicates that the frame is present in CHILD—a solid line indicating a strong presence (relative frequency $>$ 0.010) and a dotted line indicating a weak presence (relative frequency $>$ 0.005). Rounded-edge rectangles represent the presence of SCFs within CDS similarly. For example, the frame NP represents a TP in both CHILD and CDS and the frame NP-NP represents a FP within CHILD.

With reference to Figure 1, we notice that all of the SCFs present in CHILD are directly connected within the hierarchy and there is a tendency for weakly present SCFs to inherit from those strongly present. A possible explanation for this is that children are exploring SCFs—trying out frames that are slightly more complex than those already acquired (for a learning algorithm that exploits such a hypothesis in general see (Buttery, 2006)).

The SCF NP-NP is strongly present in CHILD despite being a FP. Inspection of the associated utterances reveals that some instances NP-NP are legitimate but so uncommon in adult language that they are omitted from the gold-standard (e.g. *"can i shoot us all to pieces"*. However, other instances demonstrate a misunderstanding of the semantic class of the verb; there is possible confusion with the semantic class of *send* or *throw* (e.g. *"i shoot him home"*).

The frame NP-INF is a FP in both corpora and a frequent FP in CHILD. Inspection of the associated utterances flags up a parsing problem. Frame NP-INF can be illustrated by the sentences *"he helped her bake the cake"* or *"he made her sing"*, however, within CHILD the NP-INF has been acquired from utterances such as *"i want ta shoot him"*. The RASP parser has mistagged the word *"ta"* leading to a misclassification by the SCF extraction system. This problem could be solved by augmenting RASP's current grammar with a lexical entry specifying *"ta"* as an alternative to infinitival *"to"*.

In summary, our analysis of TP and FP differences has confirmed previous studies regarding the nature of child speech (the over-extension of the *"ing"* morpheme). It has also demonstrated that TP/FP analysis can be a useful diagnostic for parsing/subcategorization extraction problems within a new data domain. Further, we suggest that analysis of FPs can provide empirical data regarding the manner in which children learn the semantic classes of

[8]For instance, the intransitive frame INTRANS is less complex than the transitive frame NP, which in turn is less complex than the di-transitive frame NP-NP. For a detailed description of all SCFs see (Korhonen, 2002).

verbs (a matter that has been much debated e.g. (Levin, 1993), (Brooks and Tomasello, 1999)).

5 Conclusion

We have reported the first experiment for automatically acquiring verbal subcategorization from both child and child-directed parts of the CHILDES database. Our results show that a state-of-the-art subcategorization acquisition system yields useful results on challenging child language data even without any domain-specific tuning. It produces data which is accurate enough to confirm and extend several previous research findings in CLA. We explore the discovery that children and adults have different relative preferences for certain verb types, and that these preferences influence the way children acquire subcategorization. Our work demonstrates the value of using NLP technology to annotate child language data, particularly where manual annotations are not readily available for research use. Our pilot study yielded useful information which will help us further improve both parsing and lexical acquisition performance on spoken/child language data. In the future, we plan to optimize the technology so that it can produce higher quality data for investigation of syntactic complexity in this domain. Using the improved technology we plan to then conduct a more thorough investigation of the interesting CLA topics discovered in this study—first concentrating on SCF differences in child speech across age ranges.

References

B. Boguraev, J. Carroll, E. J. Briscoe, D. Carter, and C. Grover. 1987. The derivation of a grammatically-indexed lexicon from the Longman Dictionary of Contemporary English. In *Proc. of the 25th Annual Meeting of ACL*, pages 193–200, Stanford, CA.

E Briscoe and J Carroll. 1997. Automatic extraction of subcategorization from corpora. In *5th ACL Conference on Applied Natural Language Processing*, pages 356–363, Washington, DC. ACL.

E. J. Briscoe, J. Carroll, and R. Watson. 2006. The second release of the rasp system. In *Proc. of the COLING/ACL 2006 Interactive Presentation Sessions*, Sydney, Australia.

P Brooks and M Tomasello. 1999. Young children learn to produce passives with nonce verbs. *Developmental Psychology*, 35:29–44.

R Brown. 1973. *A first Language: the early stages*. Harvard University Press, Cambridge, MA.

L. Burnard, 1995. *The BNC Users Reference Guide*. British National Corpus Consortium, Oxford, May.

P. Buttery and A. Korhonen. 2005. Large-scale analysis of verb subcategorization differences between child directed speech and adult speech. In *Proceedings of the Interdisciplinary Workshop on the Identification and Representation of Verb Features and Verb Classes*, Saarbrucken, Germany.

P Buttery. 2006. *Computational Models for First Language Acquisition*. Ph.D. thesis, University of Cambridge.

E. Charniak. 2000. A maximum-entropy-inspired parser. In *Proceedings of the 1st Meeting of the North American Chapter of the Association for Computational Linguistics*, Seattle, WA.

C. Fisher, G. Hall, S. Rakowitz, and L. Gleitman. 1994. When it is better to receive than to give: syntactic and conceptual constraints on vocabulary growth. *Lingua*, 92(1–4):333–375, April.

R. Grishman, C. Macleod, and A. Meyers. 1994. COMLEX Syntax: Building a Computational Lexicon. In *Proc. of COLING*, Kyoto.

A. Korhonen and Y. Krymolowski. 2002. On the Robustness of Entropy-Based Similarity Measures in Evaluation of Subcategorization Acquisition Systems. In *Proc. of the 6th CoNLL*, pages 91–97, Taipei, Taiwan.

A. Korhonen, Y. Krymolowski, and E. J. Briscoe. 2006. A large subcategorization lexicon for natural language processing applications. In *Proc. of the 5th LREC*, Genova, Italy.

A Korhonen. 2002. *Subcategorization Acquisition*. Ph.D. thesis, University of Cambridge. Thesis published as Technical Report UCAM-CL-TR-530.

E Lenneberg. 1967. *Biological Foundations of Language*. Wiley Press, New York, NY.

B Levin. 1993. *English Verb Classes and Alternations*. Chicago University Press, Chicago, IL.

B. MacWhinney. 2000. *The CHILDES Project: Tools for Analyzing Talk*. Lawrence Erlbaum, Mahwah, NJ, 3rd edition.

D. McCarthy and J. Carroll. 2003. Disambiguating nouns, verbs, and adjectives using automatically acquired selectional preferences. *Computational Linguistics*, 29(4).

L Naigles. 1990. Children use syntax to learn verb meanings. *Journal of Child Language*, 17:357–374.

S Pinker. 1994. *The Language Instinct: How the Mind Creates Language*. Harper Collins, New York, NY.

J. Preiss, E. J. Briscoe, and A. Korhonen. 2007. A system for large-scale acquisition of verbal, nominal and adjectival subcategorization frames from corpora. In *Proceedings of the 45th Annual Meeting of ACL*, Prague, Czech Republic. To appear.

K. Sagae, A. Lavie, and B. MacWhinney. 2005. Automatic measurement of syntactic development in child langugage. In *Proceedings of the 42nd Meeting of the Association for Computational Linguistics*, Ann Arbor, Michigan.

S. Schulte im Walde. 2006. Experiments on the automatic induction of german semantic verb classes. *Computational Linguistics*, 32(2):159–194.

A Cognitive Model for the Representation and Acquisition of Verb Selectional Preferences

Afra Alishahi
Department of Computer Science
University of Toronto
afra@cs.toronto.edu

Suzanne Stevenson
Department of Computer Science
University of Toronto
suzanne@cs.toronto.edu

Abstract

We present a cognitive model of inducing verb selectional preferences from individual verb usages. The selectional preferences for each verb argument are represented as a probability distribution over the set of semantic properties that the argument can possess—a *semantic profile*. The semantic profiles yield verb-specific conceptualizations of the arguments associated with a syntactic position. The proposed model can learn appropriate verb profiles from a small set of noisy training data, and can use them in simulating human plausibility judgments and analyzing implicit object alternation.

1 Introduction

Verbs have preferences for the semantic properties of the arguments filling a particular role. For example, the verb *eat* expects that the object receiving its theme role will have the property of being edible, among others. Learning verb selectional preferences is an important aspect of human language acquisition, and the acquired preferences have been shown to guide children's expectations about missing or upcoming arguments in language comprehension (Nation et al., 2003).

Resnik (1996) introduced a statistical approach to learning and use of verb selectional preferences. In this framework, a semantic class hierarchy for words is used, together with statistical tools, to induce a verb's selectional preferences for a particular argument position in the form of a distribution over all the classes that can occur in that position. Resnik's model was proposed as a model of human learning of selectional preferences that made minimal representational assumptions; it showed how such preferences could be acquired from usage data and an existing conceptual hierarchy. However, his and later computational models (see Section 2) have properties that do not match with certain cognitive plausibility criteria for a child language acquisition model. All these models use the training data in "batch mode", and most of them use information theoretic measures that rely on total counts from a corpus. Therefore, it is not clear how the representation of selectional preferences could be updated incrementally in these models as the person receives more data. Moreover, the assumption that children have access to a full hierarchical representation of semantic classes may be too strict. We propose an alternative view in this paper which is more plausible in the context of child language acquisition.

In previous work (Alishahi and Stevenson, 2005), we have proposed a usage-based computational model of early verb learning that uses Bayesian clustering and prediction to model language acquisition and use. Individual verb usages are incrementally grouped to form emergent classes of linguistic constructions that share semantic and syntactic properties. We have shown that our Bayesian model can incrementally acquire a general conception of the semantic roles of predicates based only on exposure to individual verb usages (Alishahi and Stevenson, 2007). The model forms probabilistic associations between the semantic properties of arguments, their syntactic positions, and the semantic primitives

Proceedings of the Workshop on Cognitive Aspects of Computational Language Acquisition, pages 41–48,
Prague, Czech Republic, June 2007

of verbs. Our previous experiments demonstrated that, initially, this probability distribution for an argument position yields verb-specific conceptualizations of the role associated with that position. As the model is exposed to more input, the verb-based roles gradually transform into more abstract representations that reflect the general properties of arguments across the observed verbs.

A shortcoming of the model was that, because the prediction of the semantic roles was based only on the groupings of verbs, it could not make use of verb-specific knowledge in generating expectations about a particular verb's arguments. That is, once it was exposed to a range of verbs, it no longer had access to the verb-specific information, only to generalizations over clusters of verbs.

In this paper, we propose a new version of our model that, in addition to learning general semantic roles for constructions, can use its verb-specific knowledge to predict intuitive selectional preferences for each verb argument position. We introduce a new notion, a *verb semantic profile*, as a probability distribution over the semantic properties of an argument for each verb. A verb semantic profile is predicted from both the verb-based and the construction-based knowledge that the model has learned through clustering, and reflects the properties of the arguments that are observed for that verb. Our proposed prediction model makes appropriate generalizations over the observed properties, and captures expectations about previously unseen arguments.

As in other work on selectional preferences, the semantic properties that we use in our representation of arguments are drawn from a standard lexical ontology (WordNet; Miller, 1990), but we do not require knowledge of the hierarchical structure of the WordNet concepts. From the computational point of view, this makes use of an available resource, while from the cognitive view, this avoids ad hoc assumptions about the representation of a conceptual hierarchy. However, we do require some properties to be more general (i.e., shared by more words) than others, which eventually enables the model to make appropriate generalizations. Otherwise, the selected semantic properties are not fundamental to the model, and could in the future be replaced with an approach that is deemed more appropriate to child language acquisition. Each argument contributes to the semantic profile of the verb through its (potentially large) set of semantic properties instead of its membership in a single class. As input to our model, we use an automatically parsed corpus, which is very noisy. However, as a result of our novel representation, the model can induce and use selectional preferences using a relatively small set of noisy training data.

2 Related Computational Models

A variety of computational models for verb selectional preferences have been proposed, which use different statistical models to induce the preferences of each verb from corpus data. Most of these models, however, use the same representation for verb selectional preferences: the preference can be thought of as a mapping, with respect to an argument position for a verb, of each class to a real number (Light and Greiff, 2002). The induction of a verb's preferences is, therefore, modeled as using a set of training data to estimate that number.

Resnik (1996) defines the selectional preference strength of a verb as the divergence between two probability distributions: the prior probabilities of the classes, and the posterior probabilities of the classes given that verb. The selectional association of a verb with a class is also defined as the contribution of that class to the total selectional preference strength. Resnik estimates the prior and posterior probabilities based on the frequencies of each verb and its relevant argument in a corpus.

Li and Abe (1998) model selectional preferences of a verb (for an argument position) as a set of nodes in the semantic class hierarchy with a probability distribution over them. They use the Minimum Description Length (MDL) principle to find the best set for each verb and argument based on the usages of that verb in the training data. Clark and Weir (2002) also find an appropriate set of concept nodes to represent the selectional preferences for a verb, but do so using a χ^2 test over corpus frequencies mapped to concepts to determine when to generalize from a node to its parent. Ciaramita and Johnson (2000) use a Bayesian network with the same topology as WordNet to estimate the probability distribution of the relevant set of nodes in the hierarchy. Abney and Light (1999) use a different representational approach: they train a separate hidden Markov model for each verb, and the selectional preference is represented as a probability distribution over words instead of semantic classes.

3 The Bayesian Verb-Learning Model

3.1 Overview of the Model

Our model learns the set of *argument structure frames* for each verb, and their grouping across verbs into *constructions*. An argument structure frame is a set of features of a verb usage that are both syntactic (the number of arguments, the syntactic pattern of the usage) and semantic (the semantic properties of the verb, the semantic properties of each argument). The syntactic pattern indicates the word order of the verb and arguments. A construction is a grouping of individual frames which probabilistically share syntactic and semantic features, and form probabilistic associations across verb semantic properties, argument semantic properties, and syntactic pattern. These groupings typically correspond to general constructions in the language such as transitive, intransitive, and ditransitive.

For each verb, the model associates an argument position with a probability distribution over a set of semantic properties—a semantic profile. In doing so, the model uses the knowledge that it has learned for that verb, as well as the grouping of frames for that verb into constructions.

The semantic properties of words are taken from WordNet (version 2.0) as follows. We extract all the hypernyms (ancestors) for all the senses of the word, and add all the words in the hypernym synsets to the list of the semantic properties. Figure 1 shows an example of the hypernyms for *dinner*, and its resulting set of semantic properties.[1]

The following sections review basic properties of the model from Alishahi and Stevenson (2005, 2007), and introduce extensions that give the model its ability to make verb-based predictions.

```
Sense 1
dinner
       => meal, repast
           => nutriment, nourishment, nutrition, sustenance,
              aliment, alimentation, victuals
               => food, nutrient
                   => substance, matter
                       => entity
Sense 2
dinner, dinner party
       => party
           => social gathering, social affair
               => gathering, assemblage
                   => social group
                       => group, grouping
```

dinner: {meal, repast, nutriment, nourishment, nutrition, substance, aliment, alimentation, victuals, food, nutrient, substance, matter, entity, party, social gathering, social affair, gathering, assemblage, social group, group, grouping }

Figure 1: Semantic properties for *dinner* from WordNet

3.2 Learning as Bayesian Clustering

Each argument structure frame for an observed verb usage is input to an incremental Bayesian clustering process. This process groups the new frame together with an existing group of frames—a construction—that probabilistically has the most similar semantic and syntactic properties to it. If no construction has sufficiently high probability for the new frame, then a new construction is created for it. We use the probabilistic model of Alishahi and Stevenson (2007) for learning constructions, which is itself an adaptation of a Bayesian model of human categorization proposed by Anderson (1991). It is important to note that the categories (i.e., constructions) are not predefined, but rather are created according to the patterns of similarity over observed frames.

Grouping a frame F with other frames participating in construction k is formulated as finding the k with the maximum probability given F:

$$\mathbf{BestConstruction}(F) = \underset{k}{\operatorname{argmax}}\, P(k|F) \quad (1)$$

where k ranges over the indices of all constructions, with index 0 representing recognition of a new construction.

Using Bayes rule, and dropping $P(F)$ which is constant for all k:

$$P(k|F) = \frac{P(k)P(F|k)}{P(F)} \propto P(k)P(F|k) \quad (2)$$

The prior probability, $P(k)$, indicates the degree of entrenchment of construction k, and is given by the relative frequency of its frames over all observed frames. The posterior probability of a frame F is expressed in terms of the individual probabilities of its features, which we assume are independent, thus yielding a simple product of feature probabilities:

[1] We do not remove alternate spellings of a term in WordNet; this will be seen in the profiles in the results section.

$$P(F|k) = \prod_{i \in FrameFeatures} P_i(j|k) \quad (3)$$

where j is the value of the ith feature of F, and $P_i(j|k)$ is the probability of displaying value j on feature i within construction k. Given the focus here on semantic profiles, we next focus on the calculation of the probabilities of semantic properties.

3.3 Probabilities of Semantic Properties

The probability in equation (3) of value j for feature i in construction k is estimated using a smoothed version of this maximum likelihood formula:

$$P_i(j|k) = \frac{\mathbf{count}_i^k(j)}{n_k} \quad (4)$$

where n_k is the number of frames participating in construction k, and $\mathbf{count}_i^k(j)$ is the number of those with value j for feature i.

For most features, $\mathbf{count}_i^k(j)$ is calculated by simply counting those members of construction k whose value for feature i exactly matches j. However, for the semantic properties of words, counting only the number of exact matches between the sets is too strict, since even highly similar words very rarely have the exact same set of properties. We instead use the following Jaccard similarity score to measure the overlap between the set of semantic properties, S_F, of a particular argument in the frame to be clustered, and the set of semantic properties, S_k, of the same argument in a member frame of a construction:

$$\mathbf{sem\_score}(S_F, S_k) = \frac{|S_F \cap S_k|}{|S_F \cup S_k|} \quad (5)$$

For example, assume that the new frame F represents a usage of *John ate cake*. In the construction that we are considering for inclusion of F, one of the member frames represents a usage of *Mom got water*. We must compare the semantic properties of the corresponding arguments *cake* and *water*:

cake: {baked goods,food,solid,substance,matter,entity}
water: {liquid,fluid,food,nutrient,substance,matter,entity}

The intersection of the two sets is {food, substance, matter, entity}, yielding a **sem_score** of $\frac{4}{9}$.

In general, to calculate the conditional probability for the set of semantic properties, we set $\mathbf{count}_i^k(j)$ in equation (4) to the sum of the **sem_score**'s for the new frame and every member of construction k, and normalize the resulting probability over all possible sets of semantic properties in our lexicon.

3.4 Predicting Semantic Profiles for Verbs

We represent the selectional preferences of a verb for an argument position as a semantic profile, which is a probability distribution over all the semantic properties. To predict the profile of a verb v for an argument position arg, we need to estimate the probability of each semantic property j separately:

$$\begin{aligned} P_{arg}(j|v) &= \sum_k P_{arg}(j,k|v) \quad (6) \\ &\propto \sum_k P(k,v) P_{arg}(j|k,v) \end{aligned}$$

Here, j ranges over all the possible semantic properties that an argument can have, and k ranges over all constructions. The prior probability of having verb v in construction k, or $P(k,v)$, takes into account two important factors: the relative entrenchment of the construction k, and the (smoothed) frequency with which v participates in k.

The posterior probability $P_{arg}(j|k,v)$ is calculated analogously to $P_i(j|k)$ in equation (4), but limiting the count of matching features to those frames in k that contain v:

$$P_{arg}(j|k,v) = \frac{\mathbf{verb\_count}_{arg}^k(j,v)}{n_{kv}} \quad (7)$$

where n_{kv} is the number of frames for v participating in construction k, and $\mathbf{verb\_count}_{arg}^k(j,v)$ is the number of those with semantic property j for argument arg. We use a smoothed version of the above formula, where the relative frequency of each property j among all nouns is used as the smoothing factor.

3.5 Verb-Argument Compatibility

In one of our experiments, we need to measure the compatibility of a particular noun n for an argument position arg of some verb v. That is, we need to estimate how much the semantic properties of n conform to the acquired semantic profile of v for arg. We formulate the compatibility as the conditional probability of observing n as an argument arg of v:

$$\mathbf{compatibility}(v,n) = log(P_{arg}(j_n|v)) \quad (8)$$

where j_n is the set of the semantic properties for word n, and $P_{arg}(j_n|v)$ is estimated as in equation (7). However, since j_n here is a set of properties (as opposed to j in equation (7) being a single property), $\mathbf{verb\_count}^k_{arg}$ in equation (7) should be modified as described in Section 3.3: we set $\mathbf{verb\_count}^k_{arg}(j_n, v)$ to the sum of the $\mathbf{sem\_score}$'s (equation (5)) for j_n and every frame of v that participates in construction k.

4 Experimental Results

In the following sections, we first describe the training data for our model. In accordance with other computational models, we focus here on the verb preferences for the direct object position.[2] Next, we provide a qualitative analysis of our model through examination of the semantic profiles for a number of verbs. We then evaluate our model through two tasks of simulating verb-argument plausibility judgment, and analyzing the implicit object alternation, following Resnik (1996).[3]

4.1 The Training Data

In earlier work (Alishahi and Stevenson, 2005, 2007), we used a method to automatically generate training data with the same distributional properties as the input children receive. However, this relies on manually-compiled data about verbs and their argument structure frames from the CHILDES database (MacWhinney, 1995). To evaluate the new version of our model for the task of learning selectional preferences, we need a wide selection of verbs and their arguments that is impractical to compile by hand.

The training data for our experiments here are generated as follows. We use 20,000 sentences randomly selected from the British National Corpus (BNC),[4] automatically parsed using the Collins parser (Collins, 1999), and further processed with TGrep2,[5] and an NP-head extraction software.[6] For each verb usage in a sentence, we construct a frame by recording the verb in root form, the number of the arguments for that verb, and the syntactic pattern of the verb usage (i.e., the word order of the verb and the arguments). We also record in the frame the semantic properties of the verb and each of the argument heads (each noun is also converted to root form); these properties are extracted from WordNet (as discussed in Section 3.1 and illustrated in Figure 1). This process results in 16,300 frames which serve as input data to our learning model.

4.2 Formation of Semantic Profiles for Verbs

After training our model on the above data, we use equation (7) to predict the semantic profile of the direct object position for a range of verbs. Some of these verbs, such as *write* and *sing*, have strong selectional preferences, whereas others, such as *want* and *put*, can take a wide range of nouns as direct object (as confirmed by Resnik's (1996) estimated strength of selectional preference for these verbs). The semantic profiles for *write* and *sing* are displayed in Figure 2, and the profiles for *want* and *put* are displayed in Figure 3. (Due to limited space, we only include the 25 properties that have the highest probability in each profile.)

Because we extract the semantic properties of words from WordNet, which has a hierarchical structure, the properties that come from nodes in the higher levels of the hierarchy (such as *entity* and *abstraction*) appear as the semantic property for a very large set of words, whereas the properties that come from the leaves in the hierarchy are specific to a small set of words. Therefore, the general properties are more likely to be associated with a higher probability in the semantic profiles for most verbs. In fact, a closer look at the semantic profiles for *want* and *put* reveals that the top portion of the semantic profile for these verbs consists solely of such general properties that are shared among a large group of words. However, this is not the case for the more restrictive verbs. The semantic profiles for *write* and *sing* show that the specific properties that these verbs demand from their direct object appear amongst the highest-ranked properties, even though only a small set of words share these properties (e.g., *content,*

[2]To our knowledge, the only work that considers selectional preferences of subjects and prepositional phrases as well as direct objects is Brockmann and Lapata (2003).

[3]Computational models of verb selectional preference have been evaluated through disambiguation tasks (Li and Abe, 1998; Abney and Light, 1999; Ciaramita and Johnson, 2000; Clark and Weir, 2002), but for to evaluate our cognitive model, the experiments from Resnik (1996) are the most interesting.

[4]http://www.natcorp.ox.ac.uk

[5]http://tedlab.mit.edu/~dr/Tgrep2

[6]The software was provided to us by Eric Joanis, and Afsaneh Fazly helped us in using the above-mentioned tools for generating our input corpora.

write	
(0.024)	abstraction
(0.022)	entity
(0.021)	location
(0.020)	substance
(0.019)	destination
(0.018)	relation
(0.015)	communication
(0.015)	social relation
(0.013)	content
(0.011)	message
(0.011)	subject matter
(0.011)	written communication
(0.011)	written language
(0.010)	object
(0.010)	physical object
(0.010)	writing
(0.010)	goal
(0.010)	unit
(0.009)	whole
(0.009)	whole thing
(0.009)	artifact
(0.009)	artefact
(0.009)	state
(0.009)	amount
(0.009)	measure

sing	
(0.020)	abstraction
(0.015)	relation
(0.015)	communication
(0.015)	social relation
(0.013)	act
(0.013)	human action
(0.013)	human activity
(0.013)	auditory communication
(0.012)	music
(0.010)	entity
(0.010)	piece
(0.009)	composition
(0.009)	musical composition
(0.009)	opus
(0.009)	piece of music
(0.009)	psychological feature
(0.008)	cognition
(0.008)	knowledge
(0.008)	noesis
(0.008)	activity
(0.008)	content
(0.008)	grouping
(0.008)	group
(0.008)	amount
(0.008)	measure

Figure 2: Semantic profiles of *write* and *sing* for the direct object position.

message, written communication, written language, ... for *write*, and *auditory communication, music, musical composition, opus, ...* for *sing*).

The examination of the semantic profiles for fairly frequent verbs in the training data shows that our model can use the verb usages to predict an appropriate semantic profile for each verb. When presented with a novel verb (for which no verb-based information is available), equation (7) predicts a semantic profile which reflects the relative frequencies of the semantic properties among all words (due to the smoothing factor added to equation (7)), modulated by the prior probability of each construction. The predicted profile is displayed in Figure 4. It shows similarities with the profiles for *want* and *put* in Figure 3, but the general properties in this profile have an even higher probability. Since the profile for the novel verb is predicted in the absence of any evidence (i.e., verb usage) in the training data, we later use it as the base for estimating other verbs' strength of selectional preference.

want	
(0.016)	entity
(0.015)	object
(0.015)	physical object
(0.014)	abstraction
(0.013)	act
(0.012)	human action
(0.012)	human activity
(0.012)	relation
(0.011)	unit
(0.011)	whole
(0.011)	whole thing
(0.011)	artifact
(0.011)	artefact
(0.008)	communication
(0.008)	social relation
(0.008)	activity
(0.007)	cause
(0.007)	state
(0.007)	instrumentality
(0.007)	instrumentation
(0.007)	event
(0.006)	being
(0.006)	living thing
(0.006)	animate thing
(0.006)	organism

put	
(0.015)	entity
(0.015)	object
(0.013)	physical object
(0.013)	abstraction
(0.011)	unit
(0.011)	whole
(0.011)	whole thing
(0.011)	artifact
(0.011)	artefact
(0.010)	act
(0.009)	relation
(0.008)	human action
(0.008)	human activity
(0.008)	communication
(0.008)	social relation
(0.007)	substance
(0.007)	content
(0.007)	instrumentality
(0.007)	instrumentation
(0.007)	measure
(0.006)	amount
(0.006)	quantity
(0.006)	cause
(0.006)	causal agent
(0.006)	causal agency

Figure 3: Semantic profiles of *want* and *put* for the direct object position.

4.3 Verb-Argument Plausibility Judgments

Holmes et al. (1989) evaluate verb argument plausibility by asking human subjects to rate sentences like *The mechanic warned the driver* and *The mechanic warned the engine*. Resnik (1996) used this data to assess the performance of his model by comparing its judgments of selectional fit against the plausibility ratings elicited from human subjects. He showed that his selectional association measure for a verb and its direct object can be used to select the more plausible verb-noun pair among the two (e.g., <warn,driver> vs. <warn,engine> in the previous example). That is, a higher selectional association between the verb and one of the nouns compared to the other noun indicates that the former is the more plausible pair. Resnik (1996) used the Brown corpus as training data, and showed that his model arrives at the correct ordering of more and less plausible arguments in 11 of the 16 cases.

We repeated this experiment, using the same 16 pairs of verb-noun combinations. For each pair of $<v, n_1>$ and $<v, n_2>$, we calculate the compatibility measure using equation (8); these values are shown in Figure 5. (Note that because these are

A novel verb	
(0.021)	entity
(0.017)	object
(0.017)	physical object
(0.015)	abstraction
(0.010)	act
(0.010)	human action
(0.010)	human activity
(0.010)	unit
(0.009)	whole
(0.009)	whole thing
(0.009)	artifact
(0.009)	artefact
(0.009)	being
(0.009)	living thing
(0.009)	animate thing
(0.009)	organism
(0.008)	cause
(0.008)	causal agent
(0.008)	causal agency
(0.008)	relation
(0.008)	person
(0.008)	individual
(0.008)	someone
(0.008)	somebody
(0.008)	mortal

Figure 4: Semantic profile of a novel verb for the direct object position.

log-probabilities and therefore negative numbers, a lower absolute value of **compatibility**(v, n) shows a better compatibility between the verb v and the argument n.) For example, <see,friend> has a higher compatibility score (-30.50) than <see,method> (-32.14). Similar to Resnik, our model detects 11 plausible pairs out of 16. However, these results are reached with a much smaller training corpus (around 500,000 words), compared to the Brown corpus used by Resnik (1996) which contains one million words. Moreover, whereas the Brown corpus is tagged and parsed manually, the portion of the BNC that we use is parsed automatically, and as a result our training data is very noisy. Nonetheless, the model achieves the same level of accuracy in distinguishing plausible verb-argument pairs from implausible ones.

4.4 Implicit Object Alternations

In English, some inherently transitive verbs can appear with or without their direct objects (e.g., *John ate his dinner* as well as *John ate*), but others cannot (e.g., *Mary made a cake* but not **Mary made*). It is argued that implicit object alternations involve a

Verb	**Plausible**		**Implausible**	
see	friend	-30.50	method	-32.14
read	article	-32.76	fashion	-33.33
find	label	-32.05	fever	-33.30
hear	story	-32.11	issue	-32.40
write	letter	-31.37	market	-32.46
urge	daughter	-36.73	contrast	-35.64
warn	driver	-33.68	engine	-34.42
judge	contest	-39.05	climate	-38.23
teach	language	-45.64	distance	-45.11
show	sample	-31.75	travel	-31.42
expect	visit	-33.88	mouth	-32.87
answer	request	-31.89	tragedy	-33.95
recognize	author	-32.53	pocket	-32.62
repeat	comment	-33.80	journal	-33.97
understand	concept	-32.25	session	-32.93
remember	reply	-33.79	smoke	-34.29

Figure 5: Compatibility scores for plausible vs. implausible verb-noun pairs.

particular relationship between the verb and its argument. In particular, for verbs that participate in the implicit object alternation, the omitted object must be in some sense inferable or *typical* for that verb (Levin, 1993, among others).

Resnik (1996) used his model of selectional preferences to analyze implicit object alternations, and showed a relationship between his measure of selectional preference strength and the notion of typicality of an object. He calculated this measure for two groups of Alternating and Non-alternating verbs, and showed that, on average, the Alternating verbs have a higher strength of selectional preference for the direct object than the Non-alternating verbs. However, there was no threshold separating the two groups of verbs.

To repeat Resnik's experiment, we need a measure of how "strongly constraining" a semantic profile is. We can do this by measuring the similarity between the semantic profile we generate for the object of a particular verb and some "default" notion of the argument for that position across all verbs. We use the semantic profile predicted for the object position of a novel verb, shown earlier in Figure 4, as the default profile for that argument position. Because this profile is predicted in the absence of any evidence in the training data, it makes the minimum assumptions about the properties of the argument and thus serves as a suitable default. We then assume that verbs with weaker selectional preferences have semantic profiles more similar to the default profile

Alternating verbs		Non-alternating verbs	
write	0.61	*hang*	0.56
sing	0.67	*wear*	0.71
drink	0.67	*say*	0.75
eat	0.74	*catch*	0.76
play	0.74	*show*	0.77
pour	0.76	*make*	0.78
watch	0.77	*hit*	0.78
pack	0.78	*open*	0.81
steal	0.80	*take*	0.83
push	0.80	*see*	0.87
call	0.80	*like*	0.87
pull	0.80	*get*	0.87
explain	0.81	*find*	0.87
read	0.82	*give*	0.88
hear	0.87	*bring*	0.89
		want	0.89
		put	0.90
Mean:	0.76	Mean:	0.81

Figure 6: Similarity with the base profile for Alternating and Non-alternating verbs.

than verbs with stronger preferences. We use the cosine measure to estimate the similarity between two profiles p and q:

$$\text{cosine}(p,q) = \frac{p \times q}{||p|| \times ||q||} \tag{9}$$

The similarity values for the Alternating and Non-alternating verbs are shown in Figure 6. The larger values represent more similarity with the base profile, which means a weaker selectional preference. The means for the Alternating and Non-alternating verbs were respectively 0.76 and 0.81, which confirm the hypothesis that verbs participating in implicit object alternations select more strongly for the direct objects than verbs that do not. However, like Resnik (1996), we find that it is not possible to set a threshold that will distinguish the two sets of verbs.

5 Conclusions

We have proposed a cognitively plausible model for learning selectional preferences from instances of verb usage. The model represents verb selectional preferences as a semantic profile, which is a probability distribution over the semantic properties that an argument can take. One of the strengths of our model is the incremental nature of its learning mechanism, in contrast to other approaches which learn selectional preferences in batch mode. Here we have only reported the results for the final stage of learning, but the model allows us to monitor the semantic profiles during the course of learning, and compare it with child data for different age groups, as we do with semantic roles (Alishahi and Stevenson, 2007). We have shown that the model can predict appropriate semantic profiles for a variety of verbs, and use these profiles to simulate human judgments of verb-argument plausibility, using a small and highly noisy set of training data. The model can also use the profiles to measure verb-argument compatibility, which was used in analyzing the implicit object alternation.

References

Abney, S. and Light, M. (1999). Hiding a semantic hierarchy in a Markov model. In *Proc. of the ACL Workshop on Unsupervised Learning in Natural Language Processing*.

Alishahi, A. and Stevenson, S. (2005). A probabilistic model of early argument structure acquisition. In *Proc. of the CogSci 2005*.

Alishahi, A. and Stevenson, S. (2007). A computational usage-based model for learning general properties of semantic roles. In *Proc. of the EuroCogSci 2007*.

Anderson, J. R. (1991). The adaptive nature of human categorization. *Psychological Review*, 98(3):409–429.

Brockmann, C. and Lapata, M. (2003). Evaluating and combining approaches to selectional preference acquisition. In *Proc. of the EACL 2003*.

Ciaramita, M. and Johnson, M. (2000). Explaining away ambiguity: Learning verb selectional preference with Bayesian networks. In *Proc. of the COLING 2000*.

Clark, S. and Weir, D. (2002). Class-based probability estimation using a semantic hierarchy. *Computational Linguistics*, 28(2):187–206.

Collins, M. (1999). *Head-Driven Statistical Models for Natural Language Parsing*. PhD thesis, University of Pennsylvania.

Holmes, V. M., Stowe, L., and Cupples, L. (1989). Lexical expectations in parsing complement-verb sentences. *Journal of Memory and Language*, 28:668–689.

Levin, B. (1993). *English verb classes and alternations: A preliminary investigation*. The University of Chicago Press.

Li, H. and Abe, N. (1998). Generalizing case frames using a thesaurus and the MDL principle. *Computational Linguistics*, 24(2):217–244.

Light, M. and Greiff, W. (2002). Statistical models for the induction and use of selectional preferences. *Cognitive Science*, 26(3):269–281.

MacWhinney, B. (1995). *The CHILDES project: Tools for analyzing talk*. Lawrence Erlbaum.

Miller, G. (1990). WordNet: An on-line lexical database. *International Journal of Lexicography*, 17(3).

Nation, K., Marshall, C. M., and Altmann, G. T. M. (2003). Investigating individual differences in children's real-time sentence comprehension using language-mediated eye movements. *J. of Experimental Child Psych.*, 86:314–329.

Resnik, P. (1996). Selectional constraints: An information-theoretic model and its computational realization. *Cognition*, 61:127–199.

ISA meets Lara: An incremental word space model for cognitively plausible simulations of semantic learning

Marco Baroni
CIMeC (University of Trento)
C.so Bettini 31
38068 Rovereto, Italy
marco.baroni@unitn.it

Alessandro Lenci
Department of Linguistics
University of Pisa
Via Santa Maria 36
56126 Pisa, Italy
alessandro.lenci@ilc.cnr.it

Luca Onnis
Department of Psychology
Cornell University
Ithaca, NY 14853
lo35@cornell.edu

Abstract

We introduce *Incremental Semantic Analysis*, a fully incremental word space model, and we test it on longitudinal child-directed speech data. On this task, ISA outperforms the related Random Indexing algorithm, as well as a SVD-based technique. In addition, the model has interesting properties that might also be characteristic of the semantic space of children.

1 Introduction

Word space models induce a semantic space from raw textual input by keeping track of patterns of co-occurrence of words with other words through a vectorial representation. Proponents of word space models such as HAL (Burgess and Lund, 1997) and LSA (Landauer and Dumais, 1997) have argued that such models can capture a variety of facts about human semantic learning, processing, and representation. As such, word space methods are not only increasingly useful as engineering applications, but they are also potentially promising for modeling cognitive processes of lexical semantics.

However, to the extent that current word space models are largely non-incremental, they can hardly accommodate how young children develop a semantic space by moving from virtually no knowledge of the language to reach an adult-like state. The family of models based on singular value decomposition (SVD) and similar dimensionality reduction techniques (e.g., LSA) first construct a full co-occurrence matrix based on statistics extracted from the whole input corpus, and then build a model at once via matrix algebra operations. Admittedly, this is hardly a plausible simulation of how children learn word meanings incrementally by being exposed to short sentences containing a relatively small number of different words. The lack of incrementality of several models appears conspicuous especially given their explicit claim to solve old theoretical issues about the acquisition of language (e.g., (Landauer and Dumais, 1997)). Other extant models display some degree if incrementality. For instance, HAL and Random Indexing (Karlgren and Sahlgren, 2001) can generate well-formed vector representations at intermediate stages of learning. However, they lack incrementality when they make use of stop word lists or weigthing techniques that are based on whole corpus statistics. For instance, consistently with the HAL approach, Li et al. (2000) first build a word co-occurrence matrix, and then compute the variance of each column to reduce the vector dimensions by discarding those with the least contextual diversity.

Farkas and Li (2000) and Li et al. (2004) propose an incremental version of HAL by using a a recurrent neural network trained with Hebbian learning. The networks incrementally build distributional vectors that are then used to induce word semantic clusters with a Self-Organizing Map.Farkas and Li (2000) does not contain any evaluation of the structure of the semantic categories emerged in the SOM. A more precise evaluation is instead performed by Li et al. (2004), revealing the model's ability to simulate interesting aspects of early vocabulary dynamics. However, this is achieved by using hybrid word

Proceedings of the Workshop on Cognitive Aspects of Computational Language Acquisition, pages 49–56,
Prague, Czech Republic, June 2007 ©2007 Association for Computational Linguistics

representations, in which the distributional vectors are enriched with semantic features derived from WordNet.

Borovsky and Elman (2006) also model word learning in a fairly incremental fashion, by using the hidden layer vectors of a Simple Recurrent Network as word representations. The network is probed at different training epochs and its internal representations are evaluated against a gold standard ontology of semantic categories to monitor the progress in word learning. Borovsky and Elman (2006)'s claim that their model simulates relevant aspects of child word learning should probably be moderated by the fact that they used a simplified set of artificial sentences as training corpus. From their simulations it is thus difficult to evaluate whether the model would scale up to large naturalistic samples of language.

In this paper, we introduce *Incremental Semantic Indexing* (ISA), a model that strives to be more developmentally plausible by achieving full incrementality. We test the model and some of its less incremental rivals on Lara, a longitudinal corpus of child-directed speech based on samples of child-adult linguistic interactions collected regularly from 1 to 3 years of age of a single English child. ISA achieves the best performance on these data, and it learns a semantic space that has interesting properties for our understanding of how children learn and structure word meaning. Thus, the desirability of incrementality increases as the model promises to capture specific developmental trajectories in semantic learning.

The plan of the paper is as follows. First, we introduce ISA together with its main predecessor, Random Indexing. Then, we present the learning experiments in which several versions of ISA and other models are trained to induce and organize lexical semantic information from child-directed speech transcripts. Lastly, we discuss further work in developmental computational modeling using word space models.

2 Models

2.1 Random Indexing

Since the model we are proposing can be seen as a fully incremental variation on *Random Indexing* (RI), we start by introducing the basic features of RI (Karlgren and Sahlgren, 2001). Initially, each context word is assigned an arbitrary vector representation of fixed dimensionality d made of a small number of randomly distributed +1 and -1, with all other dimensions assigned a 0 value (d is typically much smaller than the dimensionality of the full co-occurrence matrix). This vector representation is called *signature*. The context-dependent representation for a given target word is then obtained by adding the signatures of the words it co-occurs with to its *history* vector. Multiplying the history by a small constant called *impact* typically improves RI performance. Thus, at each encounter of target word t with a context word c, the history of t is updated as follows:

$$\mathbf{h}_t \mathrel{+}= i \times \mathbf{s}_c \tag{1}$$

where i is the impact constant, $\mathbf{h}_t$ is the history vector of t and $\mathbf{s}_c$ is the signature vector of c. In this way, the history of a word keeps track of the contexts in which it occurred. Similarity among words is then measured by comparing their history vectors, e.g., measuring their cosine.

RI is an extremely efficient technique, since it directly builds and updates a matrix of reduced dimensionality (typically, a few thousands elements), instead of constructing a full high-dimensional co-occurrence matrix and then reducing it through SVD or similar procedures. The model is incremental to the extent that at each stage of corpus processing the vector representations are well-formed and could be used to compute similarity among words. However, RI misses the "second order" effects that are claimed to account, at least in part, for the effectiveness of SVD-based techniques (Manning and Schütze, 1999, 15.4). Thus, for example, since different random signatures are assigned to the words *cat*, *dog* and *train*, the model does not capture the fact that the first two words, but not the third, should count as similar contexts. Moreover, RI is not fully incremental in several respects. First, on each encounter of two words, the same fixed random signature of one of them is added to the history of the other, i.e., the way in which a word affects another does not evolve with the changes in the model's knowledge about the words. Second, RI makes use of filtering and weighting procedures that rely on global statistics, i.e., statistics based on whole corpus counts. These procedures include: a) treating the most frequent words as stop words; b) cutting off the lowest frequency words as potential contexts; and c) using mutual information or entropy measures to weight the effect of a word on the other). In addition, although procedures b) and c) may have some psychological grounding, procedure a) would implausibly entail that to build semantic representations the child actively filters out high frequency words as noise from her linguistic experience. Thus, as it stands RI has some noticeable limitations as a developmental model.

2.2 Incremental Semantic Analysis

Incremental Semantic Analysis (ISA) differs from RI in two main respects. First and most importantly, when a word encounters another word, the history vector of the former is updated with a weighted sum of the signature *and* the history of the latter. This corresponds to the idea that a target word is affected not only by its context words, but also by the semantic information encoded by that their distributional histories. In this way, ISA can capture SVD-like second order effects: *cat* and *dog* might work like similar contexts because they are likely to have similar histories. More generally, this idea relies on two intuitively plausible assumptions about contextual effects in word learning, i.e., that the information carried by a context word will change as our knowledge about the word increases, and that knowing about the history of co-occurrence of a context word is an important part of the information being contributed by the word to the targets it affects.

Second, ISA does not rely on global statistics for filtering and weighting purposes. Instead, it uses a weighting scheme that changes as a function of the frequency of the context word at each update. This makes the model fully incremental and (together with the previous innovation) sensitive not only to the overall frequency of words in the corpus, but to the order in which they appear.

More explicitly, at each encounter of a target word t with a context word c, the history vector of t is updated as follows:

$$\mathbf{h}_t \mathrel{+}= i \times (m_c \mathbf{h}_c + (1 - m_c)\mathbf{s}_c) \qquad (2)$$

The constant i is the impact rate, as in the RI formula (1) above. The value m_c determines how much the history of a word will influence the history of another word. The intuition here is that frequent words tend to co-occur with a lot of other words by chance. Thus, the more frequently a word is seen, the less informative its history will be, since it will reflect uninteresting co-occurrences with all sorts of words. ISA implements this by reducing the influence that the history of a context word c has on the target word t as a function of the token frequency of c (notice that the model still keeps track of the encounter with c, by adding its signature to the history of t; it is just the history of c that is weighted down). More precisely, the m weight associated with a context word c decreases as follows:

$$m_c = \frac{1}{\exp\left(\frac{Count(c)}{k_m}\right)}$$

where k_m is a parameter determining how fast the decay will be.

3 Experimental setting

3.1 The Lara corpus

The input for our experiments is provided by the Child-Directed-Speech (CDS) section of the Lara corpus (Rowland et al., 2005), a longitudinal corpus of natural conversation transcripts of a single child, Lara, between the ages of 1;9 and 3;3. Lara was the firstborn monolingual English daughter of two White university graduates and was born and brought up in Nottinghamshire, England. The corpus consists of transcripts from 122 separate recording sessions in which the child interacted with adult caretakers in spontaneous conversations. The total recording time of the corpus is of about 120 hours, representing one of the densest longitudinal corpora available. The adult CDS section we used contains about 400K tokens and about 6K types.

We are aware that the use of a single-child corpus may have a negative impact on the generalizations on semantic development that we can draw from the experiments. On the other hand, this choice has the important advantage of providing a fairly homogeneous data environment for our computational simulations. In fact, we can abstract from the intrinsic variability characterizing any multi-child corpus, and stemming from differences in the conversation settings, in the adults' grammar and lexicon, etc. Moreover, whereas we can take our experiments to constitute a (very rough) simulation of how a particular child acquires semantic representations from her specific linguistic input, it is not clear what simulations based on an "averages" of different linguistic experiences would represent.

The corpus was part-of-speech-tagged and lemmatized using the CLAN toolkit (MacWhinney, 2000). The automated output was subsequently checked and disambiguated manually, resulting in very accurate annotation. In our experiments, we use lemma-POS pairs as input to the word space models (e.g., `go-v` rather than `going`, `goes`, etc.) Thus, we make the unrealistic assumptions that the learner already solved the problem of syntactic categorization and figured out the inflectional morphology of her language. While a multi-level bootstrapping process in which the morphosyntactic and lexical properties of words are learned in parallel is probably cognitively more likely, it seems reasonable at the current stage of experimentation to fix morphosyntax and focus on semantic learning.

3.2 Model training

We experimented with three word space models: ISA, RI (our implementations in both cases) and the SVD-based technique implemented by the *Infomap* package.[1]

Parameter settings may considerably impact the performance of word space models (Sahlgren, 2006). In a stage of preliminary investigations (not reported here, and involving also other corpora) we identified a relatively small range of values for each parameter of each model that produced promising results, and we focused on it in the subsequent, more systematic exploration of the parameter space.

For all models, we used a context window of five words to the left and five words to the right of the target. For both RI and ISA, we set signature initialization parameters (determining the random assignment of 0s, +1s and -1s to signature vectors) similar to those described by Karlgren and Sahlgren (2001). For RI and SVD, we used two stop word filtering lists (removing all function words, and removing the top 30 most frequent words), as well as simulations with no stop word filtering. For RI and ISA, we used signature and history vectors of 1,800 and 2,400 dimensions (the first value, again, inspired by Karlgren and Sahlgren's work). Preliminary experiments with 300 and 900 dimensions produced poor results, especially with RI. For SVD, we used 300 dimensions only. This was in part due to technical limitations of the implementation, but 300 dimensions is also a fairly typical choice for SVD-based models such as LSA, and a value reported to produce excellent results in the literature. More importantly, in unrelated experiments SVD with 300 dimensions and function word filtering achieved state-of-the-art performance (accuracy above 90%) in the by now standard TOEFL synonym detection task (Landauer and Dumais, 1997).

After preliminary experiments showed that both models (especially ISA) benefited from a very low impact rate, the impact parameter i of RI and ISA was set to 0.003 and 0.009. Finally, k_m (the ISA parameter determining the steepness of decay of the influence of history as the token frequency of the context word increases) was set to 20 and 100 (recall that a higher k_m correspond to a less steep decay).

The parameter settings we explored were systematically crossed in a series of experiments. Moreover, for RI and ISA, given that different random initializations will lead to (slightly) different results, each experiment was repeated 10 times.

Below, we will report results for the best performing models of each type: ISA with 1,800 dimensions, i set to 0.003 and k_m set to 100; RI with 2,400 dimensions, i set to 0.003 and no stop words; SVD with 300-dimensional vectors and function words removed. However, it must be stressed that 6 out of the 8 ISA models we experimented with outperformed the best RI model (and they all outperformed the best SVD model) in the Noun AP task discussed in section 4.1. This suggests that the results we report are not overly dependent on specific parameter choices.

3.3 Evaluation method

The test set was composed of 100 nouns and 70 verbs (henceforth, Ns and Vs), selected from the most frequent words in Lara's CDS section (word frequency ranges from 684 to 33 for Ns, and from

[1] `http://infomap-nlp.sourceforge.net/`

3501 to 89 for Vs). This asymmetry in the test set mirrors the different number of V and N types that occur in the input (2828 Ns vs. 944 Vs). As a further constraint, we verified that all the words in the test set also appeared among the child's productions in the corpus. The test words were unambiguously assigned to semantic categories previously used to model early lexical development and represent plausible early semantic groupings. Semantic categories for nouns and verbs were derived by combining two methods. For nouns, we used the ontologies from the Macarthur-Bates Communicative Development Inventories (CDI).[2] All the Ns in the test set also appear in the Toddler's List in CDI. The noun semantic categories are the following (in parenthesis, we report the number of words per class and an example): ANIMALS_REAL_OR_TOY (19; *dog*), BODY_PARTS (16; *nose*), CLOTHING (5; *hat*), FOOD_AND_DRINK (13; *pizza*), FURNITURE_AND_ROOMS (8; *table*), OUTSIDE_THINGS_AND_PLACES_TO_GO (10; *house*), PEOPLE (10; *baby*), SMALL_HOUSEHOLD_ITEMS (13; *bottle*), TOYS (6; *pen*). Since categories for verbs were underspecified in the CDI, we used 12 broad verb semantic categories for event types, partly extending those in Borovsky and Elman (2006): ACTION (11; *play*), ACTION_BODY (6; *eat*), ACTION_FORCE (5; *pull*), ASPECTUAL (6; *start*), CHANGE (12; *open*), COMMUNICATION (4; *talk*), MOTION (5; *run*), PERCEPTION (6; *hear*), PSYCH (7; *remember*), SPACE (3; *stand*), TRANSFER (6; *buy*).

It is worth emphasizing that this experimental setting is much more challenging than those that are usually adopted by state-of-the-art computational simulations of word learning, as the ones reported above. For instance, the number of words in our test set is larger than the one in Borovsky and Elman (2006), and so is the number of semantic categories, both for Ns and for Vs. Conversely, the Lara corpus is much smaller than the data-sets normally used to train word space models. For instance, the best results reported by Li et al. (2000) are obtained with an input corpus which is 10 times bigger than ours.

As an evaluation measure of the model performance in the word learning task, we adopted *Average Precision* (AP), recently used by Borovsky and Elman (2006). AP evaluates how close all members of a certain category are to each other in the semantic space built by the model.

To calculate AP, for each w_i in the test set we first extracted the corresponding distributional vector v_i produced by the model. Vectors were used to calculate the pair-wise cosine between each test word, as a measure of their distance in the semantic space. Then, for each target word w_i, we built the list r_i of the other test words ranked by their decreasing cosine values with respect to w_i. The ranking r_i was used to calculate $AP(w_i)$, the Word Average Precision for w_i, with the following formula:

$$AP(w_i) = \frac{1}{|C_{w_i}|} \sum_{w_j \in C_{w_i}} \frac{n_{w_j}(C_{w_i})}{n_{w_j}}$$

where C_{w_i} is the semantic category assigned to w_i, n_{w_j} is the set of words appearing in r_i up to the rank occupied by w_j, and $n_{w_j}(C_{w_i})$ is the subset of words in n_{w_j} that belong to category C_{w_i}.

$AP(w_i)$ calculates the proportion of words that belong to the same category of w_i at each rank in r_i, and then divides this proportion by the number of words that appear in the category. AP ranges from 0 to 1: $AP(w_i) = 1$ would correspond to the ideal case in which all the closest words to w_i in r_i belonged to the same category as w_i; conversely, if all the words belonging to categories other than C_{w_i} were closer to w_i than the words in C_{w_i}, $AP(w_i)$ would approach 0. We also defined the Class AP for a certain semantic category by simply averaging over the Word $AP(w_i)$ for each word in that category:

$$AP(C_i) = \frac{\sum_{j=1}^{j=|C_i|} AP(w_j)}{|C_i|}$$

We adopted AP as a measure of the purity and cohesiveness of the semantic representations produced by the model. Words and categories for which the model is able to converge on well-formed representations should therefore have higher AP values. If we define Recall as the number of words in n_{w_j} belonging to C_{w_i} divided by the total number of words in C_{w_i}, then all the AP scores reported in our experiments correspond to 100% Recall, since the neighbourhood we used to compute $AP(w_i)$ always included all the words in C_{w_i}. This represents a very

[2] http://www.sci.sdsu.edu/cdi/

Nouns			
Tokens	**ISA**	**RI**	**SVD**
100k	0.321	0.317	0.243
200k	0.343	0.337	0.284
300k	0.374	0.367	0.292
400k	0.400	0.393	0.306
Verbs			
100k	0.242	0.247	0.183
200k	0.260	0.266	0.205
300k	0.261	0.266	0.218
400k	0.270	0.272	0.224

Table 1: Word AP scores for Nouns (top) and Verbs (bottom). For ISA and RI, scores are averaged across 10 iterations

stringent evaluation condition for our models, far beyond what is commonly used in the evaluation of classification and clustering algorithms.

4 Experiments and results

4.1 Word learning

Since we intended to monitor the incremental path of word learning given increasing amounts of linguistic input, AP scores were computed at four "training checkpoints" established at 100K, 200K, 300K and 400K word tokens (the final point corresponding to the whole corpus).[3] Scores were calculated independently for Ns and Vs. In Table 1, we report the AP scores obtained by the best performing models of each type , as described in section 3.2. The reported AP values refer to Word AP averaged respectively over the number of Ns and Vs in the test set. Moreover, for ISA and RI we report mean AP values across 10 repetitions of the experiment.

For Ns, both ISA and RI outperformed SVD at all learning stages. Moreover, ISA also performed significantly better than RI in the full-size input condition (400k checkpoint), as well as at the 300k checkpoint (*Welch t-test*; $df = 17, p < .05$).

One of the most striking results of these experiments was the strong *N-V asymmetry* in the Word AP scores, with the Vs performing significantly worse than the Ns. For Vs, RI appeared to have a small advantage over ISA, although it was never significant at any stage. The asymmetry is suggestive of the widely attested N-V asymmetry in child word learning. A consensus has gathered in the early word learning literature that children from several languages acquire Ns earlier and more rapidly than Vs (Gentner, 1982). An influential account explains this noun-bias as a product of language-external factors such as the different complexity of the world referents for Ns and Vs. Recently, Christiansen and Monaghan (2006) found that distributional information in English CDS was more reliable for identifying Ns than Vs. This suggests that the category-bias may also be partly driven by how good certain language-internal cues for Ns and Vs are in a given language. Likewise, distributional cues to semantics may be stronger for English Ns than for Vs. The noun-bias shown by ISA (and by the other models) could be taken to complement the results of Christiansen and Monaghan in showing that English Ns are more easily discriminable than Vs on distributionally-grounded semantic terms.

[3]The checkpoint results for SVD were obtained by training different models on increasing samples from the corpus, given the non-incremental nature of this method.

4.2 Category learning

In Table 2, we have reported the Class AP scores achieved by ISA, RI and SVD (best models) under the full-corpus training regime for the nine nominal semantic categories. Although even in this case ISA and RI generally perform better than SVD (with the only exceptions of FURNITURE_AND_ROOMS and SMALL_HOUSEHOLD_ITEMS), results show a more complex and articulated situation. With BODY_PARTS, PEOPLE, and SMALL_HOUSEHOLD_ITEMS, ISA significantly outperforms its best rival RI (*Welch t-test*; $p < .05$). For the other classes, the differences among the two models are not significant, except for CLOTHING in which RI performs significantly better than ISA. For verb semantic classes (whose analytical data are not reported here for lack of space), no significant differences exist among the three models.

Some of the lower scores in Table 2 can be explained either by the small number of class members (e.g. TOYS has only 6 items), or by the class highly heterogeneous composition (e.g. in OUTSIDE_THINGS_AND_PLACES_TO_GO we find nouns like *garden*, *flower* and *zoo*). The case of PEOPLE, for which the performance of all the three models is far below their average Class AP score (ISA = 0.35; RI = 0.35; SVD = 0.27), is instead much more surprising. In fact, PEOPLE is one of the classes

Semantic class	ISA	RI	SVD
ANIMALS_REAL_OR_TOY	0.616	0.619	0.438
BODY_PARTS	0.671	0.640	0.406
CLOTHING	0.301	0.349	0.328
FOOD_AND_DRINK	0.382	0.387	0.336
FURNITURE_AND_ROOMS	0.213	0.207	0.242
OUTSIDE_THINGS_PLACES	0.199	0.208	0.198
PEOPLE	0.221	0.213	0.201
SMALL_HOUSEHOLD_ITEMS	0.208	0.199	0.244
TOYS	0.362	0.368	0.111

Table 2: Class AP scores for Nouns. For ISA and RI, scores are averaged across 10 iterations

with the highest degree of internal coherence, being composed only of nouns unambiguously denoting human beings, such as *girl*, *man*, *grandma*, etc. The token frequency of the members in this class is also fairly high, ranging between 684 and 55 occurrences. Last but not least, in unrelated experiments we found that a SVD model trained on the British National Corpus with the same parameters as those used with Lara was able to achieve very good performances with human denoting nouns, similar to the members of our PEOPLE class.

These facts have prompted us to better investigate the reasons why with Lara none of the three models was able to converge on a satisfactory representation for the nouns belonging to the PEOPLE class. We zoomed in on this semantic class by carrying out another experiment with ISA. This model underwent 8 cycles of evaluation, in each of which the 10 words originally assigned to PEOPLE have been reclassified into one of the other nominal classes. For each cycle, AP scores were recomputed for the 10 test words. The results are reported in Figure 1 (where AP refers to the average Word AP achieved by the 10 words originally belonging to the class PEOPLE). The highest score is reached when the PEOPLE nouns are re-labeled as ANIMALS_REAL_OR_TOY (we obtained similar results in a parallel experiment with SVD). This suggests that the low score for the class PEOPLE in the original experiment was due to ISA mistaking people names for animals. What *prima facie* appeared as an error could actually turn out to be an interesting feature of the semantic space acquired by the model. The experiments show that ISA (as well as the other models) groups together animals and people Ns, as

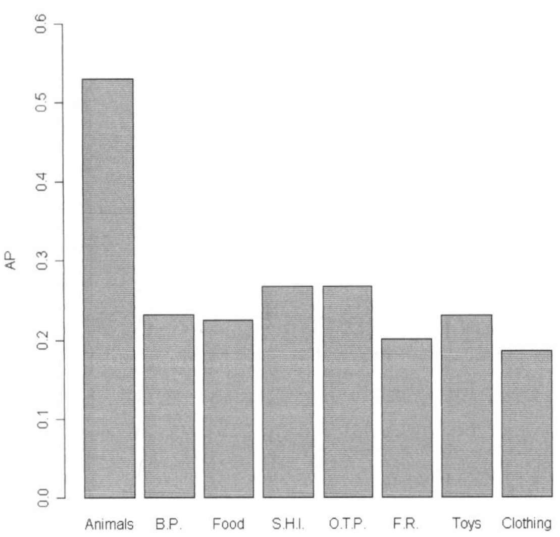

Figure 1: AP scores for Ns in PEOPLE reclassified in the other classes

it has formed a general and more underspecified semantic category that we might refer to as ANIMATE. This hypothesis is also supported by qualitative evidence. A detailed inspection of the CDS in the Lara corpus reveals that the animal nouns in the test set are mostly used by adults to refer either to toy-animals with which Lara plays or to characters in stories. In the transcripts, both types of entities display a very human-like behavior (i.e., they talk, play, etc.), as it happens to animal characters in most children's stories. Therefore, the difference between model performance and the gold standard ontology can well be taken as an interesting clue to a genuine peculiarity in children's semantic space with respect to adult-like categorization. Starting from an input in which animal and human nouns are used in similar contexts, ISA builds a semantic space in which these nouns belong to a common underspecified category, much like the world of a child in which cats and mice behave and feel like human beings.

5 Conclusion

Our main experiments show that ISA significantly outperforms state-of-the-art word space models in a learning task carried out under fairly challenging training and testing conditions. Both the incremental nature and the particular shape of the semantic representations built by ISA make it a (relatively) realistic computational model to simulate the emergence of a semantic space in early childhood.

Of course, many issues remain open. First of all, although the *Lara* corpus presents many attractive characteristics, it still contains data pertaining to a single child, whose linguistic experience may be unusual. The evaluation of the model should be extended to more CDS corpora. It will be especially interesting to run experiments in languages such as as Korean (Choi and Gopnik, 1995), where no noun-bias is attested. There, we would predict that the distributional information to semantics be less skewed in favor of nouns. All CDS corpora we are aware of are rather small, compared to the amount of linguistic input a child hears. Thus, we also plan to test the model on "artificially enlarged" corpora, composed of CDS from more than one child, plus other texts that might be plausible sources of early linguistic input, such as children's stories.

In addition, the target of the model's evaluation should not be to produce as high a performance as possible, but rather to produce performance matching that of human learners.[4] In this respect, the output of the model should be compared to what is known about human semantic knowledge at various stages, either by looking at experimental results in the acquisition literature or, more directly, by comparing the output of the model to what we can infer about the semantic generalizations made by the child from her/his linguistic production recorded in the corpus.

Finally, further studies should explore how the space constructed by ISA depends on the *order* in which sentences are presented to it. This could shed some light on the issue of how different experiential paths might lead to different semantic generalizations.

While these and many other experiments must be run to help clarifying the properties and effectiveness of ISA, we believe that the data presented here constitute a very promising beginning for this new line of research.

References

Borovsky, A. and J. Elman. 2006. Language input and semantic categories: a relation between cognition and early word learning. *Journal of Child Language*, 33: 759-790.

Burgess, C. and K. Lund. 1997. Modelling parsing constraints with high-dimensional context space. *Language and Cognitive Processes*, 12: 1-34.

Choi, S. and A. Gopnik, A. 1995. Early acquisition of verbs in Korean: a cross-linguistic study. *Journal of Child Language* 22: 497-529.

Christiansen, M.H. and P. Monaghan. 2006. Discovering verbs through multiple-cue integration. In K. Hirsh-Pasek and R.M. Golinkoff (eds.), *Action meets word: How children learn verbs*. OUP, Oxford.

Farkas, I. and P. Li. 2001. A self-organizing neural network model of the acquisition of word meaning. *Proceedings of the 4th International Conference on Cognitive Modeling*.

Gentner, D. 1982. Why nouns are learned before verbs: Linguistic relativity versus natural partitioning. In S.A. Kuczaj (ed.), *Language development, vol. 2: Language, thought and culture*. Erlbaum, Hillsdale, NJ.

Karlgren, J. and M. Sahlgren. 2001. From words to understanding. In Uesaka, Y., P. Kanerva and H. Asoh (eds.), *Foundations of real-world intelligence*, CSLI, Stanford: 294-308,

Landauer, T.K. and S.T. Dumais. 1997. A solution to Plato's problem: The Latent Semantic Analysis theory of acquisition, induction and representation of knowledge. *Psychological Review*, 104(2): 211-240.

Li, P., C. Burgess and K. Lund. 2000. The acquisition of word meaning through global lexical co-occurrences. *Proceedings of the 31st Child Language Research Forum*: 167-178.

Li, P., I. Farkas and B. MacWhinney. 2004. Early lexical acquisition in a self-organizing neural network. *Neural Networks*, 17(8-9): 1345-1362.

Manning Ch. and H. Schütze. 1999. *Foundations of statistical natural language processing* The MIT Press, Cambridge, MASS.

MacWhinney, B. 2000. *The CHILDES project: Tools for analyzing talk (3d edition)*. Erlbaum, Mahwah, NJ.

Rowland, C., J. Pine, E. Lieven and A. Theakston. 2005. The incidence of error in young children's wh-questions. *Journal of Speech, Language and Hearing Research*, 48(2): 384-404.

Sahlgren, M. 2006. *The Word-Space Model: Using distributional analysis to represent syntagmatic and paradigmatic relations between words in high-dimensional vector spaces.* Ph.D. dissertation, Department of Linguistics, Stockholm University.

[4] We thank an anonymous reviewer for this note

Simulating the acquisition of object names

Alessio Plebe and **Vivian De la Cruz**
Dept. Cognitive Science
University of Messina - Italy
{alessio.plebe,vdelacruz}@unime.it

Marco Mazzone
Lab. Cognitive Science
University of Catania - Italy
mazzonem@unict.it

Abstract

Naming requires recognition. Recognition requires the ability to categorize objects and events. Infants under six months of age are capable of making fine-grained discriminations of object boundaries and three-dimensional space. At 8 to 10 months, a child's object categories are sufficiently stable and flexible to be used as the foundation for labeling and referencing actions. What mechanisms in the brain underlie the unfolding of these capacities? In this article, we describe a neural network model which attempts to simulate, in a biologically plausible way, the process by which infants learn how to recognize objects and words through exposure to visual stimuli and vocal sounds.

1 Introduction

Humans, come to recognize an infinite variety of natural and man-made objects and make use of sounds to identify and categorize them. How do human beings arrive at this capacity? Different explanations have been offered to explain the processes, and those behind the learning of first words in particular.

Evidence has made clear that object recognition and categorization in early infancy is much more sophisticated than was previously thought. By the time children are 8 to 10 months old their object categories are sufficiently stable and flexible to be used as the foundation for labeling and referencing actions. Increasing amounts of evidence point to the growing capacity of infants at this stage to reliably map arbitrary sounds onto meanings and this mapping process is crucial to the acquisition of language. The word-learning mechanisms used at this early phase of language learning could very well involve a mapping of words onto the most perceptually interesting objects in an infant's environment (Pruden et al., 2006). There are those that claim that early word learning is not purely associative and that it is based on a sensitivity to social intent (Tomasello, 1999), through joint attention phenomena (Bloom, 2000). Pruden et al. have demonstrated that 10-month-old infants "are sensitive to social cues but cannot recruit them for word learning" and therefore, at this age infants presumably have to learn words on a simple associative basis. It is not by chance, it seems, that early vocabulary is made up of the objects infants most frequently see (Gershkoff-Stowe and Smith, 2004). Early word-learning and object recognition can thus be explained, according to a growing group of researchers, by associational learning strategies alone.

There are those such as Carey and Spelke that postulate that there must necessarily be innate constraints that have the effect of making salient certain features as opposed to others, so as to narrow the hypothesis space with respect to the kinds of objects to be categorized first (Carey and Spelke, 1996). They reject the idea that object categorization in infants could emerge spontaneously from the ability to grasp patterns of statistical regularities. Jean Mandler presents evidence that the first similarity dimensions employed in categorization processes are indeed extremely general (Mandler, 2004); in other words, these dimensions single out wide domains of objects, with further refinements coming only later. Mandler claims, however, that the early salience of

Proceedings of the Workshop on Cognitive Aspects of Computational Language Acquisition, pages 57–64,
Prague, Czech Republic, June 2007

these extremely general features could have a different explanation other than nativism: for example, that salience could emerge from physiological constraints.

Using a connectionist model with backpropagation, Rogers and McClelland have shown that quite general dimensions of similarity can emerge without appealing to either physiological or cognitive constraints, simply as the result of a coherent covariation of features, that is, as an effect of mere statistical regularities (Rogers and McClelland, 2006). What Rogers and McClelland say about the most general features obviously apply also to more specific features which become salient later on. However, interesting as it is from a computational point of view, this model is rather unrealistic as a simulation of biological categorization processes.

Linda Smith, suggests that words can contribute to category formation, in that they behave as features which co-vary with other language-independent features of objects (Smith, 1999). In general, her idea is that the relevant features simply emerge from regularities in the input. Terry Regier, building upon the proposal offered by Smith, has shown that word learning might behave in analogy with what we have said about categorization (Regier, 2005): certain features of both objects and words (i.e., phonological forms) can be made more salient than others, simply as a consequence of regularities in objects, words, and their co-variation. Regier's training sets however, are constituted by wholly "artificial phonological or semantic features", rather than by "natural features such as voicing or shape". The positions mentioned above conflict with others, such as that of Lila Gleitman and her colleagues, according to which some innate constraints are needed in order to learn words. It should be noted, however, that even in Gleitman's proposal the need for innate constraints on syntax-semantic mapping mainly concerns verbs; moreover, the possibility to apprehend a core set of concrete terms without the contribution of any syntactic constraint is considered as a precondition for verb acquisition itself (Gillette et al., 1999).

This paper describes a neural network model which attempts to simulate the process by which infants learn how to recognize objects and words in the first year of life through exposure to visual stimuli and vocal sounds. The approach here pursued is in line with the view that a coherent covariation of features is the major engine leading to object name acquisition, the attempt made however, is to rely on biological ways of capturing coherent covariation. The pre-established design of the mature functions of the organism is avoided, and the emergence of the final function of each component of the system is left to the plastic development of the neural circuits. In the cortex, there is very little differentiation in the computational capability that neural circuits will potentially perform in the mature stage. The interaction between environmental stimuli and some of the basic mechanisms of development is what drives differentiation in computational functions. This position has large empirical support (Katz and Callaway, 1992; Löwel and Singer, 2002), and is compatible with current knowledge on neural genetics (Quartz, 2003).

The model here described, can be considered an implementation of the processes that emerge around the 10 month of age period. It can also be used to consider what happens in a hypothesized subsequent period, in which the phenomenon of joint attention provides the social cueing that leads to the increased ability to focus on certain objects as opposed to others.

2 The proposed model

First the mathematics common to the modules will be described, then the model will be outlined. Details of the visual and the auditory paths will be provided along with a description of the learning procedures.

2.1 The mathematical abstraction of the cortical maps

All the modules composing this model are implemented as artificial cortical maps, adopting the LISSOM (*Laterally Interconnected Synergetically Self-Organizing Map*) architecture (Sirosh and Miikkulainen, 1997; Bednar, 2002). This architecture has been chosen because of its reproduction of neural plasticity, through the combination of Hebb's principle and neural homeostasis, and because it is a good compromise between a number of realistic features and the simplicity necessary for building complex

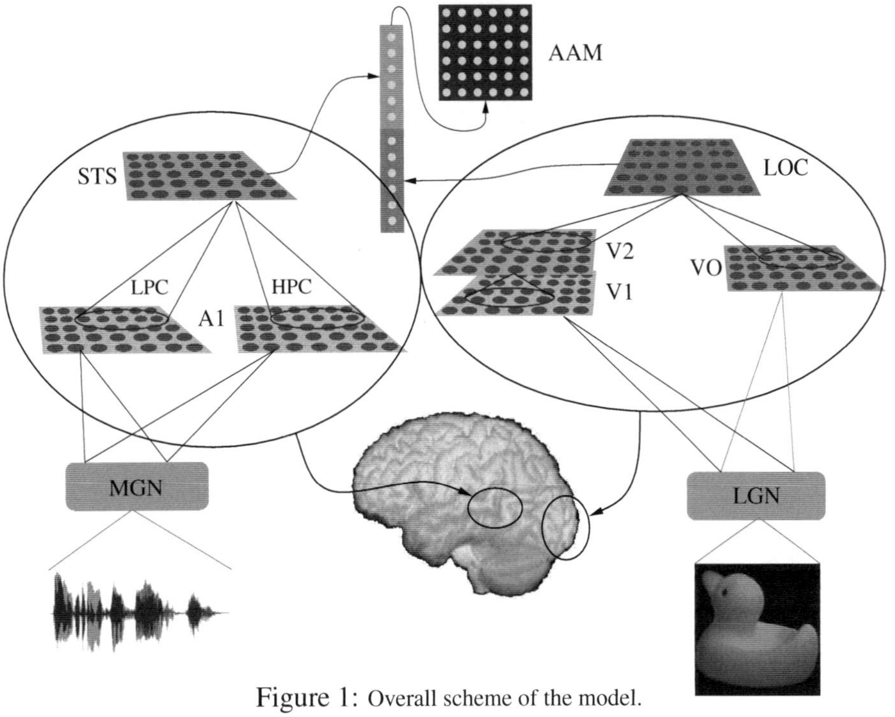

Figure 1: Overall scheme of the model.

models. The LISSOM is a two dimensional arrangement of neurons, where each cell is not only connected with the afferent input vector, but receives excitatory and inhibitory inputs from several neighbor neurons on the same map:

$$\begin{aligned} x_i^{(k)} = f\Bigg(& \frac{\gamma_{\mathrm{A}}}{1+\gamma_{\mathrm{N}}\vec{I}\cdot\vec{v}_{r_{\mathrm{A}},i}}\vec{a}_{r_{\mathrm{A}},i}\cdot\vec{v}_{r_{\mathrm{A}},i} \\ & + \gamma_{\mathrm{E}}\vec{e}_{r_{\mathrm{E}},i}\cdot\vec{x}^{(k-1)}_{r_{\mathrm{E}},i} \\ & - \gamma_{\mathrm{H}}\vec{h}_{r_{\mathrm{H}},i}\cdot\vec{x}^{(k-1)}_{r_{\mathrm{H}},i}\Bigg), \end{aligned} \tag{1}$$

where $x_i^{(k)}$ is the activation of the neuron i at time step k. All vectors are composed by a circular neighborhood of given radius around the neuron i: vectors $\vec{x}^{(k-1)}$ are activations of neurons on the same layer at the previous time step. Vector $\vec{v}_{r_{\mathrm{A}},i}$ comprises all neurons in the underlying layer, in a circular area centered on the projection of i on this layer, with radius r_{A}. Vectors $\vec{a}_{r_{\mathrm{A}},i}$, $\vec{e}_{r_{\mathrm{E}},i}$, and $\vec{h}_{r_{\mathrm{H}},i}$ are composed by all connection strengths of, afferent, excitatory or inhibitory neurons respectively, projecting to i, inside circular areas of radius r_{A}, r_{E}, r_{H}. Vector $\vec{I}$ is just a vector of 1's of the same dimension of $\vec{v}_{r_{\mathrm{A}},i}$. The scalars γ_{A}, γ_{E}, and γ_{H}, are constants modulating the contribution of afferent, excitatory and inhibitory connections. The scalar γ_{N} controls the setting of a push-pull effect in the afferent weights, allowing inhibitory effect without negative weight values. Mathematically, it represents dividing the response from the excitatory weights by the response from a uniform disc of inhibitory weights over the receptive field of neuron i. The map is characterized by the matrices $\mathbf{A}, \mathbf{E}, \mathbf{H}$, which columns are all vectors $\vec{a}$, $\vec{e}$, $\vec{h}$ for every neuron in the map. The function f is a monotonic non-linear function limited between 0 and 1. The final activation value of the neurons is assessed after settling time K.

All connection strengths to neuron i adapt by following the rules:

$$\Delta\vec{a}_{r_{\mathrm{A}},i} = \frac{\vec{a}_{r_{\mathrm{A}},i}+\eta_{\mathrm{A}}x_i\vec{v}_{r_{\mathrm{A}},i}}{\|\vec{a}_{r_{\mathrm{A}},i}+\eta_{\mathrm{A}}x_i\vec{v}_{r_{\mathrm{A}},i}\|} - \vec{a}_{r_{\mathrm{A}},i}, \tag{2}$$

$$\Delta\vec{e}_{r_{\mathrm{E}},i} = \frac{\vec{e}_{r_{\mathrm{E}},i}+\eta_{\mathrm{E}}x_i\vec{x}_{r_{\mathrm{E}},i}}{\|\vec{a}_{r_{\mathrm{E}},i}+\eta_{\mathrm{E}}x_i\vec{x}_{r_{\mathrm{E}},i}\|} - \vec{e}_{r_{\mathrm{E}},i}, \tag{3}$$

$$\Delta\vec{h}_{r_{\mathrm{H}},i} = \frac{\vec{h}_{r_{\mathrm{H}},i}+\eta_{\mathrm{A}}x_i\vec{x}_{r_{\mathrm{H}},i}}{\left\|\vec{h}_{r_{\mathrm{H}},i}+\eta_{\mathrm{A}}x_i\vec{x}_{r_{\mathrm{H}},i}\right\|} - \vec{h}_{r_{\mathrm{H}},i}, \tag{4}$$

where $\eta_{\{\mathrm{A,E,H}\}}$ are the learning rates for afferent, excitatory and inhibitory synaptic modifications. All rules are based on the Hebbian law, with an additional competitive factor, here implemented as a normalization, that maintains constant the integration of all connection strengths to the same neu-

	layer	size	r_A	r_E	r_H	γ_A	γ_E	γ_H	γ_N
LGN	Lateral Geniculated Nucleus	120×120	-	-	-	-	-	-	-
MGN	Medial Geniculated Nucleus	32×32	-	-	-	-	-	-	-
V1	Primary Visual Cortex	96×96	8.5	1.5	7.0	1.5	1.0	1.0	0.0
V2	Secondary Visual Cortex	30×30	7.5	8.5	3.5	50.0	3.2	2.5	0.7
VO	Ventral Occipital	30×30	24.5	4.0	8.0	1.8	1.0	1.0	0.0
A1	Auditory Primary Cortex	24×24	3.5	2.5	5.5	5.0	5.0	6.7	0.8
LOC	Lateral Occipital Complex	16×16	6.5	1.5	3.5	1.2	1.0	1.5	0.0
STS	Superior Temporal Sulcus	16×16	3.5	2.5	2.5	2.0	1.6	2.6	0.0

Table 1: Legend of all modules, and main parameters of the cortical layers composing the model.

ron, and to the same type (afferent, excitatory or inhibitory). This is a computational account of the biological phenomena of homeostatic plasticity, that induce neurons in the cortex to maintain an average firing rate by correcting their incoming synaptic strengths.

2.2 The overall model

An outline of the modules that make up the model is shown in Fig. 1. The component names and their dimensions are in Tab. 1. All cortical layers are implemented by LISSOM maps, where the afferent connections $\vec{v}$ in (1) are either neurons of lower LISSOM maps, or neurons in the thalamic nuclei MGN and LGN. There are two main paths, one for the visual process and another for the auditory channel. Both paths include thalamic modules, which are not the object of this study and are therefore hardwired according to what is known about their functions. The two higher cortical maps, LOC and STS, will carry the best representation coded by models on object visual features and word features. These two representations are associated in an abstract type map, called AAM (*Abstract Associative Map*). This component is implemented using the SOM (*Self Organized Map*) (Kohonen, 1995) architecture, known to provide non linear bidimensional ordering of input vectors by unsupervised mechanisms. It is the only component of the model that cannot be conceptually referred to as a precise cortical area. It is an abstraction of processes that actually involve several brain areas in a complex way, and as such departs computationally from realistic cortical architecture.

2.3 The visual pathway

As shown in Fig. 1, the architecture here used includes hardwired extracortical maps with simple on-center and off-center receptive fields. There are three pairs of sheets in the LGN maps: one connected to the intensity image plane, and the other two connected to the medium and long wavelength planes. In the color channels the internal excitatory portion of the receptive field is connected to the channel of one color, and the surrounding inhibitory part to the opposite color. The cortical process proceeds along two different streams: the achromatic component is connected to the primary visual map V1 followed by V2, the two spectral components are processed by map VO, the color center, also called hV4 or V8 (Brewer et al., 2005). The two streams rejoin in the cortical map LOC, the area recently suggested as being the first involved in object recognition in humans (Malach et al., 1995; Kanwisher, 2003). Details of the visual path are in (Plebe and Domenella, 2006).

2.4 The auditory pathway

The hardwired extracortical MGN component is just a placeholder for the spectrogram representation of the sound pressure waves, which is extracted with tools of the *Festival* software (Black and Taylor, 1997). It is justified by evidence of the spectro-temporal process performed by the cochlear-thalamic circuits (Escabi and Read, 2003). The auditory primary cortex is simulated by a double sheet of neurons, taking into account a double population of cells found in this area (Atzori et al., 2001), where the so-called LPC (*Low-Probability Connections*) is sensitive to the stationary component of the sound signal and the HPC (*High-Probability Connections*) population responds to transient inputs mainly. The next map in the auditory path of the model is STS, because the superior temporal sulcus is believed to be the main brain area responsive to vocal sounds (Belin et al., 2002).

2.5 The Abstract Associative Map

The upper AAM map in the model reflects how the system associates certain sound forms with the visual appearance of objects, and has the main purpose of showing what has been achieved in the cortical part of the model. It is trained using the outputs of the STS and the LOC maps of the model. After training, each neuron x in AAM is labeled, according to different test conditions X. The labeling function $l(\cdot)$ associates the neuron x with an entity e, which can be an object o of the COIL set $\mathcal{O}$, when $X \in \{\mathrm{A}, \mathrm{B}\}$ or a category c of the set $\mathcal{C}$ for the test condition $X \in \{\mathrm{C}, \mathrm{D}\}$. The general form of the labeling function is:

$$l^{(X)}(x) = \arg\max_{e \in \mathcal{E}} \left\{ \left| \mathcal{W}_x^{(e)} \right| \right\} \tag{5}$$

where $\mathcal{W}_x^{(e)}$ is a set of sensorial stimuli related to the element $e \in \mathcal{E}$, such that their processing in the model activate x as winner in the AMM map. The set $\mathcal{E}$ can be $\mathcal{O}$ or $\mathcal{C}$ depending on X. The neuron x elicited in the AAM map as the consequence of presenting a visual stimulus v_o of an object o and a sound stimulus s_c of a tagory c is given by the function $x = w(v_o, s_c)$ with the convention that $w(v, \epsilon)$ computes the winning neuron in AAM comparing only the LOC portion of the coding vector, and $w(\epsilon, s)$ only the STS portion. The function $b(o) : \mathcal{O} \to \mathcal{C}$ associates an object o to its category. Here four testing conditions are used:

- A object recognition by vision and audio
- B object recognition by vision only
- C category recognition by vision and audio
- D category recognition by audio only

corresponding to the following $\mathcal{W}$ sets in (5):

$$\begin{aligned} \mathrm{A} &: \{v_o : x = w(v_o, s_{c(o)})\} && (6) \\ \mathrm{B} &: \{v_o : x = w(v_o, \epsilon)\} && (7) \\ \mathrm{C} &: \{v_o : c = b(o) \wedge x = w(\epsilon, s_c)\} && (8) \\ \mathrm{D} &: \{s_c : x = w(\epsilon, s_c)\} && (9) \end{aligned}$$

From the labeling functions the possibility of estimating the accuracy of recognition immediately follows, simply by weighing the number of cases where the category or the object has been classified as the prevailing one in each neuron of the AAM SOM.

2.6 Exposure to stimuli

The visual path in the model develops in two stages. Initially the inputs to the network are synthetic random blobs, simulating pre-natal waves of spontaneous activity, known to be essential in the early development of the visual system (Sengpiel and Kind, 2002). In the second stage, corresponding to the period after eye opening, natural images are used. In order to address one of the main problems in recognition, the identifying of an object under different views, the COIL-100 collection has been used (Nayar and Murase, 1995) where 72 different views are available for each of the 100 objects. Using natural images where there is only one main object is cleary a simplification in the vision process of this model, but it does not compromise the realism of the conditions. It always could be assumed that the single object analysis corresponds to a foval focusing as consequence of a saccadic move, cued by any attentive mechanism.

In the auditory path there are different stages as well. Initially, the maps are exposed to random patches in frequency-time domain, with shorter duration for HPC and longer for LPC. Subsequently, all the auditory maps are exposed to the 7200 most common English words (from `http://www.bckelk.uklinux.net/menu.html`) with lengths between 3 and 10 characters. All words are converted from text to waves using *Festival* (Black and Taylor, 1997), with cepstral order 64 and a unified time window of 2.3 seconds. Eventually, the last stage of training simulates events when an object is viewed and a word corresponding to its basic category is heard simultaneously. The 100 objects have been grouped manually into 38 categories. Some categories, such as `cup` or `medicine` count 5 exemplars in the object collection, while others, such as `telephone`, have only one exemplar.

3 Results

3.1 Developed functions in the cortical maps

At the end of development each map in the model has evolved its own function. Different functions have emerged from identical computational architectures. The differences are due to the different positions of a maps in the modules hierarchy, to different exposure to environmental stimuli, and different structural parameters. The functions obtained in the experiment are the following. In the visual path orientation selectivity emerged in the model's V1 map as demonstrated in (Sirosh and Miikkulainen, 1997) and (Plebe and Domenella, 2006). Orientation selectivity is the main organization in primary visual cortex, where the responsiveness of neurons to oriented segments is arranged over repeated patterns of gradually changing orientations, broken by few discontinuities (Vanduffel et al., 2002). Angle selectivity emerged in the model's V2 map. In the secondary visual cortex the main recently discovered phenomena is the selectivity to angles (Ito and Komatsu, 2004), especially in the range between 60 and 150 degrees. The essential features of color constancy are reproduced in the model's VO map, which is the ability of neurons to respond to specific hues, regardless of intensity. Color constancy is the tendency of the color of a surface to appear more constant that it is in reality. This property is helpful in object recognition, and develops sometime between two and four months of age. (Dannemiller, 1989). One of the main functions shown by the LOC layer in the model is visual invariance, the property of neurons to respond to peculiar object features despite changes in the object's appearance due to different points of view. Invariance indeed is one of the main requirements for an object-recognition area, and is found in human LOC (Grill-Spector et al., 2001; Kanwisher, 2003). Tonotopic mapping is a known feature of the primary auditory cortex that represents the dimensions of frequency and time sequences in a sound pattern (Verkindt et al., 1995). In the model it is split into a sheet where neurons have receptive fields that are more elongated along the time dimension (LPC) and another where the resulting receptive fields are more elongated along the frequency dimension (HPC). The spectrotemporal mapping obtained in STS is a population coding of features, in frequency and time domains, representative of the sound patterns heard during the development phase. It therefore reflects the statistical phonemic regularities in common spoken English, extracted from the 7200 training samples.

category	test A	test B	test C	test D
medicine	0.906	0.803	1.0	1.0
fruit	1.0	0.759	1.0	1.0
boat	0.604	0.401	1.0	1.0
tomato	1.0	0.889	1.0	1.0
sauce	1.0	1.0	1.0	1.0
car	0.607	0.512	0.992	1.0
drink	0.826	0.812	1.0	1.0
soap	0.696	0.667	1.0	1.0
cup	1.0	0.919	1.0	0.0
piece	0.633	0.561	1.0	1.0
kitten	1.0	0.806	1.0	1.0
bird	1.0	1.0	1.0	1.0
truck	0.879	0.556	1.0	1.0
dummy	1.0	0.833	1.0	1.0
tool	0.722	0.375	1.0	1.0
pottery	1.0	1.0	1.0	1.0
jam	1.0	1.0	1.0	1.0
frog	1.0	0.806	1.0	1.0
cheese	0.958	0.949	1.0	1.0
bottle	0.856	0.839	1.0	1.0
hanger	1.0	0.694	1.0	1.0
sweets	1.0	0.701	1.0	1.0
tape	1.0	0.861	1.0	1.0
mug	0.944	0.889	1.0	1.0
spoon	1.0	0.680	1.0	1.0
cigarettes	0.972	0.729	0.972	1.0
ring	1.0	1.0	1.0	1.0
pig	1.0	0.778	1.0	1.0
dog	1.0	0.917	1.0	1.0
toast	1.0	0.868	1.0	1.0
plug	1.0	0.771	1.0	1.0
pot	1.0	0.681	1.0	1.0
telephone	1.0	0.306	1.0	1.0
pepper	1.0	0.951	1.0	1.0
chewinggum	0.954	0.509	1.0	1.0
chicken	1.0	0.944	1.0	1.0
jug	1.0	0.917	1.0	1.0
can	1.0	0.903	1.0	1.0

Table 2: Accuracy in recognition measured by labeling in the AAM, for objects grouped by category.

3.2 Recognition and categorization in AAM

The accuracy of object and category recognition under several conditions is shown in Table 2. All tests clearly prove that the system has learned an efficient capacity of object recognition and naming, with respect to the small world of object and names used in the experiment. Tests C and D demonstrate that the recognition of categories by names is almost complete, both when hearing a name or when seeing an object and hearing its name. In tests A and B, the recognition of individual objects is also very high. In several cases, it can be seen that names also help in the recognition of individual objects. One of the clearest cases is the category `tool` (shown in Fig. 2),

shape	test A	test B	Δ
h-parallelepiped	0.921	0.712	0.209
round	1.0	0.904	0.096
composed	0.702	0.565	0.137
q-cylindrical	0.884	0.861	0.023
q-h-parallelepiped	0.734	0.513	0.221
cylindrical	0.926	0.907	0.019
cup-shaped	0.975	0.897	0.078
q-v-parallelepiped	0.869	0.754	0.115
body	1.0	0.869	0.131
conic	1.0	1.0	0.0
parallelepiped	0.722	0.510	0.212
q-parallelepiped	1.0	0.634	0.366

Table 3: Accuracy in recognition measured by labeling in the AAM, for objects grouped by their visual shape, Δ is the improvement gained with naming.

where the accuracy for each individual object doubles when using names. It seems to be analogous to the situation described in (Smith, 1999), where the word contributes to the emergence of patterns of regularity. The 100% accuracy for the category, in this case, is better accounted for as an emergent example of synonymy, where coupling with the same word is accepted, despite the difference in the output of the visual process.

In table 3 accuracy results for individual objects are listed, grouped by object shape. In this case category accuracy cannot be computed, because shapes cross category boundaries. It can be seen that the improvement Δ is proportional to the salience in shape: it is meaningless for common, obvious shapes, and higher when object shape is uncommon. This result is in agreement with findings in (Gershkoff-Stowe and Smith, 2004).

4 Conclusions

The model here described attempts to simulate lexical acquisition from auditory and visual stimuli from a brain processes point of view. It models these processes in a biologically plausible way in that it does not begin with a predetermined design of mature functions, but instead allows final functions of the components to emerge as a result of the plastic development of neural circuits. It grounds this choice and its design principles in what is known of the cerebral cortex. In this model, the overall important result achieved so far, is the emergence of naming and recognition abilities exclusively through exposure of the system to environmental stimuli, in terms of activities similar to pre-natal spontaneous activities, and later to natural images and vocal sounds. This result has interesting theoretical implications for developmental psychologists and may provide a useful computational tool for future investigations on phenomena such as the effects of shape on object recognition and naming.

In conclusion this model represents a first step in simulating the interaction of the visual and the auditory cortex in learning object recognition and naming, and being a model of high level complex cognitive functions, it necessarily lacks several details of the biological cortical circuits. It lacks biological plausibility in the auditory path because of the state of current knowledge of the processes going on there. Future developments of the model will foresee the inclusion of backprojections between maps in the hierarchy, trials on preliminary categorization at the level of phonemes and syllables in the auditory path, as well as exposure to images with multiple objects in the scene.

References

Marco Atzori, Saobo Lei, D. Ieuan P. Evans, Patrick O. Kanold, Emily Phillips-Tansey, Orinthal McIntyre, and Chris J. McBain. 2001. Differential synaptic processing separates stationary from transient inputs to the auditory cortex. *Neural Networks*, 4:1230–1237.

James A. Bednar. 2002. *Learning to See: Genetic and Environmental Influences on Visual Development*. Ph.D. thesis, University of Texas at Austin. Tech Report AI-TR-02-294.

Pascal Belin, Robert J. Zatorre, and Pierre Ahad. 2002. Human temporal-lobe response to vocal sounds. *Cognitive Brain Research*, 13:17–26.

Alan W. Black and Paul A. Taylor. 1997. The festival speech synthesis system: System documentation. Technical Report HCRC/TR-83, Human Communciation Research Centre, University of Edinburgh, Edinburgh, UK.

Paul Bloom. 2000. *How children learn the meanings of words*. MIT Press, Cambridge (MA).

Alyssa A. Brewer, Junjie Liu, Alex R. Wade, and Brian A. Wandell. 2005. Visual field maps and stimulus selectivity in human ventral occipital cortex. *Nature Neuroscience*, 8:1102–1109.

Susan Carey and Elizabeth Spelke. 1996. Science and core knowledge. *Journal of Philosophy of Science*, 63:515–533.

James L. Dannemiller. 1989. A test of color constancy in 9- and 20-weeks-old human infants following simulated illuminant changes. *Developmental Psychology*, 25:171–184.

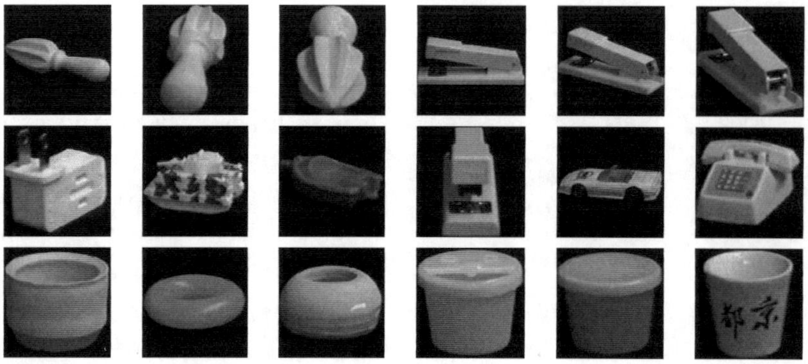

Figure 2: Objects mentioned in the discussion on recognition results. In the upper row views of the two objects of the category `tool`. In the middle row objects with difficult shapes (`q-h-parallelepiped`, `q-parallelepiped`). In the lower row objects with easy shapes (`cylindrical`, `round`, and `conic`).

Monty A. Escabi and Heather L. Read. 2003. Representation of spectrotemporal sound information in the ascending auditory pathway. *Biological Cybernetics*, 89:350–362.

Lisa Gershkoff-Stowe and Linda B. Smith. 2004. Shape and the first hundred nouns. *Child Development*, 75:1098–1114.

Jane Gillette, Henry Gleitman, Lila Gleitman, and Anne Lederer. 1999. Human simulations of vocabulary learning. *Cognition*, 73:135–176.

Kalanit Grill-Spector, Zoe Kourtzi, and Nancy Kanwisher. 2001. The lateral occipital complex and its role in object recognition. *Vision Research*, 41:1409–1422.

Minami Ito and Hidehiko Komatsu. 2004. Representation of angles embedded within contour stimuli in area V2 of macaque monkeys. *Journal of Neuroscience*, 24:3313–3324.

Nancy Kanwisher. 2003. The ventral visual object pathway in humans: Evidence from fMRI. In Leo Chalupa and John Werner, editors, *The Visual Neurosciences*. MIT Press, Cambridge (MA).

Lawrence C. Katz and Edward M. Callaway. 1992. Development of local circuits in mammalian visual cortex. *Annual Review Neuroscience*, 15:31–56.

Teuvo Kohonen. 1995. *Self-Organizing Maps*. Springer-Verlag, Berlin.

Siegrid Löwel and Wolf Singer. 2002. Experience-dependent plasticity of intracortical connections. In Manfred Fahle and Tomaso Poggio, editors, *Perceptual Learning*. MIT Press, Cambridge (MA).

R. Malach, J. B. Reppas, R. R. Benson, K. K. Kwong, H. Jiang, W. A. Kennedy, P. J. Ledden, T. J. Brady, B. R. Rosen, and R. B.H. Tootell. 1995. Object-related activity revealed by functional magnetic resonance imaging in human occipital cortex. *Proceedings of the Natural Academy of Science USA*, 92:8135–8139.

Jean Matter Mandler. 2004. *The Foundations of Mind*. Oxford University Press, Oxford (UK).

Shree Nayar and Hiroshi Murase. 1995. Visual learning and recognition of 3-d object by appearence. *International Journal of Computer Vision*, 14:5–24.

Alessio Plebe and Rosaria Grazia Domenella. 2006. Early development of visual recognition. *BioSystems*, 86:63–74.

Shannon M. Pruden, Kathy Hirsh-Pasek, Roberta Michnick Golinkoff, and Elizabeth A. Hennon. 2006. The birth of words: Ten-month-olds learn words through perceptual salience. *Child Development*, 77:266–280.

Steven R. Quartz. 2003. Innateness and the brain. *Biology and Philosophy*, 18:13–40.

Terry Regier. 2005. The emergence of words: Attentional learning in form and meaning. *Cognitive Science*, 29:819–865.

Timothy T. Rogers and James L. McClelland. 2006. *Semantic Cognition - A Parallel Distributed Processing Approach*. MIT Press, Cambridge (MA).

Frank Sengpiel and Peter C. Kind. 2002. The role of activity in development of the visual system. *Current Biology*, 12:818–826.

Joseph Sirosh and Risto Miikkulainen. 1997. Topographic receptive fields and patterned lateral interaction in a self-organizing model of the primary visual cortex. *Neural Computation*, 9:577–594.

Linda B. Smith. 1999. Children's noun learning: How general learning processes make specialized learning mechanisms. In Brian MacWhinney, editor, *The Emergence of Language*. Lawrence Erlbaum Associates, Mahwah (NJ). Second Edition.

Michael Tomasello. 1999. *The cultural origins of human cognition*. Harvard University Press, Cambridge (MA).

Wim Vanduffel, Roger B.H. Tootell, Anick A. Schoups, and Guy A. Orban. 2002. The organization of orientation selectivity throughout the macaque visual cortex. *Cerebral Cortex*, 12:647–662.

Chantal Verkindt, Olivier Bertrand, Franqis Echallier, and Jacques Pernier. 1995. Tonotopic organization of the human auditory cortex: N100 topography and multiple dipole model analysis. *Electroencephalography and Clinical Neurophisiology*, 96:143–156.

Rethinking the syntactic burst in young children

Christophe Parisse
INSERM-Modyco
Paris X Nanterre University
CNRS
parisse@vjf.cnrs.fr

Abstract

A testing procedure is proposed to re-evaluate the syntactic burst in children over age two. The experimentation is based on the children's capacities in perception, memory, association and cognition, and does not presuppose any specific innate grammatical capacities. The procedure is tested using the large Manchester corpus in the CHILDES database. The results showed that young children grammatical capabilities (before age three) could be the results of simple mechanisms and that complex linguistic mastery does not need to be available so early in the course of language development.

1 Introduction

Between the ages of two and three, most children go through a syntactic burst. In other words, they progress from uttering one word at a time to constructing utterances with a mean length of more than three words, and frequently longer, and they do this without any negative evidence and with limited input data (Ritchie & Bhatia, 1999). This represents quite a mystery, which is often explained by postulating the existence of innate constraints on the grammar of the human languages and the human mind (Pinker, 1984; Wexler, 1982). This report uses an iterative procedure to demonstrate that what appears to be near magical could result mostly from mechanisms that do not require the existence of innate principles of grammar, as they are based on children's inherent capacities for perception, memory and association (Jusczyk & Hohne, 1997; Saffran, Johnson, Aslin, & Newport, 1999). The acquisition of complex 'across the board' grammar does not appear to be necessary to explain children's behavior before age three or more. At that age, much more complex and structured input data will be available to children, thereby increasing their learning capacities and reducing the limitations on knowledge they may acquire.

2 A testing procedure in three parts

The testing procedure for grammatical development that will be implemented in this report is made of three parts.

The goal of the first and the second part is to determine the basic elements that children use to construct language. Two assumptions are made about young children's perceptive and mnemonic capacities: anything they have once produced, they can produce again; and, when their language exactly reproduces an adult's, this can be explained as a simple copy of their input.

Part 1: All single-word utterances produced by children are meaningful to them; they are directly derived from adults' output. They are the basic elements that children use to build language.

Part 2: Children's multi-word utterances containing only one word already produced in isolation (words produced in part 1), along with other words never produced in isolation (never produced at part 1), are also basic elements that children use to speak. They are also directly derived from children's input; this is facilitated by the children's knowledge of isolated words. These multi-word utterances are manipulated and understood by chil-

Proceedings of the Workshop on Cognitive Aspects of Computational Language Acquisition, pages 65–72,
Prague, Czech Republic, June 2007

dren as single blocks, just as isolated words are. They may also be called frozen forms.

The goal of the third part is to check whether the basic elements identified in part 1 and 2 are sufficient to account for the children's multiword utterances.

Part 3: Children link utterances produced at parts 1 and 2 to produce multi-word utterances with more than one word already produced in isolation (words produced in part 1). They do this using a simple concatenation mechanism and the fact that the utterances they create have a pertinent meaning prevents them from producing aberrant utterances.

Since the productions of children and their adult partners are easy to record, it is possible to test whether the testing procedure has sufficient generative power to account for all children's productions. However, some points could make such a demonstration more difficult than it appears. First of all, the assumption made in part 1 is not always true, as it is quite possible for a child to reproduce any sequence of sounds while playing with language. This uncertainty about part 1 is only important in conjunction with part 2, as isolated words are the key used to parse the elements of part 2. To decide that a word has meaning in isolation for a child, it has been assumed that it must first have meaning in isolation for an adult. Words in the categories of determiner and auxiliary produced in isolation have been considered as not having meaning in isolation and have therefore been removed from the elements gathered at part 1. Analysis of language data demonstrated that this assumption is quite reasonable, as the use of these words in isolation is often the result of unfinished utterances, with incomplete prosody.

Measuring the generative power of the testing procedure implies evaluating the accuracy of the assumptions made in parts 1, 2 and 3. These assumptions are quite easy to accept for very young children, at the time of the first multi-word utterances, i.e. before age two. The question is: to what extent is this true and until what age? Two experiments have been carried out in order to answer this question.

3 Experiment 1

The experiment 1 used a corpus extracted from the CHILDES database (MacWhinney, 2000). It is referred to as the Manchester corpus (Theakston, Lieven, Pine, & Rowland, 1999) and consists of recordings of 12 children from the age of 1;10 to 2;9. Their mean length of utterance varies from 1.5 to 2.9 words. Each child was seen 34 times and each recording lasted one hour. This results in a total production of 537,811 words in token and 7,840 in type. For each child, the average is 44,817 words in token (SD = 9,653) and 1,913 in type (SD = 372).

The testing procedure was run in three steps in an iterative way. Each step from the experiment corresponds to one of the parts described above.

Step 1: For each transcript, the child's single-word utterances are extracted and added to a cumulative list of words uttered in isolation, referred to as L1. It is possible to measure at this point whether the words on L1 can be derived from the adult's output. In order to do this, a cumulative list, L-adult, of all adult utterances is also maintained.

Step 2: For each multi-word utterance in the transcript, the number of words previously uttered in isolation is computed using list L1. Multi-word utterances with only one word uttered in isolation are added to a list called L2. It is possible to measure at this point whether the utterances on L2 can be derived from the adult's output (list L-adult above).

Step 3: the remaining utterances (list L3), which contain more than one word previously uttered in isolation, are used to test the final step of the algorithm. The test consists in trying to reconstruct these utterances using a catenation of the utterances from lists L1 and L2 only. Two measurements can be obtained: the percentage of utterances on list L3 that can be fully reconstructed (referred to below as the 'percentage of exact reconstruction') and the percentage of words in the utterances on list L3 that contribute to a reconstruction (referred to below as the 'percentage of reconstruction covering'). For example, for the utterance 'The boy has gone to school', if L1 and L2 contain 'the boy' and 'has gone' but not 'to school', only 'the boy has gone' can be reconstructed, thus leading to a percentage of reconstruction covering of 66%. Thus, the percentage of exact reconstruction is the percentage of utterances with a 100% reconstruction covering. The percentages of list L3 that are reconstructed or recovered do not include utterances from L1 and L2 lists.

The testing procedure is iterative because it is performed in turn for each of the transcripts of the corpus. List L1, L2 and L-adult are cumulative, which means that the list obtained with transcript 1 are used as a starting point for the analysis of transcript 2, and so on. This presupposes that children can reuse data they heard only once a long time after they heard it.

In Step 1 it was found that the percentage of words on L1 present in adult speech has a mean value of 91% (SD = 0.03). Step 2 revealed that the percentage of elements of L2 present in adult speech has a mean value of 67% (SD = 0.05). These two results are stable across ages—even though lists L1, L2 and L-adult are growing continuously. After two transcripts, for all 12 children, lists L1 + L2 represent 11,979 words in token and L-adult contains 82,255 words in token. After 17 transcripts, these totals are 89,479 and 688,802, respectively. After 34 transcripts, they total 167,149 and 1,370,565. The ratio comparing the size of L1 + L2 and L-adult does not evolve much, varying between 6 and 8.

Figure 1: Percentage of utterances exactly reconstructed

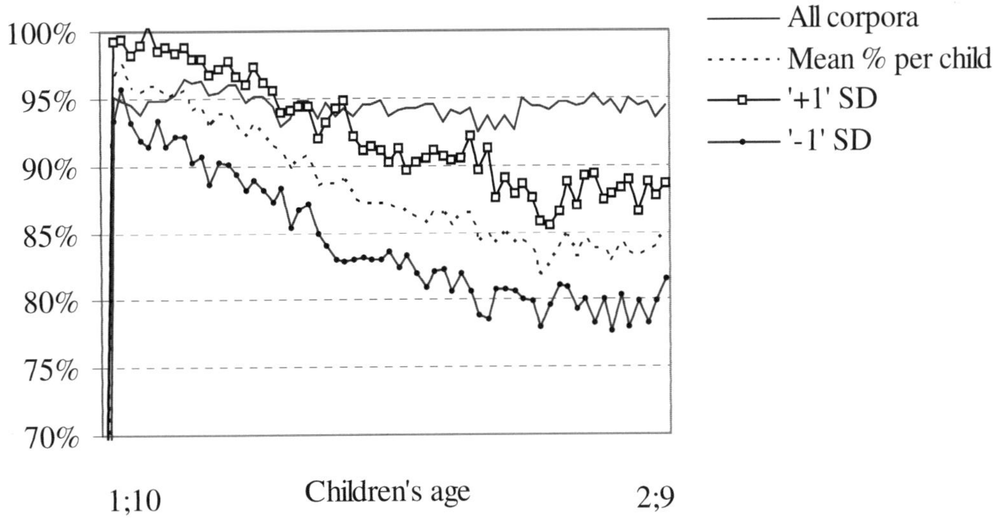

Figure 2: Percentage of reconstruction covering in all utterances

The results for Step 3 are presented in Figures 1 and 2. Each point in the series corresponds to the nth iteration performed with the nth transcript. The mean value is the mean of the percentage for all children considered as individuals (reconstruction between a child's corpus and his/her parents' corpus only). The algorithm is also applied to all corpora: for each point in the series of recordings, the 12 files corresponding to 12 children are gathered into a single file used to run the nth iteration of the algorithm. Percentages for all corpora are shown with a bold line. The percentages are clearly higher for the aggregated corpora, although the number of unknown utterances (list L3) increased more than the number of known utterances (lists L1 and L2). After two transcripts, there are half as many elements in list L3 as in L1 + L2. But after 17 transcripts, L3 is 42% larger than L1 + L2, and after 34 transcripts, it is 127% larger. As children grow older, there is a decrease in the scores for exact reconstruction and reconstruction covering. This decrease is greater in individuals than for the children as a group, which suggests a size effect.

4 Experiment 2

The second experiment uses the same corpus and reproduces the same tests but assumes that children have knowledge of the syntactic categories Noun and Verb. The conditions of step 2 and step 3 are more easily fulfilled if the children have a certain amount of syntactic class knowledge. As described by Maratsos and Chalkley (1980), it is possible for children to learn syntactic classes from the contexts in which words occur. However, knowledge of part of speech is unlikely in very young children on the basis of syntactic distribution. Semantic knowledge can also help to construct syntactic knowledge (Bloom, 1999) for classes such as common nouns, proper nouns and verbs, and perhaps also adjectives and adverbs. To simulate the fact that children are able to construct the classes of common nouns, proper nouns and non-auxiliary verbs, it suffices to substitute every occurrence of common or proper nouns in the Manchester corpus by the symbol 'noun' and every occurrence of non-auxiliary verbs by the symbol 'verb'. This is easy to realize because the Manchester corpus has been fully tagged for part of speech, as described in the MOR section of the CHILDES manual (MacWhinney, 2000). The result is that list L1 now includes all nouns, all verbs plus all words occurring in isolation, as in the first experiment. In list L2, in utterances that include a word from the categories Noun or Verb, this word is substituted by the symbol 'noun' or 'verb'. These utterances now form rule-like productive patterns known as formulaic frames (Peters, 1995) or slot-and-frame structures (Lieven, Pine, & Baldwin, 1997) — for example, 'my + NOUN'.

When we reproduce the first experiment under these conditions, the new results obtained at steps 2 and 3 should be better, in the sense that they should correspond more closely to the adult input, and should hold up longer on the age scale.

The results for Step 1 and Step 2 are indeed better than before. The percentage of utterances on L2 present in adult speech has a mean value of 91% (SD = 0.02).

The results for Step 3 are presented in Figure 3 (for exact reconstruction) and Figure 4 (for reconstruction covering). In each of these figures, two results are presented for the whole Manchester corpus: one assuming no category knowledge, and one assuming the knowledge of the three categories proper noun, common noun and verb. The percentages of reconstruction become markedly higher, as any combination that contains some of three categories proper noun, common noun and verb is known for all occurrences of words from these categories. The mean for exact reconstruction with 'no category' knowledge is 67% (SD = 5.7) and 87% (SD = 2.0) for reconstruction covering. These values increase to 83% (SD = 5.2) and 95% (SD = 2.6) for 'noun and verb' knowledge.

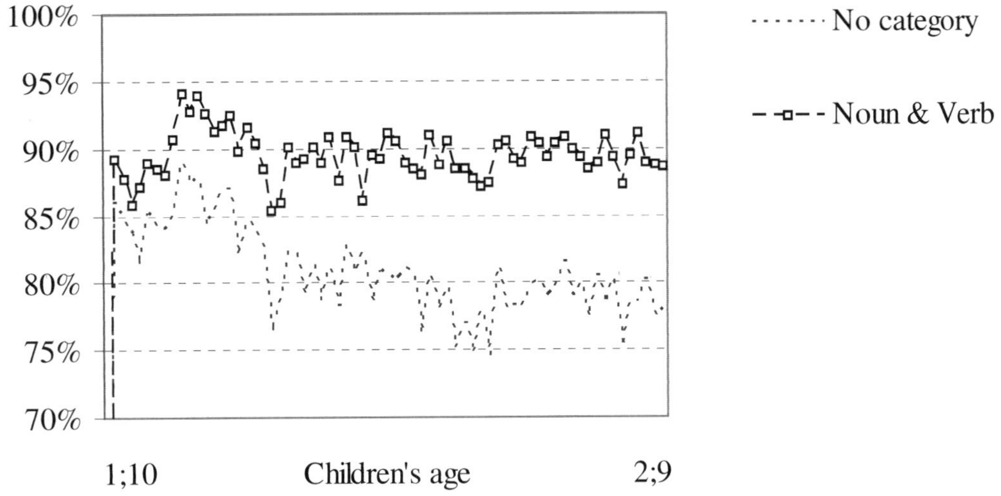

Figure 3: Percentage of utterances exactly reconstructed, depending on the degree of knowledge of noun and verb categories

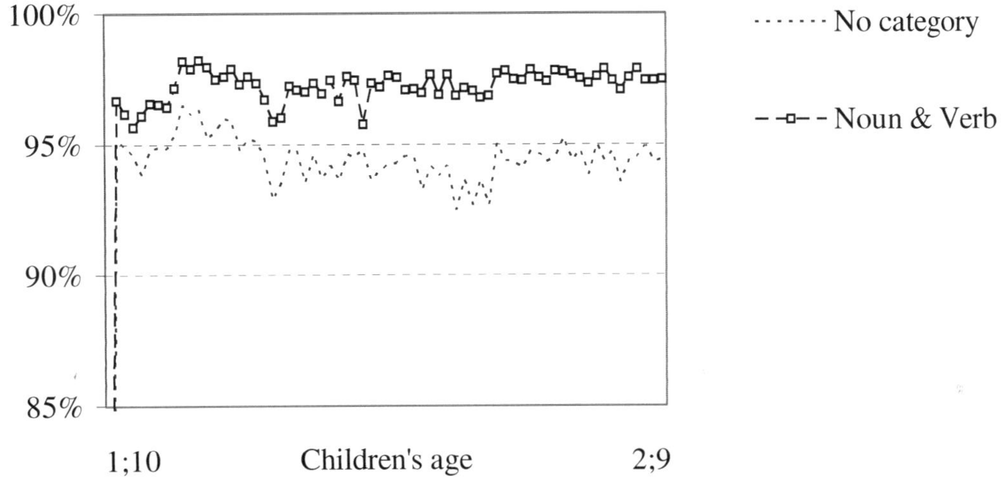

Figure 4: Percentage of reconstruction covering in all utterances, depending on the degree of knowledge of noun and verb categories

5 Experiment 3

A limit of experiments 1 and 2 is that nothing indicates how long the three-step mechanisms would remain efficient and appropriate. We supposed that these mechanisms would remain operational at an older age. This can be checked using other material from the CHILDES database with recordings spanning a longer period. The corpus chosen for the test is Brown's (1973) Sarah corpus, which ranges from age 2;3 to age 5;1; with its 139 different transcripts, it follows the development of the child's language quite well and is well suited for the purposes of this study, which requires lengthy corpora. The mean length of utterance varies from 1.47 to 4.85 words. This results in a total production of 99,918 words in token and 3,990 in type.

Step 1 found the percentage of words on L1 present in adult speech to have a mean value of 77% (SD = 14.5). Step 2 revealed that the percentage of elements of L2 present in adult speech had a mean value of 38% (SD = 11.5). These two results are stable across ages. With the assumption of a knowledge of the Noun and Verb categories, results for Step 1 and 2 are, respectively, 83% (SD = 13.8) and 55% (SD = 16.6).

The results for Step 3 are presented in Figure 5 (for exact reconstruction) and Figure 6 (for reconstruction covering). In each of these figures, two results are presented: one assuming no category knowledge and one assuming knowledge of the three categories Proper Noun, Common Noun and Verb. The mean for exact reconstruction with "no category" knowledge is 54% (SD = 17.6) and 84% (SD = 6.6) for reconstruction covering. These values increase 72% (SD = 11.9) and 93% (SD = 4.0) for "Noun and Verb" knowledge.

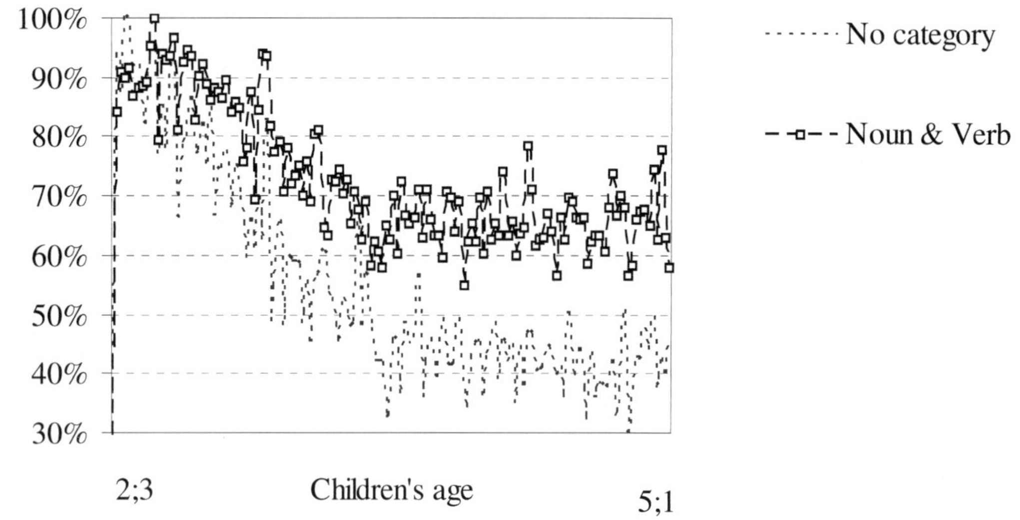

Figure 5: Percentage of utterances in the Sarah corpus exactly reconstructed, depending on the degree of knowledge of vocabulary and syntactic categories

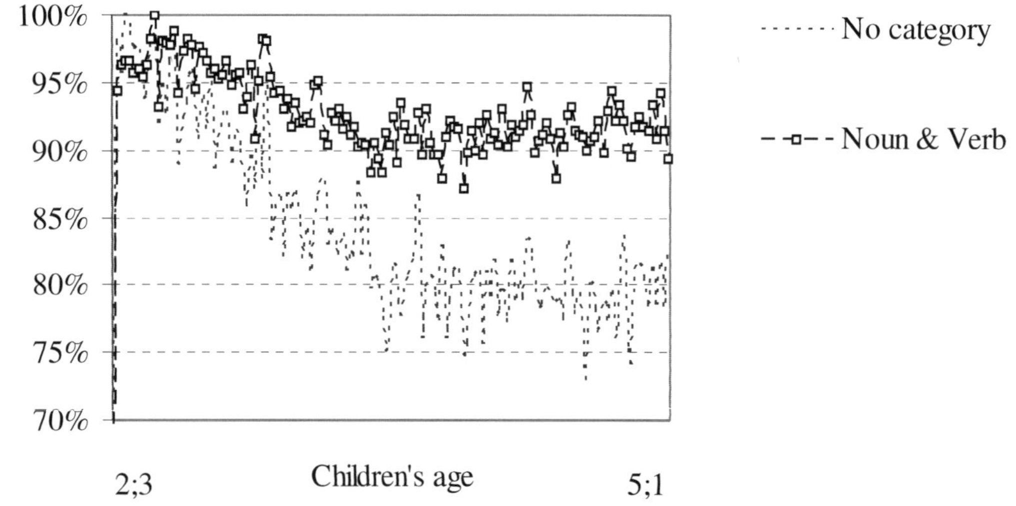

Figure 6: Percentage of reconstruction covering in all utterances in the Sarah corpus, depending on the degree of knowledge of vocabulary and syntactic categories

The average percentages of reconstruction are lower for the Sarah corpus than for the Manchester corpus. Comparing Figures 3 and 6 and Figures 4 and 7, one can see that there is a drop in the reconstruction performances in the third year. The percentages for Sarah in her second year were as high as those for the Manchester corpus children. Part of this drop in performance may be attributed to the smaller corpus. Indeed, comparing Figures 1 and 3 and Figures 2 and 4, it appears that the drop in performance that became visible when single child corpora were used was not in evidence when all the corpora were amalgamated into one big corpus. It is also possible that the drop in performance found in the Sarah corpus reflects a progressive decrease in the systematic use of a simple concatenation procedure by the child.

6 Discussion

The testing procedure does not achieve a full 100% reconstruction in the test conditions described above, where the database consists of only 34 one-hour recordings for each of the 12 children in the corpus. This corresponds globally to a pseudo-corpus of 408 hours, which amounts to 8 to 10 weeks of speech. With a larger corpus, the results would probably be better, as indicated by the increase in percentage of recovery when one moves from children in isolation to children as a group (see Figures 1 and 2). In addition, there are bound to be words that children utter for the first time in multi-word utterances even though they could have been produced as isolated utterances. The percentage of reconstruction, however, is still quite high, as was the case for results obtained using a similar methodology with Hungarian children (MacWhinney, 1975). With the assumption of a benefit from the use of the Noun and Verb categories, which somewhat circumvents the limited size of the corpus, the results are very high.

A problem with the second experiment is that it is not sure that children can have a knowledge of part of speech (even very general part of speech such as noun and verb) with semantic knowledge only. However, the experiment 2 is interesting as it can be viewed as a way to extend artificially a limited corpus. Instead of saying that children have the knowledge of part of speech, we propose that noun and verb as so common in adult speech that an extended corpus will contain all basic utterances with a single content word and the appropriate grammatical context. In other words, list L2 will contain all the most basic syntactic constructions. Although this will not be the case in reality, it is indeed possible that a full corpus covering all utterances produced by adults will contains a very large number of L2 structures. In this way, experiment 2 provides a measure of the upper limit that can be reached by the crude mechanism presented in this article (L3 constructions).

The testing procedure does not cover all language acquisition processes before the age of three. Its rather crude mechanisms would, on their own, produce many aberrant utterances if they were not regulated by other mechanisms. The first of these regulatory mechanisms is semantics, as children produce language that, for them, makes sense. They will articulate thoughts with two or three elements that complement each other logically and thus create utterances interpretable by adults. Strange utterances may be produced on occasion but none will sound alien. Secondly, even though children sometimes join words or groups of words randomly when very young, they soon start to follow a systematic order probably copied from adults' utterances (Sinclair & Bronckart, 1972). To do this, they merely have to concentrate on the words or groups of words that they already master, having previously uttered them as single words. Indeed, form-function mapping is easier with single-word utterances than with multi-word utterances and this helps to manipulate single-word forms consciously. Thus, single-word utterances are better candidates than most to become the first elements in a combinatorial system and to undergo representational redescription (Karmiloff-Smith, 1992). Their semantic values allow one to perform semantic combinations. By the age of two, associations words or frozen forms may be sufficient to allow children to produce and control language.

The fact that children can learn to produce complex speech patterns quickly without complex grammatical knowledge casts a whole new light on the problem of the acquisition of syntax. The testing procedure relies heavily on semantics because it is assumed that what children understand, they will remember and manipulate. This does not necessarily contradict all the theories that claim that there are some innate principles specific to grammar acquisition (Pinker, 1984; Wexler, 1982). If children acquire high-level grammatical rules at a later period of their development than is usually admitted in these theories, then the structure of their input—the couple 'base phrase marker' plus 'surface sentence' (Wexler, 1982) — will be more complex. The more complex these structures, the lower the innate conditions on grammars. It would then be possible to progress from a simple system such as the association of frozen elements to a more complex one. Late grammatical acquisition is a very important notion as it goes a long way towards explaining why there do not seem to be any neuronal structures specific to language or grammar (Elman et al., 1996; Muller, 1996). Late grammatical acquisition is also highly compatible with constructivist proposals such as Tomasello's (2003) and Goldberg's (2006).

It has often been said that children already master syntax by the age of three, which is quite remarkable considering the complexity of what they are acquiring. This report suggests that some simple generative mechanisms can explain the explosive acquisition of an apparent mastery of language observed in young children. It demonstrates once again that, as already shown for other linguistic developmental features (Elman et al., 1996), an apparently complex output may be the product of a simple system. The need for large-scale corpora to better tackle the problem of language acquisition with improved tools is also highlighted here.

References

Bloom, P. (1999). Theories of word learning: Rationalist alternatives to associationism. In W. C. Ritchie & T. K. Bhatia (Eds.), Handbook of language acquisition . San Diego: Academic Press.

Elman, J. L., Bates, E., Johnson, M., Karmiloff-Smith, A., Parisi, D., & Plunkett, K. (1996). Rethinking innateness: A connectionist perspective on development. Cambridge, MA: MIT Press/Bradford Books.

Goldberg, A. (2006). Constructions at Work: the nature of generalization in language. Oxford University Press.

Jusczyk, P. W., & Hohne, E. A. (1997). Infants' memory for spoken words [see comments]. Science, 277(5334), 1984-6.

Karmiloff-Smith, A. (1992). Beyond modularity: a developmental perspective on cognitive science. Cambridge, Mass.: MIT Press/Bradford Books.

Lieven, E. V., Pine, J. M., & Baldwin, G. (1997). Lexically-based learning and early grammatical development. Journal of Child Language, 24(1), 187-219.

MacWhinney, B. (1975). Rules, rote, and analogy in morphological formations by Hungarian children. Journal of Child Language, 2, 65-77.

MacWhinney, B. (2000). The CHILDES project : Tools for analyzing talk (3rd). Hillsdale, N.J, Lawrence Erlbaum.

Maratsos, M. P., & Chalkley, M. A. (1980). The internal language of children's syntax: The ontogenesis and representation of syntactic categories. In K. E. Nelson (Ed.), Children's language. Vol: 2 . New York, NY: Gardner Press.

Muller, R.-A. (1996). Innateness, autonomy, universality? Neurobiological approaches to language. Behavioral and Brain Sciences, 19(4), 611-675.

Peters, A. M. (1995). Strategies in the acquisition of syntax. In P. Fletcher & B. MacWhinney (Eds.), The handbook of child language . Oxford, UK: Blackwell.

Pinker, S. (1984). Language learnability and language development. Cambridge, MA: Harvard University Press.

Ritchie, W. C., & Bhatia, T. K. (1999). Child language acquisition: Introduction, foundations, and overview. In W. C. Ritchie & T. K. Bhatia (Eds.), Handbook of language acquisition . San Diego: Academic Press.

Saffran, J. R., Johnson, E. K., Aslin, R. N., & Newport, E. L. (1999). Statistical learning of tone sequences by human infants and adults. Cognition, 70(1), 27-52.

Sinclair, H., & Bronckart, J. P. (1972). S.V.O. A linguistic universal? A study in developmental psycholinguistics. Journal of Experimental Psychology, 14(3), 329-348.

Theakston, A. L., Lieven, E. V. M., Pine, J. M., & Rowland, C. F. (1999). The role of performance limitations in the acquisition of 'mixed' verb-argument structure at stage 1. In M. Perkins & S. Howard (Eds.), New directions in language development and disorders : Plenum Press.

Tomasello, M. (2003). Constructing a language: A usage-based theory of language acquisition. Cambridge: MA, Harvard.

Wexler, K. (1982). A principle theory for language acquisition. In E. Wanner & L. R. Gleitman (Eds.), Language acquisition - the state of the art. New York: Cambridge University Press.

The Topology of Synonymy and Homonymy Networks

James Gorman and James R. Curran
School of Information Technologies
University of Sydney
NSW 2006, Australia
{jgorman2,james}@it.usyd.edu.au

Abstract

Semantic networks have been used successfully to explain access to the mental lexicon. Topological analyses of these networks have focused on acquisition and generation. We extend this work to look at models that distinguish semantic relations. We find the scale-free properties of association networks are not found in synonymy-homonymy networks, and that this is consistent with studies of childhood acquisition of these relationships. We further find that distributional models of language acquisition display similar topological properties to these networks.

1 Introduction

Semantic networks have played an important role in the modelling of the organisation of lexical knowledge. In these networks, words are connected by graph edges based on their semantic relations. In recent years, researchers have found that many semantic networks are *small-world*, *scale-free* networks, having a high degree of structure and a short distance between nodes (Steyvers and Tenenbaum, 2005).

Early models were taxonomic and explained some aspects of human reasoning (Collins and Quillian, 1969) (and are still used in artificial reasoning systems), but were replaced by models that focused on general graph structures (e.g. Collins and Loftus, 1975). These better modelled many observed phenomena but explained only the searching of semantic space, not its generation or properties that exist at a whole-network level.

Topological analyses, looking at the statistical regularities of whole semantic networks, can be used to model phenomena not easily explained from the smaller scale data found in human experiments. These networks are typically formed from corpora, expert compiled lexical resources, or human word-association data.

Existing work has focused language acquisition (Steyvers and Tenenbaum, 2005) and generation (Cancho and Solé, 2001). These models use the general notion of semantic *association* which subsumes all specific semantic relations, e.g. synonymy.

There is evidence that there are distinct cognitive processes for different semantic relations (e.g. Casenhiser, 2005). We perform a graph analysis of *synonymy*, nearness of meaning, and *homonymy*, shared lexicalisation.

We find that synonymy and homonymy produce graphs that are topologically distinct from those produced using association. They still produce small-world networks with short path lengths but lack scale-free properties. Adding edges of different semantic relations, in particular hyponymy, produces graphs more similar to the association networks. We argue our analyses consistent with other semantic network models where nodes of a common type share edges of different types (e.g. Collins and Loftus, 1975).

We further analyse the distributional model of language acquisition. We find that it does not well explain whole-language acquisition, but provides a model for synonym and homonym acquisition.

Proceedings of the Workshop on Cognitive Aspects of Computational Language Acquisition, pages 73–80,
Prague, Czech Republic, June 2007

2 Graph Theory

Our overview of graph theory follows Watts (1999). A graph consists of a set of *n vertices* (*nodes*) and a set of *edges*, or *arcs*, which join pairs of vertices. Edges are *undirected* and arcs are *directed*. Edges and arcs can be *weighted* or *unweighted*, with weights indicating the relative strength or importance of the edges. We will only consider unweighted, undirected networks. Although there is evidence that semantic relations are both directed (Tversky, 1977) and weighted (Collins and Loftus, 1975), we do not have access to this information in a consistent and meaningful format for all our resources.

Two vertices connected by an edge are called *neighbours*. The *degree k* of a vertex is the count of it neighbours. From this we measure the average degree $\langle k \rangle$ for the graph and the degree distribution $P(k)$ for all values of k. The degree distribution is the probability of a vertex having a degree k.

The *neighbourhood* Γ_v of a vertex v is the set of all neighbours of v not including v. The neighbourhood Γ_S of a subgraph S is the set of all neighbours of S, not including the members of S.

The *distance* between any two vertices is the *shortest path length*, or the minimum number of edges that must be traversed, to reach the first from the second. The *characteristic path length L* is the average distance between vertices.[1] The *diameter* D of a graph is the maximum shortest path length between any two vertices. At most D steps are required to reach any vertex from any other vertex but, on average, only L are required.

For very large graphs, calculating the values for L and D is computationally difficult. We instead sample $n' \ll n$ nodes and find the mean values of L and D across the samples. The diameter produced will always be less than or equal to the true diameter. We found $n' = 100$ to be most efficient.

It is not a requirement that every vertex be reachable from every other vertex and in these cases both L and D will be infinite. In these cases we analyse the largest connected subgraph.

[1] Here we follow Steyvers and Tenenbaum (2005) as it is more commonly used in the cognitive science literature. Watts (1999) defines the characteristic path length as the *median* of the means of shortest path lengths for each vertex.

2.1 Small-world Networks

Traditional network models assume that networks are either completely random or completely regular. Many natural networks are somewhere between these two extremes. These *small-world* networks a have the high degree of clustering of a regular *lattice* and the short average path length of a random network (Watts and Strogatz, 1998). The clustering is indicative of organisation, and the short paths make for easier navigation.

The *clustering coefficient* C_v is used to measure the degree of clustering around a vertex v:

$$C_v = \frac{|E(\Gamma_v)|}{\binom{k_v}{2}}$$

where $|E(\Gamma_v)|$ is the number of edges in the neighbourhood Γ_v and $\binom{k_v}{2}$ is the total number of possible edges in Γ_v. The clustering coefficient C of a graph is the average over the coefficients of all the vertices.

2.2 The Scale of Networks

Amaral et al. (2000) describe three classes of small world networks based on their degree distributions:

Scale-free networks are characterised by their degree distribution decaying as a power law, having a small number of vertices with many links (*hubs*) and many vertices with few links. Networks in this class include the internet (Faloutsos et al., 1999) and semantic networks (Steyvers and Tenenbaum, 2005).

Broad-scale networks are characterised by their degree distribution decaying as a power law followed by a sharp cut-off. This class includes collaborative networks (Watts and Strogatz, 1998).

Single-scale networks are characterised by fast decaying degree distribution, such exponential or Gaussian, in which hubs are scarce or nonexistent. This class includes power grids (Watts and Strogatz, 1998) and airport traffic (Amaral et al., 2000).

Amaral et al. (2000) model these differences using a constrained preferential attachment model, where new nodes prefer to attach to highly connected nodes. Scale-free networks result when there are no constraints. Broad-scale networks are produced when ageing and cost-to-add-link constraints are added, making it more difficult to produce very high degree hubs. Single-scale networks occur when these constraints are strengthened. This is one of several models for scale-free network generation, and different models will result in different internal structures and properties (Keller, 2005).

3 Semantics Networks

Semantic networks represent the structure of human knowledge through the connections of words. Collins and Quillian (1969) proposed a taxonomic representation of knowledge, where words are connected by hyponym relations, like in the WordNet noun hierarchy (Fellbaum, 1998). While this structure predicted human reaction times for verifying facts it allows only a limited portion of knowledge to be expressed. Later models represented knowledge as semi-structured networks, and focused on explaining performance in memory retrieval tasks. One such model is *spreading-activation*, in which the degree to which a concept is able to be recalled is related to its similarity both to other concepts in general and to some particular *prime* or primes (Collins and Loftus, 1975). In this way, if one is asked to name a red vehicle, fire truck is more likely response than car: while both are strongly associated with vehicle, fire truck is more strongly associated with red than is car.

More recently, graph theoretic approaches have examined the topologies of various semantic networks. Cancho and Solé (2001) examine graphs of English modelled from the British National Corpus. Since co-occurrence is non-trivial — words in a sentence must share some semantic content for the sentence to be coherent — edges were formed between adjacent words, with punctuation skipped. Two graphs were formed: one from all co-occurrences and the other from only those co-occurrences with a frequency greater than chance. Both models produced scale-free networks. They find this model compelling for word choice during speech, noting function words are the most highly connected. These give structure without conveying significant meaning, so can be omitted without rendering a sentence incoherent, but when unavailable render speech non-fluent. This is consistent with work by Albert et al. (2000) showing that scale-free networks are tolerant to random deletion but sensitive to targeted removal of highly connected vertices.

Sigman and Cecchi (2002) investigate the structure of WordNet to study the effects of nounal polysemy on graph navigation. Beginning with synsets and the hyponym tree, they find adding polysemy both reduces the characteristic path length and increases the clustering coefficient, producing a small-world network. They propose, citing word priming experiments as evidence, that these changes in structure give polysemy a role in metaphoric thinking and generalisation by increasing the navigability of semantic networks.

Steyvers and Tenenbaum (2005) examine the growth of semantic networks using graphs formed from several resources: the free association index collected by Nelson et al. (1998), Wordnet and the 1911 Roget's thesaurus. All these produced scale-free networks, and, using an age of acquisition and frequency weighted preferential attachement model, show that this corresponds to age-of-acquisition norms for a small set of words. This is compared to networks produced by Latent Semantic Analysis (LSA, Landauer and Dumais, 1997), and conclude that LSA is an inadequate model for language growth as it does not produce the same scale-free networks as their association models.

3.1 Synonymy and Homonymy

While there have been many studies using human subjects on the acquisition of particular semantic relations, there have been no topological studies differentiating these from the general notion of semantic *association*. This is interesting as psycholinguistic studies have shown that semantic relationships are distinguishable (e.g. Casenhiser, 2005). Here we consider *synonymy* and *homonymy*.

There are very few cases of true synonymy, where two words are substitutable in all contexts. Near-synonymy, where two words share some close common meaning, is more common. Sets of synonyms can be grouped together into *synsets*, representing a common idea.

Homonymy occurs when a word has multiple meanings. Formally, homonymy is occurs when words do not share an etymological root (in linguistics) or when the distinction between meanings is coarse (in cognitive science). When the words share a root or meanings are close, the relationship is called *polysemy*. This distinction is significant in language acquisition, but as yet little research has been performed on the learning of polysemes (Casenhiser, 2005). It is also significant for Natural Language Processing. The effect of disambiguating homonyms is markedly different from polysemes in Information Retrieval (Stokoe, 2005).

We do not have access to these distinctions, as they are not available in most resources, nor are there techniques to automatically acquire these distinctions (Kilgarriff and Yallop, 2000). For simplicity, will conflate the categories under homonymy.

There have been several studies into synonymy and homonymy acquisition in children, and these have shown that it lags behind vocabulary growth (Doherty and Perner, 1998; Garnham et al., 2000). A child will associate both rabbit and bunny with the same concept, but before the age of four, most children have difficulty in choosing the word bunny if they have already been presented with the word rabbit. Similarly, a young child asked to point to two pictures that have the same name but mean different things will have difficulty, despite knowing each of the things independently.

Despite this improvement with age, there are tendencies for language to avoid synonyms and homonyms as a more general principle of economy (Casenhiser, 2005). This is balanced by the utility of ambiguous relations for mental navigation (Sigman and Cecchi, 2002) which goes some way to explaining why they still play such a large role in language.

4 The Topology of Synonymy and Homonymy Relations

For each of our resources we form a graph based on the relations between lexical items. This differs to the earlier work of Sigman and Cecchi (2002), who use synsets as vertices, and Steyvers and Tenenbaum (2005) who use both lexical items and synsets..

This is motivated largely by our automatic acquisition techniques, and also by human studies, in which we can only directly access relationships between words. This also allows us to directly compare resources where we have information about synsets to those without. We distinguish parts of speech as disambiguation across them is relatively easy psychologically (Casenhiser, 2005) and computationally (e.g. Ratnaparkhi, 1996).

4.1 Lexical Semantic Resources

A typical resource for providing this information are manually constructed lexical semantic resources. We will consider three: Roget's, WordNet and Moby

Roget's thesaurus is a common language thesaurus providing a hierarchy of synsets. Synsets with the same general or overlapping meaning and part of speech are collected into paragraphs. The parts of speech covered are nouns, verbs, adjectives, adverbs, prepositions, phrases, pronouns, interjections, conjunctions, and interrogatives. Paragraphs with similar meaning are collated by part of speech into labeled categories. Categories are then collected into classes using a three-tiered hierarchy, with the most general concept at the top. Where a word has several senses, it will appear in several synsets. Several editions of Roget's have been released representing the change in language since the first edition in 1852. The last freely available edition is the 1911, which uses outdated vocabulary, but the global topology has not changed with more recent editions (Old, 2003). As our analysis is not concerned with the specifics of the vocabulary, this is the edition we will use. It consists of a vocabulary of 29,460 nouns, 15,173 verbs, 13,052 adjectives and 3,005 adverbs.

WordNet (Fellbaum, 1998) is an electronic lexical database. Like Roget's, it main unit of organisation is the synset, and a word with several senses will appear in several synsets. These are divided into four parts of speech: nouns, verbs, adjectives and adverbs. Synsets are connected by semantic relationships, e.g antonymy, hyponymy and meronym. WordNet 2.1 provides a vocabulary of 117,097 nouns, 11,488 verbs, 22,141 adjectives and 4,601 adverbs.

The Moby thesaurus provides synonymy lists for over 30,000 words, with a total vocabulary of 322,263 words. These lists are not distinguished by part of speech. A separate file is supplied containing part of speech mappings for words in the vocabulary. We extracted separate synonym lists for nouns, verbs, adjectives and adverbs using this list combined with WordNet part of speech information.[2] This produces a vocabulary of 42,821 nouns, 11,957 verbs, 16,825 adjectives and 3,572 adverbs.

Table 1 presents the statistics for the largest con-

[2] http://aspell.sourceforge.net/wl/

	Roget's				WordNet				Moby			
	Noun	Verb	Adj	Adv	Noun	Verb	Adj	Adv	Noun	Verb	Adj	Adv
n	15,517	8,060	6,327	626	11,746	6,506	4,786	62	42,819	11,934	16,784	3501
$\langle k \rangle$	8.97	8.46	7.40	7.17	4.58	6.34	5.16	4.97	34.65	51.98	39.26	16.07
L	6.5	6.0	6.4	10.5	9.8	6.0	9.5	5.6	3.7	3.1	3.4	3.7
D	21.4	17	17	31	27	15.3	26.4	14	9.6	9.8	9.3	9.8
C	0.74	0.68	0.69	0.77	0.63	0.62	0.66	0.57	0.60	0.49	0.57	0.55
L_r	4.7	4.5	4.6	3.5	6.3	5.0	5.9	3.3	3.4	2.8	2.9	3.2
D_r	8.5	8.4	9.0	7	13.3	10.1	11.8	8	5.5	5	5	6
C_r	0.00051	0.0011	0.0012	0.0090	0.00036	0.00099	0.00094	0.028	0.00081	0.0043	0.0023	0.0047

Table 1: Topological statistics for nouns, verbs, adjectives and adverbs for our three gold standard resources

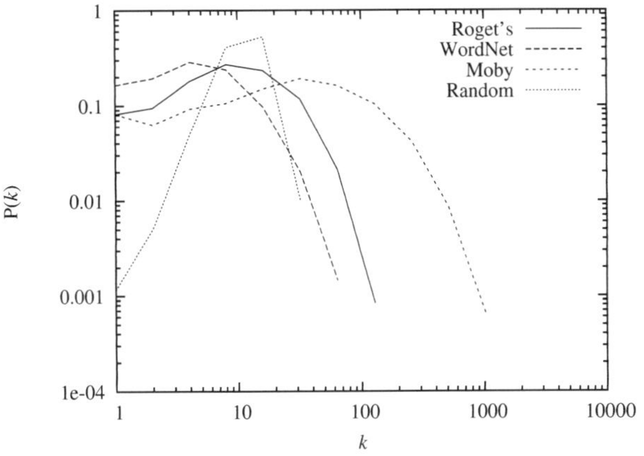

Figure 1: Degree distributions for nouns

nected subgraph for the four parts of speech considered, along with statistics for random graphs of equivalent size and average degree (subscript r). In all cases the clustering coefficient is significantly higher than that for the random graph. While the characteristic path length and diameter are larger than for the random graphs, they are still short in comparison to an equivalent latice. This, combined with the high clustering coefficient, indicates that they are producing small-world networks. The diameter is larger still than for the random graphs. Together these indicate a more lattice like structure, which is consistent with the intuition that dissimilar words are unlikely to share similar words. This is independent of part of speech.

Figure 1 shows the degree distributions for nouns, and for a random graph plotted on log-log axes. Other parts of speech produce equivalent graphs. These clearly show that we have not produced scale-free networks as we are not seeing straight line power law distributions. Instead we are seeing what is closer to single- or broad-scale distributions.

The differences in the graphs is explained by the

	WordNet		Roget's		
		Hyp	Synset	Para	Cat
n	11,746	118,264	15,517	27,989	29,431
$\langle k \rangle$	4.58	6.61	8.97	26.84	140.36
L	9.8	6.3	6.5	4.3	2.9
D	27	16.4	21.4	12.6	7
C	0.63	0.74	0.74	0.85	0.86

Table 2: Effect of adding hyponym relations

granularity of the synonymy relations presented, as indicated by the characteristic path length. WordNet has fine grained synsets and the smallest characteristic path length, while Moby has coarse grained synonyms and the largest characteristic path length.

4.2 Synonymy-Like Relations

Having seen that synonymy and homonymy alone do not produce scale-free networks, we investigate the synonymy-like relations of *hyponymy* and topic relatedness. Hyponymy is the IS-A class subsumption relationship and occurs between noun synsets in WordNet. Topic relatedness occurs in the grouping of synsets in Roget's in paragraphs and categories.

Table 2 compares adding hyponym edges to the graph of WordNet nouns and increasing the granularity of Roget's synsets using edges between all words in a paragraph or category. Adding hyponymy relations increases the connectivity of the graph significantly and there are no longer any disconnected subgraphs. At the same time the diameter is nearly halved and characteristic path length reduce one third, but average degree only increases by one third. To achieving the same reduction in path length and diameter by the granularity of Roget's requires the average degree to increase by nearly three times.

Figure 2 shows the degree distributions when hyponyms are added to WordNet nouns and the granularity of Roget's is increased. Roget's category level graph is omitted for clarity. We can see that the orig-

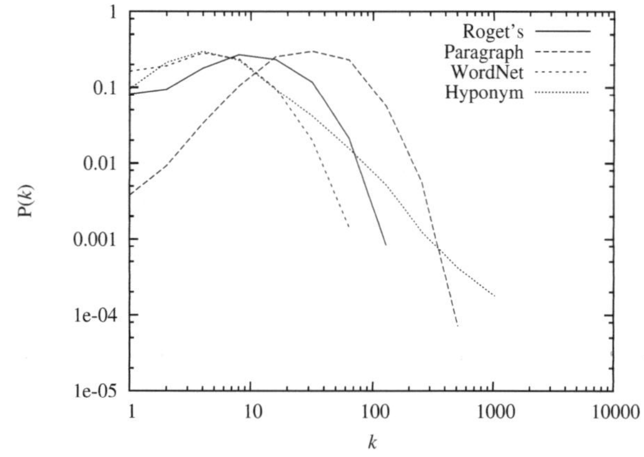

Figure 2: Degree distributions adding hyponym relations to nouns

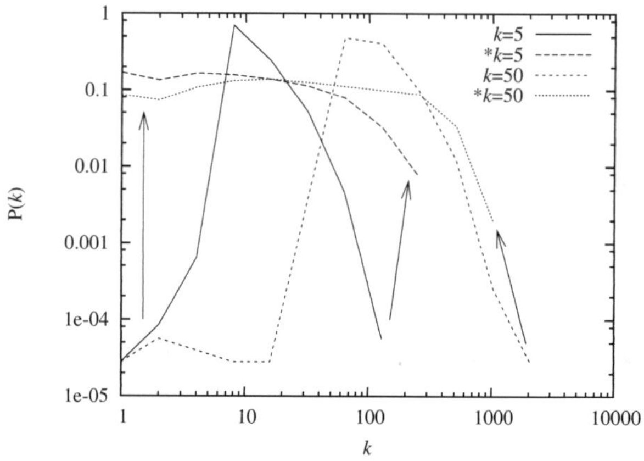

Figure 3: Degree distributions of Jaccard

inally broad-scale structure of the Roget's distribution is tending to have a more gaussian distribution. The addition of hyponyms produces a power law distribution for $k > 10$ of $P(k) \approx k^{-1.7}$.

Additional constraints on attachment reduce the ability of networks to be scale-free (Amaral et al., 2000). The difference between synonymy-homonymy networks and association networks can be explained by this. Steyvers and Tenenbaum (2005) propose a plausible attachment model for their association networks which has no additional constraint function. If we use the tendency for languages to avoid lexical ambiguity from synonymy and homonymy as a constraint to the production of edges we will produce broad-scale networks rather than scale-free networks.

As hyponymy is primarily semantic and does not produce lexical ambiguity, adding hyponym edges weakens the constraint on ambiguity, producing a scale-free network. Generalising synonymy to include topicality weakens the constraints, but at the same time reduces preference in attachment. The results of this is the gaussian-like distribution with very few low degree nodes. The difference between this thesaurus based topicality and that found in human association data is that human association data only includes the most similar words.

5 Distributional Similarity Networks

Lexical semantic resources can be automatically extracted using distributional similarity. Here words are projected into a vector space using the contexts in which they appear as axes. Contexts can be as wide as document (Landauer and Dumais, 1997) or close as grammatical dependencies (Grefenstette, 1994). The distance between words in this space approximates the similarity measured by synonymy.

We use the noun similarities produced by Gorman and Curran (2006) using the *weighted Jaccard* measure and the *t-test* weight and grammatical relations extracted from their LARGE corpus, the method found to perform best against their gold-standard evaluation. Only words with a corpus frequency higher than 100 are included. This method is comparable to that used in LSA, although using grammatical relations as context produces similarity much more like synonymy than those taken at a document level (Kilgarriff and Yallop, 2000).

Distributional similarity produces a list of vocabulary words, their similar neighbours and the similarity to the neighbours. These lists approximate synonymy by measuring substitutability in context, and do not only find synonyms as near neighbours as both antonyms and hyponyms are frequently substitutable in a grammatical context (Weeds, 2003). From this we generate graphs by taking either the k nearest neighbours to each word (k-NN), or by using a threshold. To produce a threshold we take the mean similarity of the kth neighbour of all words (*k-NN). We compare both these methods.

Figure 3 compares the degree distributions of these. Using k-NN produces a degree distribution that is close to a Gaussian, where as *k-NN produces a distribution much more like that of our expert compiled resources. This is unsurprising when the distribution of distributional distances is considered. Some words will have many near neighbours,

	Roget's	WordNet	Hyp	k-NN	*k-NN
n	15,517	11,746	118,264	35,592	19,642
$\langle k \rangle$	8.97	4.58	6.61	8.26	13.86
L	6.5	9.8	6.3	6.2	6.4
D	21.4	27	16.4	12	25.6
C	0.74	0.63	0.74	0.18	0.37

Table 3: Comparing nouns in expert and distributional resources

and other few. In the first case, k-NN will fail to include some near neighbours, and in the second will include some distant neighbours that are note semantically related. This result is consistent between $k = 5$ and 50. Introduction of random edges from the noise of distant neighbours reduces the diameter and missing near neighbours reduces the clustering coefficient (Table 3).

In Table 3 we also compare these to noun synonymy in Roget's, and to synonymy and hyponymy in WordNet. Distributional similarity (*k-NN) produces a network with similar degree, characteristic path length and diameter. The clustering coefficient is much less than that from expert resources, is still several orders of magnitude larger than an equivalent random graph (Table 1).

Figure 4 compares a distributional network to networks WordNet and Moby. We can see the same broad-scale in the distributional and synonym networks, and a distinct difference with the scale-free WordNet hyponym distribution.

The distributional similarity distribution is similar to that found in networks formed from LSA by Steyvers and Tenenbaum (2005). Steyvers and Tenenbaum hypothesise that the distributions produced by LSA might be due more to frequency distribution effects that correct language modelling.

In light of our analysis of synonymy relations, we propose a new explanation. Given that: distributional similarity has been shown to approximate the semantic similarity in synonymy relations found in thesaurus type resources (Curran, 2004); distributional similarity produces networks with similar statistical properties to those formed by synonym and homonymy relations; and, the synonym and homonymy relations found in thesauri produce networks with different statistical properties to those found in the association networks analysed by Steyvers and Tenenbaum; it can be plausibly

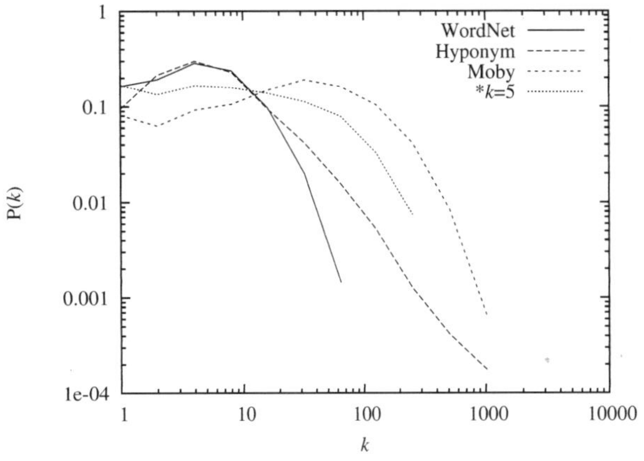

Figure 4: Degree distributions for nouns

hypothesised that distributional techniques are modeling the acquisition of synonyms and homonyms, rather than all semantic relationships.

This is given further credence by experimental findings that acquisition of homonyms occurs at a different rate to the acquisition of vocabulary. This indicates that there are different mechanisms for learning the meaning of lexical items and learning to relate the meanings of lexical items. Any whole-language model would then be composed of a common set of lexical items related by disparate relations, such as synonymy, homonymy and hyponymy. This type of model is predicted by spreading activation (Collins and Loftus, 1975).

It is unfortunate that there is a lack of data with which to validate this model, or our constraint model, empirically. This should not prevent further analysis of network models that distiguish semantic relations, so long as this limitation is understood.

6 Conclusion

Semantic networks have been used successfully to explain access to the mental lexicon. We use both expert-compiled and automatically extracted semantic resources, we compare the networks formed from semantic association and synonymy and homonymy. These relations produce small-world networks, but do not share the same scale-free properties as for semantic association.

We find that this difference can be explained using a constrained attachment model informed by childhood language acquisition experiments. It is also predicted by spreading-activation theories of semantic access where a common set of lexical items is connected by a disparate set of relations. We further find that distributional models of language acquisition produce relations that approximate synonymy and networks topologically similar to synonymy-homonymy networks.

7 Acknowledgements

We would like to thank the anonymous reviewers for their helpful feedback and corrections. This work has been supported by the Australian Research Council under Discovery Projects DP0453131 and DP0665973.

References

Réka Albert, Hawoong Jeong, and Albert-László Barabási. 2000. Error and attack tolerance of complex networks. *Nature*, 406:378–381.

Luís A. Nunes Amaral, Antonio Scala, Marc Barthélémy, and H. Eugene Stanley. 2000. Classes of small-world networks. *Proceedings of the National Academy of Sciences*, 97(21):11149–11152, October 10.

Ramon F. i Cancho and Ricard V. Solé. 2001. The small world of human language. *Proceedings of The Royal Society of London. Series B, Biological Sciences*, 268(1482):2261–2265, November.

Devin M. Casenhiser. 2005. Children's resistance to homonymy: an experimental study of pseudohomonyms. *Journal of Child Language*, 32:319–343.

Allan M. Collins and Elizabeth F. Loftus. 1975. A spreading-activation theory of semantic processing. *Psychological review*, 82(6):407–428.

Allan M. Collins and M. Ross Quillian. 1969. Retrieval time from semantic memory. *Journal of Verbal Learning and Verbal Behavior*, 8:240–247.

James R. Curran. 2004. *From Distributional to Semantic Similarity*. Ph.D. thesis, University of Edinburgh.

Martin Doherty and Josef Perner. 1998. Metalinguistic awareness and theory of mind: just two words for the same thing? *Congitive Development*, 13:279–305.

Michalis Faloutsos, Petros Faloutsos, and Christos Faloutsos. 1999. On power-law relationships of the internet topology. In *Proceedings of the conference on Applications, technologies, architectures, and protocols for computer communication*, pages 251–262.

Christiane Fellbaum, editor. 1998. *WordNet: an electronic lexical database*. The MIT Press, Cambridge, MA, USA.

Wendy A. Garnham, Julie Brooks, Alan Garnham, and Anne-Marie Ostenfeld. 2000. From synonyms to homonyms: exploring the role of metarepresentation in language understanding. *Developmental Science*, 3(4):428–441.

James Gorman and James R. Curran. 2006. Scaling distributional similarity to large corpora. In *Proceedings of the 44th Annual Meeting of the Association for Computational Linguistics*, Sydney, Australia, 17–21 July.

Gregory Grefenstette. 1994. *Explorations in Automatic Thesaurus Discovery*. Kluwer Academic Publishers, Boston.

Evelyn F. Keller. 2005. Revisiting "scale-free" networks. *Bioessays*, 27(10):1060–1068, October.

Adam Kilgarriff and Colin Yallop. 2000. What's in a thesaurus? In *Proceedings of the Second International Conference on Language Resources and Evaluation*, pages 1371–1379.

Thomas K. Landauer and Susan T. Dumais. 1997. A solution to plato's problem: The latent semantic analysis theory of acquisition, induction, and representation of knowledge. *Psychological Review*, 104(2):211–240, April.

Douglas L. Nelson, Cathy L. McEvoy, and Thomas A. Schreiber. 1998. The university of south florida word association, rhyme, and word fragment norms. http://www.usf.edu/FreeAssociation/.

L. John Old. 2003. *The Semantic Structure of Roget's, a Whole-Language Thesaurus*. Ph.D. thesis, Indiana University.

Adwait Ratnaparkhi. 1996. A maximum entropy part-of-speech tagger. In *Proceedings of the Conference on Empirical Methods in Natural Language Processing*, pages 133–142, 17–18 May.

Mariano Sigman and Guillermo A. Cecchi. 2002. Global organization of the WordNet lexicon. *Proceedings of the National Academy of Sciences*, 99(3):1742–1747.

Mark Steyvers and Joshua B. Tenenbaum. 2005. The large-scale structure of semantic networks: statistical analyses and a model of semantic growth. *Cognitive Science*, 29(1):41–78.

Christopher Stokoe. 2005. Differentiating homonymy and polysemy in information retrieval. In *Proceedings of the Conference on Human Language Technology and Empirical Methods in Natural Language Processing*, pages 403–410.

Amos Tversky. 1977. Features of similarity. *Psychological Review*, 84(4):327–352, July.

Duncan J. Watts and Steven H. Strogatz. 1998. *Collective dynamics of small-world networks*, 393:440–442, 4 June.

Duncan J. Watts. 1999. *Small Worlds: The Dynamics of Networks between Order and Randomness*. Princeton University Press, Princeton, NJ, USA.

Julie E. Weeds. 2003. *Measures and Applications of Lexical Distributional Similarity*. Ph.D. thesis, University of Sussex.

The Benefits of Errors:
Learning an OT Grammar with a Structured Candidate Set

Tamás Biró
ACLC, Universiteit van Amsterdam
Spuistraat 210
Amsterdam, The Netherlands
t.s.biro@uva.nl

Abstract

We compare three recent proposals adding a topology to OT: McCarthy's *Persistent OT*, Smolensky's ICS and Bíró's SA-OT. To test their learnability, constraint rankings are learnt from SA-OT's output. The errors in the output, being more than mere noise, follow from the topology. Thus, the learner has to reconstructs her *competence* having access only to the teacher's *performance*.

1 Introduction: topology and OT

The year 2006 witnessed the publication of several novel approaches within Optimality Theory (OT) (Prince and Smolensky, 1993 aka 2004) introducing some sort of *neighbourhood structure* (topology, geometry) on the candidate set. This idea has been already present since the beginnings of OT but its potentialities had never been really developed until recently. The present paper examines the learnability of such an enriched OT architecture.

Traditional Optimality Theory's GEN function generates a huge *candidate set* from the underlying form (UF) and then EVAL finds the candidate w that optimises the *Harmony function* $H(w)$ on this *unrestricted* candidate set. $H(w)$ is derived from the violation marks assigned by a ranked set of constraints to w. The surface form SF corresponding to UF is the (globally) optimal element of *GEN*(*UF*):

$$SF(UF) = \text{argopt}_{w \in GEN(UF)} H(w) \qquad (1)$$

Yet, already Prince and Smolensky (1993/2004:94-95) mention the possibility of restricting GEN, creating an alternative closer to standard derivations. Based the iterative syllabification in Imdlawn Tashlhiyt Berber, they suggest: "*some general procedure (Do-α) is allowed to make a certain single modification to the input, producing the candidate set of all possible outcomes of such modification.*" The outputs of Do-α are "neighbours" of its input, so Do-α defines a *topology*. Subsequently, EVAL finds the most harmonic element of this *restricted* candidate set, which then serves again as the input of Do-α. Repeating this procedure again and again produces a sequence of neighbouring candidates with increasing Harmony, which converges toward the surface form.

Calling Do-α a restricted GEN, as opposed to the freedom of analysis offered by the traditional GEN, McCarthy (2006) develops this idea into the *Persistent OT architecture* (aka. *harmonic serialism*, cf. references in McCarthy 2006). He demonstrates on concrete examples how repeating the GEN $\rightarrow$ EVAL $\rightarrow$ GEN $\rightarrow$ EVAL $\rightarrow$... cycle until reaching some *local* optimum will produce a more restrictive language typology that conforms rather well to observation. Importantly for our topic, learnability, he claims that Persistent OT "*can impose stricter ranking requirements than classic OT because of the need to ensure harmonic improvement in the intermediate forms as well as the ultimate output*".

In two very different approaches, both based on the traditional concept of GEN, Smolensky's *Integrated Connectionist/Symbolic* (ICS) *Cognitive Architecture* (Smolensky and Legendre, 2006) and the strictly symbolic *Simulated Annealing for Optimality Theory Algorithm* (SA-OT) proposed by

Proceedings of the Workshop on Cognitive Aspects of Computational Language Acquisition, pages 81–88,
Prague, Czech Republic, June 2007

Bíró (2005a; 2005b; 2006a), use *simulated annealing* to find the best candidate w in equation (1). Simulated annealing performs a random walk on the search space, moving to a similar (neighbouring) element in each step. Hence, it requires a topology on the search space. In SA-OT this topology is directly introduced on the candidate set, based on a linguistically motivated symbolic representation. At the same time, connectionist OT makes small changes in the state of the network; so, to the extent that states correspond to candidates, we obtain again a neighbourhood relation on the candidate set.

Whoever introduces a neighbourhood structure (or a restricted GEN) also introduces *local optima*: candidates more harmonic than all their neighbours, independently of whether they are globally optimal. Importantly, each proposal is prone to be stuck in local optima. McCarthy's model repeats the generation-evaluation cycle as long as the first local optimum is not reached; whereas simulated annealing is a heuristic optimisation algorithm that sometimes fails to find the global optimum and returns another local optimum. How do these proposals influence the OT "philosophy"?

For McCarthy, the first local optimum reached from UF *is* the grammatical form (the surface form predicted by the linguistic competence model), so he rejects equation (1). Yet, Smolensky and Bíró keep the basic idea of OT as in (1), and Bíró (2005b; 2006a) shows the errors made by simulated annealing can mimic performance errors (such as stress shift in fast speech). So mainstream Optimality Theory remains the model of linguistic competence, whereas its cognitively motivated, though imperfect implementation with simulated annealing becomes a model of linguistic performance. Or, as Bíró puts it, a model of the dynamic language production process in the brain. (See also Smolensky and Legendre (2006), vol. 1, pp. 227-229.)

In the present paper we test the learnability of an OT grammar enriched with a neighbourhood structure. To be more precise, we focus on the latter approaches: how can a learner acquire a grammar, that is, the constraint hierarchy defining the Harmony function $H(w)$, if the learning data are produced by a performance model prone to make errors? What is the consequence of seeing errors not simply as mere noise, but as the result of a specific mechanism?

2 Walking in the candidate set

First, we introduce the production algorithms (section 2) and a toy grammar (section 3), before we can run the learning algorithms (section 4).

Equation (1) defines Optimality Theory as an optimisation problem, but finding the optimal candidate can be NP-hard (Eisner, 1997). Past solutions—chart parsing (Tesar and Smolensky, 2000; Kuhn, 2000) and finite state OT (see Biro (2006b) for an overview)—require conditions met by several, but not by all linguistic models. They are also "too perfect", not leaving room for performance errors and computationally too demanding, hence cognitively not plausible. Alternative approaches are heuristic optimization techniques: genetic algorithms and simulated annealing.

These heuristic algorithms do not always find the (globally) optimal candidate, but are simple and still efficient because they exploit the structure of the candidate set. This structure is realized by a *neighbourhood relation*: for each candidate w there exists a set $\texttt{Neighbours}(w)$, the set of the neighbours of w. It is often supposed that neighbours differ only *minimally*, whatever this means. The neighbourhood relation is usually symmetric, irreflexive and results in a connected structure (any two candidates are connected by a finite chain of neighbours).

The topology (neighbourhood structure) opens the possibility to a (random) *walk* on the candidate set: a series $w_0, w_1, w_2, ..., w_L$ such that for all $0 \leq i < L$, candidate w_{i+1} is w_i or a neighbour of w_i. (Candidate w_0 will be called w_{init}, and w_L will be w_{final}, henceforth.) Genetic algorithms start with a random population of w_{init}'s, and employ OT's EVAL function to reach a population of w_{final}'s dominated by the (globally) optimal candidate(s) (Turkel, 1994). In what follows, however, we focus on algorithms using a single walk only.

The simplest algorithm, *gradient descent*, comes in two flavours. The version on Fig. 1 defines w_{i+1} as the best element of set $\{w_i\} \cup \texttt{Neighbours}(w_i)$. It runs as long as w_{i+1} differs from w_i, and is deterministic for each w_{init}. Prince and Smolensky's and McCarthy's serial evaluation does exactly this: w_{init} is the underlying form, Do-α (the restricted GEN) creates the set $\{w\} \cup \texttt{Neighbours}(w)$, and EVAL finds its best element.

```
ALGORITHM Gradient Descent: OT with restricted GEN
 w := w_init;
 repeat
        w_prev := w;
        w      := most_harmonic_element( {w_prev} U Neighbours(w_prev) );
 until w = w_prev
 return w                         # w is an approximation to the optimal solution
```

Figure 1: Gradient Descent: iterated Optimality Theory with a restricted GEN (Do-α).

```
ALGORITHM Randomized Gradient Descent
 w := w_init ;
 repeat
          Randomly select w' from the set Neighbours(w);
          if  (w' not less harmonic than w)    then   w := w';
 until stopping condition = true
 return w                         # w is an approximation to the optimal solution
```

Figure 2: Randomized Gradient Descent

The second version of *gradient descent* is stochastic (Figure 2). In step i, a random $w' \in \texttt{Neighbours}(w_i)$ is chosen using some pre-defined probability distribution on $\texttt{Neighbours}(w_i)$ (often a constant function). If neighbour w' is not worse than w_i, then the next element w_{i+1} of the random walk will be w'; otherwise, w_{i+1} is w_i. The stopping condition requires the number of iterations reach some value, or the average improvement of the target function in the last few steps drop below a threshold. The output is w_{final}, a local optimum if the walk is long enough.

Simulated annealing (Fig. 3) plays with this second theme to increase the chance of finding the global optimum and avoid unwanted local optima. The idea is the same, but if w' is worse than w_i, then there is still a chance to move to w'. The *transition probability* of moving to w' depends on the target function E at w_i and w', and on 'temperature' T: $P(w_i \to w'|T) = \exp\left(-\frac{E(w')-E(w_i)}{T}\right)$. Using a random r, we move to w' iff $r < P(w_i \to w'|T)$. Temperature T is gradually decreased following the *cooling schedule*. Initially the system easily climbs larger hills, but later it can only descend valleys. Importantly, the probability w_{final} is globally optimal converges to 1 as the number of iterations grows.

But the target function is not real-valued in Optimality Theory, so how can we calculate the transition probability? ICS (Smolensky and Legendre, 2006) approximates OT's harmony function with a real-valued target function, while Bíró (2006a) introduces a novel algorithm (SA-OT, Figure 4) to guarantee the principle of *strict domination* in the constraint ranking. The latter stays on the purely symbolic level familiar to the linguist, but does not always display the convergence property of traditional simulated annealing.

Temperature in the SA-OT Algorithm is a pair (K, t) with $t > 0$, and is diminished in two, embedded loops. Similarly, the difference in the target function (Harmony) is not a single real number but a pair (C, d). Here C is the *fatal constraint*, the highest ranked constraint by which w_i and w' behave differently, while d is the difference of the violations of this constraint. (For $H(w_i) = H(w')$ let the difference be $(0, 0)$.) Each constraint is assigned a real-valued rank (most often an integer; we shall call it a *K-value*) such that a higher ranked constraint has a higher K-value than a lower ranked constraint (hierarchies are fully ranked). The K-value of the fatal constraint corresponds to the first component of the temperature, and the second component of the difference in the target function corresponds to the second component of the temperature. The transition probability from w_i to its neighbour w' is 1 if w' is not less harmonic than w_i; otherwise, the originally exponential transition probability becomes

$$P\left(w_i \to w' | \,(K, t)\right) = \begin{cases} 1 & \text{if K-value of C} < K \\ e^{-\frac{d}{t}} & \text{if K-value of C} = K \\ 0 & \text{if K-value of C} > K \end{cases}$$

```
ALGORITHM Simulated Annealing
 w := w_init ;       T := T_max   ;
 repeat
         CHOOSE  random w' in Neighbours(w);
         Delta :=  E(w') - E(w);
         if   ( Delta < 0 )   then   w := w';
         else        # move to w' with transition probability P(Delta;T) = exp(-Delta/T):
                     generate random r uniformly in range (0,1);
                     if   ( r < exp(-Delta / T) )   then   w := w';
         T := alpha(T);        # decrease T according to some cooling schedule
 until stopping condition = true
 return w                      # w is an approximation to the minimal solution
```

Figure 3: *Minimizing* a real-valued energy function $E(w)$ with simulated annealing.

Again, w_{i+1} is w' if the random number r generated between 0 and 1 is less than this transition probability; otherwise $w_{i+1} = w_i$. Bíró (2006a, Chapt. 2-3) argues that this definition fits best the underlying idea behind both OT and simulated annealing.

In the next part of the paper we focus on SA-OT, and return to the other algorithms afterwards only.

3 A string grammar

To experiment with, we now introduce an abstract grammar that mimics real phonological ones.

Let the set of candidates generated by GEN for any input be $\{0, 1, ..., P-1\}^L$, the set of strings of length L over an alphabet of P phonemes. We shall use $L = P = 4$. Candidate w' is a neighbour of candidate w if and only if a single minimal operation (a *basic step*) transforms w into w'. A minimal operation naturally fitting the structure of the candidates is to change one phoneme only. In order to obtain a more interesting search space and in order to meet some general principles—the neighbourhood relation should be symmetric, yielding a connected graph but be minimal—a basic step can only change the value of a phoneme by 1 modulo P. For instance, in the $L = P = 4$ case, neighbours of 0123 are among others 1123, 3123, 0133 and 0120, but not 1223, 2123 or 0323. If the four phonemes are represented as a pair of binary features ($0 = [--]$, $1 = [+-]$, $2 = [++]$ and $3 = [-+]$), then this basic step alters exactly one feature.

We also need constraints. Constraint No-n counts the occurrences of phoneme n ($0 \leq n < P$) in the candidate (i.e., assigns one violation mark per phoneme n). Constraint No-initial-n punishes phoneme n word initially only, whereas No-final-n does the same word finally. Two more constraints sum up the number of dissimilar and similar pairs of adjacent phonemes. Let $w_{(i)}$ be the ith phoneme in string w, and let $[b] = 1$ if b is true and $[b] = 0$ if b is false; then we have $3P + 2$ markedness constraints:

No-n:	non(w)	$= \sum_{i=0}^{L-1} [w_{(i)} = n]$
No-initial-n:	nin(w)	$= [w_{(0)} = n]$
No-final-n:	nfn(w)	$= [w_{(L-1)} = n]$
Assimilate:	ass(w)	$= \sum_{i=0}^{L-2} [w_{(i)} \neq w_{(i+1)}]$
Dissimilate:	dis(w)	$= \sum_{i=0}^{L-2} [w_{(i)} = w_{(i+1)}]$

Grammars also include faithfulness constraints punishing divergences from a reference string σ, usually the input. Ours sums up the distance of the phonemes in w from the corresponding ones in σ:

$$\text{FAITH}_\sigma(w) = \sum_{i=0}^{L-1} d(\sigma_{(i)}, w_{(i)})$$

where $d(a, b) = \min((a-b) \bmod P, (b-a) \bmod P))$ is the minimal number of basic steps transforming phoneme a into b. In our case, faithfulness is also the number of differing binary features.

To illustrate SA-OT, we shall use grammar $\mathcal{H}$:

$\mathcal{H}$: no0 $\gg$ ass $\gg$ Faith$_{\sigma=0000}$ $\gg$ ni1 $\gg$ ni0 $\gg$ ni2 $\gg$ ni3 $\gg$ nf0 $\gg$ nf1 $\gg$ nf2 $\gg$ nf3 $\gg$ no3 $\gg$ no2 $\gg$ no1 $\gg$ dis

A quick check proves that the global optimum is candidate 3333, but there are many other local optima: 1111, 2222, 3311, 1333, etc. Table 1 shows the frequencies of the outputs as a function of `t_step`, all other parameters kept unchanged.

Several characteristics of SA-OT can be observed. For high `t_step`, the thirteen local optima ($\{1, 3\}^4$ and 2222) are all produced, but as the number of

```
ALGORITHM Simulated Annealing for Optimality Theory
 w := w_init ;
 for K = K_max to K_min step K_step
     for t = t_max to t_min step t_step
                CHOOSE   random w' in Neighbours(w);
                COMPARE  w' to w:  C := fatal constraint
                                   d := C(w') - C(w);
                if d <= 0 then w := w';
                else           w := w' with transition probability
                            P(C,d;K,t) = 1           , if K-value(C) < K
                                       = exp(-d/t)  , if K-value(C) = K
                                       = 0           , if K-value(C) > K
     end-for
 end-for
 return w                         # w is an approximation to the optimal solution
```

Figure 4: The Simulated Annealing for Optimality Theory Algorithm (SA-OT).

iterations increases (parameter `t_step` drops), the probability of finding the globally optimal candidate grows. In many grammars (e.g., ni1 and ni3 moved to between no0 and ass in $\mathcal{H}$), the global optimum is the only output for small `t_step` values. Yet, $\mathcal{H}$ also yields *irregular forms*: 1111 and 2222 are not globally optimal but their frequencies grow together with the frequency of 3333.

4 Learning grammar from performance

To summarise, given a grammar, that is, a constraint hierarchy, the SA-OT Algorithm produces performance forms, including the grammatical one (the global optimum), but possibly also irregular forms and performance errors. The exact distribution depends on the parameters of the algorithm, which are *not* part of the grammar, but related to external (physical, biological, pragmatic or sociolinguistic) factors, for instance, to speech rate.

Our task of learning a *grammar* can be formulated thus: given the output distribution of SA-OT based on the target OT hierarchy (the *target grammar*), the learner seeks a hierarchy that produces a similar performance distribution using the same SA-OT Algorithm. (See Yang (2002) on grammar learning as parameter setting in general.) Without any information on grammaticality, her goal is not to mimic competence, not to find a hierarchy with the same *global* optima. The grammar learnt can diverge from the target hierarchy, as long as their performance is comparable (see also Apoussidou (2007), p. 203). For instance, if ni1 and ni3 change place in grammar $\mathcal{H}$, the grammaticality of 1111 and 3333 are reversed, but the performance stays the same. This resembles two native speakers whose divergent grammars are revealed only when they judge differently forms otherwise produced by both.

We suppose that the learner employs the same SA-OT parameter setting. The acquisition of the parameters is deferred to future work, because this task is not part of language acquisition but of social acculturation: given a grammar, how can one learn which situation requires what speed rate or what level of care in production? Consequently, fine-tuning the output frequencies, which can be done by fine-tuning the parameters (such as `t_step`) and not the grammar, is not our goal here. But language learners do not seem to do it, either.

Learning algorithms in Optimality Theory belong to two families: off-line and on-line algorithms. Off-line algorithms, the prototype of which is *Recursive Constraint Demotion* (RCD) (Tesar, 1995; Tesar and Smolensky, 2000), first collect the data and then attempt to build a hierarchy consistent with them. On-line algorithms, such as Error Driven Constraint Demotion (ECDC) (Tesar, 1995; Tesar and Smolensky, 2000) and Gradual Learning Algorithm (GLA) (Boersma, 1997; Boersma and Hayes, 2001), start with an initial hierarchy and gradually alter it based on discrepancies between the learning data and the data produced by the learner's current hierarchy.

Since infants gather statistical data on their mother tongue-to-be already in pre-linguistic stages (Saffran et al., 1996; Gervain et al., submitted), an off-line algorithm created our initial grammar. Then, on-line learning refined it, modelling child language

output	t_step $= 1$	t_step $= 0.1$	t_step $= 0.01$	t_step $= 0.001$
3333	0.1174 ± 0.0016	0.2074 ± 0.0108	0.2715 ± 0.0077	0.3107 ± 0.0032
1111	0.1163 ± 0.0021	0.2184 ± 0.0067	0.2821 ± 0.0058	0.3068 ± 0.0058
2222	0.1153 ± 0.0024	0.2993 ± 0.0092	0.3787 ± 0.0045	0.3602 ± 0.0091
1133	0.0453 ± 0.0018	0.0485 ± 0.0038	0.0328 ± 0.0006	0.0105 ± 0.0014
3311	0.0436 ± 0.0035	0.0474 ± 0.0054	0.0344 ± 0.0021	0.0114 ± 0.0016
others	0.5608	0.1776	< 0.0002	–

Table 1: Outputs of SA-OT for hierarchy $\mathcal{H}$. "Others" are twelve forms, each with a frequency between 2% and 8% for t_step $= 1$, and lower than 4.5% for t_step $= 0.1$. (Forms produced in 8% of the cases at t_step $= 1$ are not produced if t_step $= 0.01$!) An experiment consisted of running 4096 simulations and counting relative frequencies; each cell contains the mean and standard deviation of three experiments.

development. (Although on-line algorithms require virtual production only, not necessarily uttered in communication, we suppose the two go together.) We defer for future work issues as parsing hidden structures, learning underlying forms and biases for ranking markedness above faithfulness.

4.1 Learning SA-OT

We first implemented Recursive Constraint Demotion with SA-OT. To begin with, RCD creates a *winner/loser table*, in which rows correspond to pairs (w, l) such that winner w is a learning datum, and loser l is less harmonic than w. Column *winner marks* contains the constraints that are more severely violated by the winner than by the loser, and vice-versa for column *loser marks*. Subsequently, RCD builds the hierarchy from top. It repeatedly collects the constraints not yet ranked that do not occur as winner marks. If no such constraint exists, then the learning data are inconsistent. These constraints are then added to the next stratum of the hierarchy in a random order, while the rows in the table containing them as loser marks are deleted (because these rows have been accounted for by the hierarchy).

Given the complexity of the learning data produced by SA-OT, it is an advantage of RCD that it recognises inconsistent data. But how to collect the winner-loser pairs for the table? The learner has no information concerning the grammaticality of the learning data, and only knows that the forms produced are local optima for the target (unknown) hierarchy and the universal (hence, known) topology. Thus, we constructed the winner-loser table from all pairs (w, l) such that w was an observed form, and l was a neighbour of w. To avoid the noise present in real-life data, we considered only w's with a frequency higher than $\sqrt{N}$, where N was the number of learning data. Applying then RCD resulted in a hierarchy that produced the observed local optima—and most often also many others, depending on the random constraint ranking in a stratum. These unwanted local optima suggest a new explanation of some "child speech forms".

Therefore, more information is necessary to find the target hierarchy. As learners do not use negative evidence (Pinker, 1984), we did not try to remove extra local optima directly. Yet, the learners do collect statistical information. Accordingly, we enriched the winner/loser table with pairs (w, l) such that w was a form observed significantly more frequently than l; l's were observed forms and the extra local optima. (A difference in frequency was significant if it was higher than $\sqrt{N}$.) The assumption that frequency reflects harmony is based on the heuristics of SA-OT, but is far not always true. So RCD recognised this new table often to be inconsistent.

Enriching the table could also be done gradually, adding a new pair only if enough errors have supported it (*Error-Selective Learning*, Tessier (2007). The pair is then removed if it proves inconsistent with stronger pairs (pairs supported by more errors, or pairs of observed forms and their neighbours).

Yet, we instead turned to real on-line algorithms, namely to Boersma's Gradual Learning Algorithm (GLA) (Boersma, 1997). (*Error Driven Constraint Demotion* is not robust, and gets stuck for inconsistent data.) Similarly to Error-Selective Learning, GLA accumulates gradually the arguments for reranking two constraints. The GLA Algorithm assigns a real-valued *rank* r to each constraint, so that a higher ranked constraint has a higher r. Then, in each learning step the learning datum (the winner) is compared to the output produced by the learner's actual hierarchy (the loser). Every constraint's rank is decreased by a small value (the plasticity) if the winner violates it more than the loser, and it is increased by the same value if the loser has more violations than the winner. Often—still, not always (Pater, 2005)—these small steps accumulate to converge towards the correct constraint ranking.

When producing an output (the winner) for the target hierarchy and another one (the loser) for the learner's hierarchy, Boersma uses Stochastic OT (Boersma, 1997). But one can also employ traditional OT evaluation, whereas we used SA-OT with `t_step` = 0.1. The learner's actual hierarchy in GLA is stored by the real-valued ranks r. So the fatal constraint in the core of SA-OT (Fig. 4) is the constraint that has the highest r among the constraints assigning different violations to w and w'. (A random one of them, if more constraints have the same r-values, but this is very rare.). The K-values were the *floor* of the r-values. (Note the possibility of more constraints having the same K-value.) The r-values could also be directly the K-values; but since parameters `K_max`, `K_min` and `K_step` are integers, this would cause the temperature not enter the domains of the constraints, which would skip an important part of simulated annealing.

Similarly to Stochastic OT, our model also displayed different convergence properties of GLA. Quite often, GLA reranked its initial hierarchy (the output of RCD) into a hierarchy yielding the same or a similar output distribution to that produced by the target hierarchy. The simulated child's performance converged towards the parent's performance, and "child speech forms" were dropped gradually.

In other cases, however, the GLA algorithm turned the performance worse. The reason for that might be more than the fact that GLA does not always converge. Increasing or decreasing the constraints' rank by a plasticity in GLA is done in order to make the winners gradually better and the losers worse. But in SA-OT the learner's hierarchy can produce a form that is indeed more harmonic (but not a local optimum) for the target ranking than the learning datum; then the constraint promotions and demotions miss the point. Moreover, unlike in Stochastic OT, these misguided moves might be more frequent than the opposite moves.

Still, the system performed well with our grammar $\mathcal{H}$. Although the initial grammars returned by RCD included local optima ("child speech forms", e.g., 0000), learning with GLA brought the learner's performance most often closer to the teacher's. Still, final hierarchies could be very diverse, with different global optima and frequency distributions.

In another experiment the initial ranking was the target hierarchy. Then, 13 runs returned the target distribution with some small changes in the hierarchy; in five cases the frequencies changed slightly, but twice the distribution became qualitatively different (e.g., 2222 not appearing).

4.2 Learning in other architectures

Learning in the ICS architecture involves similar problems to those encountered with SA-OT. The learner is faced again with performance forms that are local optima and not always better than unattested forms. The learning differs exclusively as a consequence of the connectionist implementation.

In McCarthy's Persistent OT, the learner only knows that the observed form is a local optimum, *i. e.*, it is better than all its neighbours. Then, she has to find a path backwards, from the surface form to the underlying form, such that in each step the candidate closer to the SF is better than all other neighbours of the candidate closer to the UF. Hence, the problem is more complex, but it results in a similar winner/loser table of locally close candidates.

5 Conclusion and future work

We have tested the learnability of an OT grammar enriched with a neighbourhood structure. The learning data were produced by a performance model (*viz.*, SA-OT), so the learner only had access to the teacher's *performance*. But by knowing the mechanism distorting production, she still could learn the target *competence* more or less. (Minor differences in competence are possible, as long as the performance is very similar.) She made use of the structure (the topology) of the candidate set, but also of the observed error patterns. Future work may exploit the fact that different parameter settings of SA-OT yield different distributions.

Not correctly reconstructed grammars often lead to different grammaticality judgements, but also to quantitative differences in the performance distribution, despite the qualitative similarity. This fact can explain diachronic changes and why some grammars are evolutionarily more stable than others.

Inaccurate *reconstruction*, as opposed to exact *learning*, is similar to what Dan Sperber and others said about symbolic-cultural systems: "*The tacit knowledge of a participant in a symbolic-cultural system is neither taught nor learned by rote. Rather each new participant [...] reconstructs the rules which govern the symbolic-cultural system in question. These reconstructions may differ considerably, depending upon such factors as the personal history of the individual in question. Consequently, the products of each individual's symbolic mechanism are idiosyncratic to some extent.*" (Lawson and McCauley, 1990, p. 68, italics are original). This observation has been used to argue that cultural learning is different from language learning; now we turn the table and claim that acquiring a language is indeed similar in this respect to learning a culture.

References

Diana Apoussidou. 2007. *The Learnability of Metrical Phonology*. Ph.D. thesis, University of Amsterdam.

Tamás Bíró. 2005a. How to define Simulated Annealing for Optimality Theory? In *Proc. 10th FG and 9th MoL*, Edinburgh. Also ROA-897[1].

Tamás Bíró. 2005b. When the hothead speaks: Simulated Annealing Optimality Theory for Dutch fast speech. In C. Cremers et al., editor, *Proc. of the 15th CLIN*, pages 13–28, Leiden. Also ROA-898.

Tamás Bíró. 2006a. *Finding the Right Words: Implementing Optimality Theory with Simulated Annealing*. Ph.D. thesis, University of Groningen. ROA-896.

Tamás Bíró. 2006b. Squeezing the infinite into the finite. In A. Yli-Jyr et al., editor, *Finite-State Methods and Natural Language Processing, FSMNLP 2005, Helsinki*, LNAI-4002, pages 21–31. Springer.

Paul Boersma and Bruce Hayes. 2001. Empirical tests of the Gradual Learning Algorithm. *Linguistic Inquiry*, 32:45–86. Also: ROA-348.

[1]ROA: *Rutgers Optimality Archive* at http://roa.rutgers.edu

Paul Boersma. 1997. How we learn variation, optionality, and probability. *Proceedings of the Institute of Phonetic Sciences, Amsterdam (IFA)*, 21:43–58.

Jason Eisner. 1997. Efficient generation in primitive optimality theory. In *Proc. of the 35th Annual Meeting of the Association for Computational Linguistics and 8th EACL*, pages 313–320, Madrid.

Judit Gervain, Marina Nespor, Reiko Mazuka, Ryota Horie, and Jacques Mehler. submitted. Bootstrapping word order in prelexical infants: a japanese-italian cross-linguistic study. *Cognitive Psychology*.

Jonas Kuhn. 2000. Processing optimality-theoretic syntax by interleaved chart parsing and generation. In *Proc.ACL-38, Hongkong*, pages 360–367.

E. Thomas Lawson and Robert N. McCauley. 1990. *Rethinking Religion: Connecting Cognition and Culture*. Cambridge University Press, Cambridge, UK.

John J. McCarthy. 2006. Restraint of analysis. In E. Baković et al., editor, *Wondering at the Natural Fecundity of Things: Essays in Honor of A. Prince*, pages 195–219. U. of California, Santa Cruz. ROA-844.

Joe Pater. 2005. Non-convergence in the GLA and variation in the CDA. ms., ROA-780.

Steven Pinker. 1984. *Language Learnability & Language Development*. Harvard UP, Cambridge, Mass.

Alan Prince and Paul Smolensky. 1993 aka 2004. *Optimality Theory: Constraint Interaction in Generative Grammar*. Blackwell, Malden, MA, etc. Also: RuCCS-TR-2, 1993; ROA Version: 537-0802, http://roa.rutgers.edu, 2002.

Jenny R. Saffran, Richard N. Aslin, and Elissa L. Newport. 1996. Statistical learning by 8-month-old infants. *Science*, 274(5294):1926–1928.

Paul Smolensky and Géraldine Legendre. 2006. *The Harmonic Mind: From Neural Computation to Optimality-Theoretic Grammar*. MIT P., Cambridge.

Bruce Tesar and Paul Smolensky. 2000. *Learnability in Optimality Theory*. MIT Press, Cambridge, MA.

Bruce Tesar. 1995. *Computational Optimality Theory*. Ph.D. thesis, University of Colorado. Also: ROA-90.

Anne-Michelle Tessier. 2007. *Biases and Stages in Phonological Acquisition*. Ph.D. thesis, University of Massachusetts Amherst. Also: ROA-883.

Bill Turkel. 1994. The acquisition of Optimality Theoretic systems. m.s., ROA-11.

Charles D. Yang. 2002. *Knowledge and Learning in Natural Language*. Oxford U. P., Oxford–New York.

Learning to interpret novel noun-noun compounds: evidence from a category learning experiment

Barry Devereux & Fintan Costello
School of Computer Science and Informatics, University College Dublin,
Belfield, Dublin 4, IRELAND
{barry.devereux, fintan.costello}@ucd.ie

Abstract

The ability to correctly interpret and produce noun-noun compounds such as WIND FARM or CARBON TAX is an important part of the acquisition of language in various domains of discourse. One approach to the interpretation of noun-noun compounds assumes that people make use of distributional information about how the constituent words of compounds tend to combine; another assumes that people make use of information about the two constituent concepts' features to produce interpretations. We present an experiment that examines how people acquire both the distributional information and conceptual information relevant to compound interpretation. A plausible model of the interpretation process is also presented.

1 Introduction

People frequently encounter noun-noun compounds such as MEMORY STICK and AUCTION POLITICS in everyday discourse. Compounds are particularly interesting from a language-acquisition perspective: children as young as two can comprehend and produce noun-noun compounds (Clark & Barron, 1988), and these compounds play an important role in adult acquisition of the new language and terminology associated with particular domains of discourse. Indeed, most new terms entering the English language are combinations of existing words (Cannon, 1987; consider FLASH MOB, DESIGNER BABY, SPEED DATING and CARBON FOOTPRINT).

These noun-noun compounds are also interesting from a computational perspective, in that they pose a significant challenge for current computational accounts of language. This challenge arises from the fact that the semantics of noun-noun compounds are extremely diverse, with compounds utilizing many different relations between their constituent words (consider the examples at the end of the previous paragraph). Despite this diversity, people typically interpret even completely novel compounds extremely quickly, in the order of hundredths of seconds in reaction time studies.

One approach that has been taken in both cognitive psychology and computational linguistics can be termed the relation-based approach (e.g. Gagné & Shoben, 1997; Kim & Baldwin, 2005). In this approach, the interpretation of a compound is represented as the instantiation of a relational link between the modifier and head noun of the compound. Such relations are usually represented as a set of taxonomic categories; for example the meaning of STUDENT LOAN might be specified with a POSSESSOR relation (Kim & Baldwin, 2005) or MILK COW might be specified by a MAKES relation (Gagné & Shoben, 1997). However, researchers are not close to any agreement on a taxonomy of relation categories classifying noun-noun compounds; indeed a wide range of typologies have been proposed (e.g. Levi, 1977; Kim & Baldwin, 2005).

In these relation-based approaches, there is often little focus on how the meaning of the relation interacts with the intrinsic properties of the constituent concepts. Instead, extrinsic information about concepts, such as distributional information about how often different relations are associated with a concept, is used. For example, Gagné & Shoben's CARIN model utilizes the fact that the modifier MOUNTAIN is frequently associated with the LOCATED relation (in compounds such as MOUNTAIN CABIN or MOUNTAIN GOAT); the model does not utilize the fact that the concept MOUNTAIN has in-

Proceedings of the Workshop on Cognitive Aspects of Computational Language Acquisition, pages 89–96,
Prague, Czech Republic, June 2007

trinsic properties such as *is large* and *is a geological feature*: features which may in general precipitate the LOCATION relation.

An approach that is more typical of psychological theories of compound comprehension can be termed the concept-based approach (Wisniewski, 1997; Costello and Keane, 2000). With such theories, the focus is on the intrinsic properties of the constituent concepts, and the interpretation of a compound is usually represented as a modification of the head noun concept. So, for example, the compound ZEBRA FISH may involve a modification of the FISH concept, by asserting a feature of the ZEBRA concept (e.g. *has stripes*) for it; in this way, a ZEBRA FISH can be understood as a fish with stripes. Concept-based theories do not typically use distributional information about how various relations are likely to be used with concepts.

The information assumed relevant to compound interpretation is therefore quite different in relation-based and concept-based theories. However, neither approach typically deals with the issue of how people acquire the information that allows them to interpret compounds. In the case of the relation-based approaches, for example, how do people acquire the knowledge that the modifier MOUNTAIN tends to be used frequently with the LOCATED relation and that this information is important in comprehending compounds with that modifier? In the case of concept-based approaches, how do people acquire the knowledge that features of ZEBRA are likely to influence the interpretation of ZEBRA FISH?

This paper presents an experiment which examines how both distributional information about relations and intrinsic information about concept features influence compound interpretation. We also address the question of how such information is acquired. Rather than use existing, real world concepts, our experiment used laboratory generated concepts that participants were required to learn during the experiment. As well as learning the meaning of these concepts, participants also built up knowledge during the experiment about how these concepts tend to combine with other concepts via relational links. Using laboratory-controlled concepts allows us to measure and control various factors that might be expected to influence compound comprehension; for example, concepts can be designed to vary in their degree of similarity to one another, to be associated with potential relations with a certain degree of frequency, or to have a feature which is associated with a particular relation. It would be extremely difficult to control for such factors, or investigate the aquisition process, using natural, real world concepts.

2 Experiment

Our experiment follows a category learning paradigm popular in the classification literature (Medin & Shaffer, 1978; Nosofsky, 1984). The experiment consists of two phases, a training phase followed by a transfer phase. In the training phase, participants learned to identify several laboratory generated categories by examining instances of these categories that were presented to them. These categories were of two types, conceptual and relational. The conceptual categories consisted of four "plant" categories and four "beetle" categories, which participants learned to distinguish by attending to differences between category instances. The relational categories were three different ways in which a beetle could eat a plant. Each stimulus consisted of a picture of a beetle instance and a picture of a plant instance, with a relation occurring between them. The category learning phase of our experiment therefore has three stages: one for learning to distinguish between the four beetle categories, one for learning to distinguish between the four plant categories, and one for learning to distinguish between the three relation categories.

The training phase was followed by a transfer phase consisting of two parts. In the first part participants were presented with some of the beetle-plant pairs that they had encountered in the training phase together with some similar, though previously unseen, pairs. Participants were asked to rate how likely each of the three relations were for the depicted beetle-plant pair. This part of the transfer phase therefore served as a test of how well participants had learned to identify the appropriate relation (or relations) for pairs of conceptual category exemplars and also tested their ability to generalize their knowledge about the learned categories to previously unseen exemplar pairs. In the second part of the transfer phase, participants were presented with pairs of category names (rather than pairs of category items), presented as noun-noun compounds, and were asked to rate the appropriateness of each relation for each compound.

In the experiment, we aim to investigate three issues that may be important in determining the most appropriate interpretation for a compound. Firstly, the experiment aims to investigate the influence of concept salience (i.e. how important to participants information about the two constituent concepts are, or how relevant to finding a relation that information is) on the interpretation of compounds. For example, if the two concepts referenced in a compound are identical with respect to the complexity of their representation, how well they are associated with various alternative relations (and so on), but are of differing levels of animacy, we might expect the relation associated with the more animate concept to be selected by participants more often than a different relation associated equally strongly with the less animate concept. In our experiment, all three relations involve a beetle eating a plant. Since in each case the beetle is the agent in the EATS(BEETLE,PLANT) scenario, it is possible that the semantics of the beetle concepts might be more relevant to relation selection than the semantics of the plant concepts.

Secondly, the experiment is designed to investigate the effect of the ordering of the two nouns within the compound: given two categories named A and B, our experiment investigates whether the compound "A B" is interpreted in the same way as the compound "B A". In particular, we were interested in whether the relation selected for a compound would tend to be dependent on the concept in the head position or the concept in the modifier position. Also of interest was whether the location of the more animate concept in the compound would have an effect on interpretation. For example, since the combined concept is an instance of the head concept, we might hypothesize that compounds for which the head concept is more animate than the modifier concept may be easier to interpret correctly.

Finally, were interested in the effect of concept similarity: would compounds consisting of similar constituent categories tend to be interpreted in similar ways?

learn	*trans.*	Nr	Rel	Bcat	Pcat	B1	B2	B3	P1	P2	P3
l		1	1	1	3	4	1	1	3	2	3
l		2	1	1	3	4	4	1	2	3	3
l	*t*	3	1	1	3	1	1	1	3	3	2
l	*t*	4	1	1	3	4	1	2	3	3	3
l	*t*	5	2	2	2	2	2	2	2	2	3
l		6	2	2	2	2	2	1	2	3	2
l		7	2	2	2	2	3	2	2	2	1
l	*t*	8	2	2	2	2	2	3	2	2	2
l	*t*	9	3	3	1	3	3	3	4	1	2
l	*t*	10	3	3	1	3	3	2	1	1	1
l		11	3	3	1	2	3	3	4	4	1
l		12	3	3	1	3	2	3	4	1	1
l	*t*	13	1	4	4	1	1	4	4	4	4
l	*t*	14	2	4	4	4	1	4	4	1	4
l	*t*	15	3	4	4	4	4	4	1	1	4
	t	16	-	1	1	4	1	1	4	1	1
	t	17	-	3	3	3	3	3	3	3	3
	t	18	-	2	4	2	2	2	4	1	4
	t	19	-	4	2	4	1	4	2	2	2

Table 1: The experiment's abstract category structure

2.1 Method

2.1.1 Participants

The participants were 42 university students.

2.1.2 Materials

The abstract category structure used in the experiment is presented in Table 1. There are 19 items in total; the first and second columns in the table indicate if the item in question was one of the 15 items used in the learning phase of the experiment (l) or as one of the 13 items used in the transfer stage of the experiment (t). There were four beetle categories (Bcat), four plant categories (Pcat) and three relation categories used in the experiment. Both the beetle and plant categories were represented by features instantiated on three dimensions (B1, B2 & B3 and P1, P2 & P3, respectively). The beetle and plant categories were identical with respect to their abstract structure (so, for example, the four exemplars of Pcat1 have the same abstract features as the four exemplars of Bcat1).

Beetles and plants were associated with particular relations; Bcat1, Bcat2 and Bcat3 were associated with Relations 1, 2 and 3, respectively, whereas Pcat1, Pcat2 and Pcat3 were associated with Relations 3, 2 and 1, respectively. Bcat4 and Pcat4 were not associated with any relations; the three exemplar instances of these categories in the learning phase appeared once with each of the three relations. The features of beetles and plants were sometimes diagnostic of a category (much as the feature *has three wheels* is diagnostic for TRICYCLE); for example, a particular feature associated with Bcat1 is a 1 on the B3 dimension: 3 of the 4 Bcat1 training phase exemplars have a 1 on dimension B3 while only one of the remaining 11 training phase exemplars do. Also, the intrinsic features of beetles and plants are sometimes diagnostic of a relation category (much as the intrinsic feature *has a flat surface raised off the ground* is diagnostic for the relational scenario *sit on*); values on dimensions B1, P1, B2 and P2 are quite diagnostic of relations. Participants learned to identify the plant, beetle and relation categories used in the experiment by attending to the associations between beetle, plant and relation categories and feature diagnosticity for those categories.

The beetle and plant categories were also designed to differ in terms of their similarity. For example, categories Bcat1 and Bcat4 are more similar to each other than Bcat3 and Bcat4 are: the features for Bcat1 and Bcat4 overlap to a greater extent than the features for Bcat3 and Bcat4 do. The aim of varying categories with respect to their similarity was to investigate whether similar categories would yield similar patterns of relation likelihood ratings. In particular, Bcat4 (and Pcat4) occurs equally often with the three relations; therefore if category similarity has no effect we would expect people to select each of the relations equally often for this category. However, if similarity influences participants' relation selection, then we would expect that Relation 1 would be selected more often than Relations 2 or 3.

The abstract category structure was mapped to concrete features in a way that was unique for each participant. Each beetle dimension was mapped randomly to the concrete dimensions of beetle shell color, shell pattern and facial expression. Each plant dimension was randomly mapped to the concrete dimensions of leaf color, leaf shape, and stem color. The three relations were randomly mapped to *eats from leaf*, *eats from top*, and *eats from trunk*.

2.1.3 Procedure

The experiment consisted of a training phase and a transfer phase. The training phase itself consisted of three sub-stages in which participants learned to distinguish between the plant, beetle and relation categories. During each training sub-stage, the 15 training items were presented to participants sequentially on a web-page in a random order. Underneath each item, participants were presented with a question of the form "What kind of plant is seen in this picture?", "What type of beetle is seen in this picture?" and "How does this $\langle Bcat \rangle$ eat this $\langle Pcat \rangle$?" in the plant learning, beetle learning, and relation learning training sub-stages, respectively (e.g. Figure 1). Underneath the question were radio buttons on which participants could select what they believed to be the correct category; after participants had made their selection, they were given feedback about whether their guess had been correct (with the correct eating relation shown taking place). Each of the three substages was repeated until participants had correctly classified 75% or more of the items. Once they had successfully completed the training phase they moved on to the transfer phase.

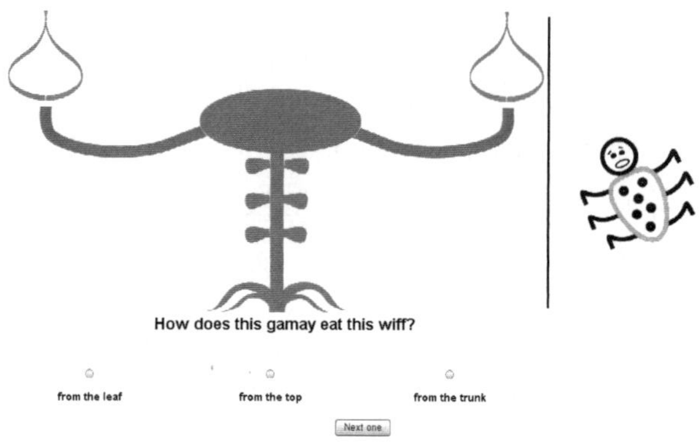

Figure 1: Example of a relation learning stimulus

The transfer phase consisted of two stages, an exemplar transfer stage and a compound transfer stage. In the exemplar transfer stage, participants were presented with 13 beetle-plant items, some of which had appeared in training and some of which were new items (see Table 1). Underneath each picture was a question of the form "How does this $\langle Bcat \rangle$ eat this $\langle Pcat \rangle$?" and three 5-point scales for the three relations, ranging from 0 (unlikely) to 4 (likely).

The materials used in the compound transfer stage of the experiment were the 16 possible noun-noun compounds consisting of a beetle and plant category label. Participants were presented with a sentence of the form "There are a lot of $\langle Pcat \rangle$ $\langle Bcat \rangle$s around at the moment." and were asked "What kind of eating activity would you expect a $\langle Pcat \rangle$ $\langle Bcat \rangle$ to have?". Underneath, participants rated the likelihood of each of the three relations on 5-point scales. One half of participants were presented with the compounds in the form "$\langle Bcat \rangle$ $\langle Pcat \rangle$" whereas the other half of participants saw the compounds in the form "$\langle Pcat \rangle$ $\langle Bcat \rangle$".

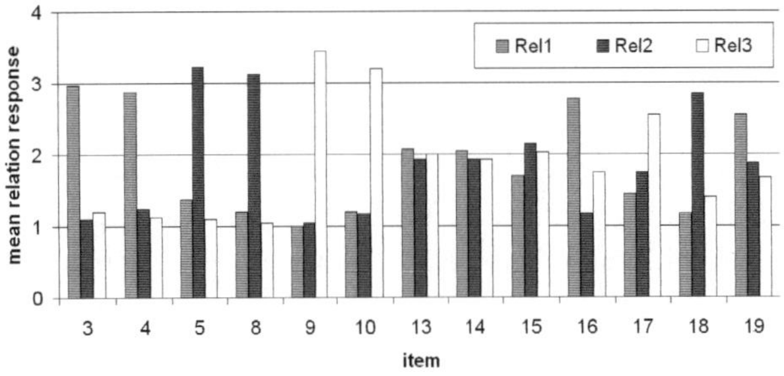

Figure 2: Participants' mean responses for the exemplar transfer items.

2.2 Results

2.2.1 Performance during training

Two of the participants failed to complete the training phase. For the remaining 40 participants, successful learning took on average 5.8 iterations of the training items for the plant categories, 3.9 iterations for the beetle categories, and 2.1 iterations for the relation categories. The participants therefore learned to distinguish between the categories quite quickly, which is consistent with the fact that the categories were designed to be quite easy to learn.

2.2.2 Performance during the exemplar transfer stage

Participants' mean ratings of relation likelihood for the nine previously seen exemplar items is presented in Figure 2 (items 3 to 15). For each of these items there was a correct relation, namely the one that the item was associated with during training. The difference between the mean response for the correct relation ($M = 2.76$) and the mean response for the two incorrect relations ($M = 1.42$) was significant ($t_s(39) = 7.50$, $p < .01$; $t_i(8) = 4.07$, $p < .01$). These results suggest that participants were able to learn which relations tended to co-occur with the items in the training phase.

Participants' mean ratings of relation likelihood for the four exemplar items not previously seen in training are also presented in Figure 2 (items 16 to 19). Each of these four items consisted of a prototypical example of each of the four beetle categories and each of the four plant categories (with each beetle and plant category appearing once; see Table 1 for details). For these four items there was no correct answer; indeed, the relation consistent with the beetle exemplar was always different to the relation suggested by the plant exemplar. For each trial, then, one relation is consistent with the beetle exemplar (r_b), one is consistent with the plant exemplar (r_p) and one is neutral (r_n). One-way repeated measures ANOVAs with response type (r_b, r_p or r_n) as a fixed factor and either subject or item as a random factor were used to investigate the data. There was a significant effect of response type in both the by-subjects and by-items analysis ($F_s(2, 39) = 19.10$, $p < .01$; $F_i(2, 3) = 24.14, p < .01$). Pairwise differences between the three response types were investigated using planned comparisons in both the by-subject and by-items analyses (with paired t-tests used in both cases). The difference between participants' mean response for the relation associated with the beetle exemplar, r_b ($M = 2.68$), and their mean response for the neutral relation, r_n ($M = 1.44$) was significant ($t_s(39) = 5.63$, $p < .001$; $t_i(3) = 5.34$, $p = .01$). These results suggest that participants were strongly influenced by the beetle exemplar when making their category judgments. However, the difference between participants' mean response for the relation associated with the plant exemplar, r_p ($M = 1.62$), and their mean response for the neutral relation was not significant ($t_s(39) = 1.11$, $p = .27$; $t_i(3) = 0.97$, $p = .40$). These results suggest that participants were not influenced by the plant exemplar when judging relation likelihood. Since the beetle and plant categories have identical abstract structure, these results suggest that other factors (such as the animacy of a concept or the role it plays in the relation) are important to interpretation.

The data from all 13 items were also analysed taken together. To investigate possible effects of category similarity, a repeated measures ANOVA with beetle category and response relation taken as within subject factors and subject taken as a random factor was undertaken. There was a significant effect of the category that the beetle exemplar belonged to on participants' responses for the three relations (the interaction between beetle category and response relation was significant; $F(6, 39) = 26.83$, $p < .01$. Planned pairwise comparisons (paired t-tests) were conducted to investigate how ratings for the correct relation (i.e. the relation consistent with training) differed for the ratings for the other two relations. For Bcat1, Bcat2 and Bcat3, the ratings for the relation consistent with learning was higher than the two alternative relations ($p < .01$ in all cases). However, for the Bcat4 items, there was no evidence that participants we more likely to rate Relation 1 ($M = 2.09$) higher than either Relation 2 ($M = 1.97$; $t(39) = 0.54$, $p = .59$) or Relation 3 ($M = 1.91$; $t(39) = 0.69$, $p > .50$). Though the difference is in the direction predicted by Bcat4's similarity to Bcat1, there is no evidence that participants made use of Bcat4's similarity to Bcat1 when rating relation likelihood for Bcat4.

In summary, the results suggest that participants were capable of learning the training items. Participants appeared to be influenced by the beetle exemplar but not the plant exemplar. There was some evidence that conceptual similarity played a role in participants' judgments of relation likelihood for Bcat4 exemplars (e.g. the responses for item 19) but over all Bcat4 exemplars this effect was not significant.

2.2.3 Performance on the noun-noun compound transfer stage

In the noun-noun compound transfer stage, each participant rated relation likelihood for each of the 16 possible noun-noun compounds that could be formed from combinations of the beetle and plant category names. Category name order was a between subject factor: half of the participants saw the compounds with beetle in the modifier position and plant in the head position whilst the other half of participants saw the reverse. First of all, we were interested in whether or not the training on exemplar items would transfer to noun-noun compounds. Another question of interest is whether or not participants' responses would be affected by the order in which the categories were presented. For example, perhaps it is the concept in the modifier position that is most influential in determining the likelihood of different relations for a compound. Alternatively perhaps it is the concept in the head position that is most influential.

To answer such questions a $4 \times 4 \times 3 \times 2$ repeated measures ANOVA with beetle category, plant category and response relation as within subject factors and category label ordering as a between subject factor was used to analyze the data. The interaction between beetle category and response relation was significant ($F(6, 38) = 59.79$, $p < .001$). Therefore, the beetle category present in the compound tended to influence participants' relation selections. The interaction between plant category and response relation was weaker, but still significant ($F(6, 38) = 5.35$, $p < 0.01$). Therefore, the plant category present in the compound tended to influence participants' relation selections. These results answer the first question above; training on exemplar items was transferred to the noun-noun compounds. However, there were no other significant interactions found. In particular, the interaction between category ordering, beetle category and response relation was not significant ($F(6, 38) = 1.82$, $p = .09$). In other words, there is no evidence that the influence of beetle category on participants' relation selections when the beetle was in the modifier position differed from the influence of beetle category on participants' relation selections when the beetle was in the head-noun position. Similarly, the interaction between noun ordering, plant category and response relation was not significant ($F(6, 38) = 0.68$, $p = .67$); there is no evidence that the influence of the plant category on relation selection differed depending on the location of the plant category in the compound.

Planned pairwise comparisons (paired t-tests) were used to investigate the significant interactions further: for Bcat1, Bcat2 and Bcat3, the ratings for the relation consistent with learning was significantly higher than the two alternative relations ($p < .001$ in all cases). However, for Bcat4, there were no significant differences between the ratings for the three relations ($p > .31$ for each of the three comparisons). For the plants, however, the only significant differences were between the response for Relation 1 and Relation 2 for Pcat2 ($t(39) = 2.12$,

$p = .04$[1]) and between Relation 2 and Relation 3 for Pcat2 ($t(39) = 3.08$, $p = .004$), although the differences for Pcat1 and Pcat3 are also in the expected direction.

In summary, the results of the noun-noun compound stage of the experiment show that participants' learning of the relations and their associations with beetle and plant categories during training transferred to a task involving noun-noun compound interpretation. This is important as it demonstrates how the interpretation of compounds can be derived from information about how concept exemplars tend to co-occur together.

2.3 Modelling relation selection

One possible hypothesis about how people decide on likely relations for a compound is that the mention of the two lexemes in the compound activates stored memory traces (i.e. exemplars) of the concepts denoted by those lexemes. Exemplars differ in how typical they are for particular conceptual categories and we would expect the likelihood of an exemplar's activation to be in proportion to its typicality for the categories named in the compound. As concept instances usually do not happen in isolation but rather in the context of other concepts, this naturally results in extensional relational information about activated exemplars also becoming activated. This activated relational information is then available to form a basis for determining the likely relation or relations for the compound. A strength of this hypothesis is that it incorporates both intensional information about concepts' features (in the form of concept typicality) and also extrinsic, distributional information about how concepts tend to combine (in the form of relational information associated with activated exemplars). In this section, we present a model instantiating this hybrid approach.

The hypothesis proposed above assumes that extensional information about relations is associated with exemplars in memory. In the context of our experiment, the extensional, relational information about beetle and plant exemplars participants held in memory is revealed in how they rated relational likelihood during the exemplar transfer stage of the experiment. For each of the 13 beetle and plant exemplars, we therefore assume that the average ratings for each of the relations describes our participants' knowledge about how exemplars combine with other exemplars. Also, we can regard the three relation likelihood ratings as being a 3-dimensional vector. Given that category ordering did not appear to have an effect on participants' responses in the compound transfer phase of the experiment, we can calculate the relation vector $\vec{r}_{B,P}$ for the novel compounds "B P" or "P B" as

$$\vec{r}_{B,P} = \frac{\sum\limits_{e \in U} (typ(e_b, B) + typ(e_p, P))^{\alpha} \cdot \vec{r}_e}{\sum\limits_{e \in U} (typ(e_b, B) + typ(e_p, P))^{\alpha}}$$

where e denotes one of the 13 beetle-plant exemplar items rated in the exemplar transfer stage, $typ(e_b, B)$ denotes the typicality of the beetle exemplar present in item e in beetle category B and $typ(e_p, P)$ denotes the typicality of the plant exemplar present in item e in plant category P. U is the set of 13 beetle-plant exemplar pairs and α is a magnification parameter to be estimated empirically which describes the relative importance of exemplar typicality.

In this model, we require a measure of how typical of a conceptual category an exemplar is (i.e. a measure of how good a member of a category a particular category instance is). In our model, we use the Generalized Context Model (GCM) to derive measures of exemplar typicality. The GCM is a successful model of category learning that implements an an exemplar-based account of how people make judgments of category membership in a category learning task. The GCM computes the probability Pr of an exemplar e belonging in a category C as a function of pairwise exemplar similarity according to:

$$Pr(e, C) = \frac{\sum\limits_{i \in C} sim(e, i)}{\sum\limits_{i \in U} sim(e, i)}$$

where U denotes the set of all exemplars in memory and $sim(e, i)$ is a measure of similarity between exemplars e and i. Similarity between exemplars is in turn defined as a negative-exponential transforma-

[1]This is not significant if Bonferroni correction is used to control the familywise Type I error rate amongst the multiple comparisons

tion of distance:

$$sim(i,j) = e^{-cdist(i,j)} \quad (1)$$

where c is a free parameter, corresponding to how quickly similarity between the exemplars diminishes as a function of their distance. The distance between two exemplars is usually computed as the city-block metric summed over the dimensions of the exemplars, with each term weighted by empirically estimated weighting parameters constrained to sum to one. According to the GCM, the probability that a given exemplar belongs to a given category increases as the average similarity between the exemplar and the exemplars of the category increases; in other words, as it becomes a more typical member of the category. In our model, we use the probability scores produced by the GCM as a means for computing concept typicality (although other methods for measuring typicality could have been used).

We compared the relation vector outputted by the model for the 16 possible compounds to the relation vectors derived from participants' ratings in the compound transfer phase of the experiment. The agreement between the model and the data was high across the three relations (for Relation 1, $r = 0.84$, $p < 0.01$; for Relation 2, $r = 0.90$, $p < 0.01$; for Relation 3, $r = 0.87$, $p < 0.01$), using only one free parameter, α, to fit the data[2].

3 Conclusions

The empirical findings we have described in this paper have several important implications. Firstly, the findings have implications for relation-based theories. In particular, the finding that only beetle exemplars tended to influence relation selection suggest that factors other than relation frequency are relevant to the interpretation process (since the beetle and plants in our experiment were identical in their degree of association with relations). Complex interactions between concepts and relations (e.g. agency in the EATS(AGENT,OBJECT) relation) is information that is not possible to capture using a taxonomic approach to relation meaning.

Secondly, the fact that participants could learn to identify the relations between exemplars and also transfer that knowledge to a task involving compounds has implications for concept-based theories of compound comprehension. No concept-based theory of conceptual combination has ever adopted an exemplar approach to concept meaning; models based on concept-focused theories tend to represent concepts as frames or lists of predicates. Our approach suggests an exemplar representation is a viable alternative. Also, distributional knowledge about relations forms a natural component of an exemplar representation of concepts, as different concept instances will occur with instances of other concepts with varying degrees of frequency. Given the success of our model, assuming an exemplar representation of concept semantics would seen to offer a natural way of incorporating both information about concept features and information about relation distribution into a single theory.

[2]In the GCM, c was set equal to 1 and the three dimensional weights in the distance calculation were set equal to $1/3$

References

G. Cannon. 1987. *Historical change and English word formation.* New York: Lang.

E. V. Clark and B.J. Barron. 1988. A thrower-button or a button-thrower? Children's judgments of grammatical and ungrammatical compound nouns. *Linguistics*, 26:3–19.

F. J. Costello & M.T. Keane. 2000. Efficient creativity: Constraint guided conceptual combination.. *Cognitive Science*, 24(2):299–349.

C. L. Gagné and E.J. Shoben. 1997. Influence of thematic relations on the comprehension of modifier noun combinations. *Journal of Experimental Psychology: Learning, Memory, and Cognition*, 23:71–78.

S. N. Kim and T. Baldwin. 2005. Automatic Interpretation of Noun Compounds Using WordNet Similarity. *Lecture Notes in Computer Science*, 3651:945–956.

J. N. Levi. 1978. *The Syntax and Semantics of Complex Nominals.* New York: Academic Press.

D. L. Medin & M.M. Schaffer. 1978. Context theory of classification learning. *Psychological Review*, 85:207–238.

R. N. Nosofsky. 1984. Choice, similarity, and the context theory of classification.. *Journal of Experimental Psychology: Learning, Memory, and Cognition*, 10(1):104–114.

E. J. Wisniewski 1997. When concepts combine. *Psychonomic Bulletin & Review*, 4(2):167–183.